Human Desire and
Economic Satisfaction

Human Desire and Economic Satisfaction

Essays on the Frontiers of Economics

Tibor Scitovsky

Professor of Economics Emeritus
Stanford University

NEW YORK UNIVERSITY PRESS
Washington Square, New York

First published in the U.S.A. in 1986 by
NEW YORK UNIVERSITY PRESS
Washington Square, New York, N.Y. 10003

Library of Congress Cataloging-in-Publication Data

Scitovsky, Tibor
  Human desire and economic satisfaction:

  Bibliography: p.
  Includes index.
  1. Economics. 2. Psychology. 3. Sociology.
I. Title
HB74.P8S37   1986   330   86-12674
ISBN 0-8147-7862-3

Typeset in Times 10/12pt by Quality Phototypesetting Ltd
Printed in Great Britain by
Biddles Ltd, Guildford and King's Lynn

Contents

Preface

It is becoming the custom of economists to preface volumes of their collected papers by explaining how and why they have become economists. To conform to that custom, the appropriate introduction to this volume, which presents my essays on the borderline of economics, must explain why I have ceased being or never became an economist as fully and wholeheartedly sticking to the subject as my colleagues.

Indeed, I never felt an irresistible call to economics and only took it up because I was anxious to stand on my own feet, prove my own worth, and avoid the banking career my family mapped out and wanted to ease me into. Academia seemed the best place to accomplish that and economics the most accessible and interesting among the academic subjects with which I had a nodding acquaintance. In short, academic economics seemed my best way to earn a living and earn it my own way.

Compared to my fellow economists, therefore, I have chosen my profession in a rather pedestrian fashion, neither pursuing lofty ideals nor pushed towards economics by the pressing problems of the day or environment. It was a selfish choice, exactly as economic textbooks model the individual's choice of occupation. It is something of a paradox therefore that it should be I of all people, whose own motivation has been so narrowly economic, who should try to bring man's non-economic motivations and choice behaviour into the realm of economic theory.

My having come to economics the way I did, from a non-intellectual, non-puritanical background, with parents preoccupied with art, beautiful things, and all the other good things the world has to offer, explains perhaps why my interests have been and always remained much broader than my work. I never forgot that there is life beyond work and good things other than economics that are no less important and often much more enjoyable. It is only natural that my abiding concern with those other things should also show up in my economics, manifest in my questioning some of the excessively narrow assumptions of the discipline and my attempts to broaden its scope.

I resigned my job and abandoned my incipient banking career to enrol in the London School of Economics and prepare myself for my chosen profession somewhat late in life, while the world was still in the throes of the Great Depression. My fellow students and I were shocked and bewildered by the faculty's teaching us a curriculum that centred around a theory of full-employment equilibrium at the very time when the rate of unemployment was 15 per cent in Britain, 20 per cent and higher in the United States and Australia, around 30 per cent in Denmark and Norway and close to 50 per cent in Germany. (Most other countries prudently published no unemployment statistics.) We felt that something to bridge the gaping gulf between beautiful economic theory and ugly economic reality was badly missing, perhaps an altogether different approach, which clearly eluded the faculty, but which we felt morally obligated to look for on our own. I worked terribly hard, not so much in doing the required reading to prepare for exams as in sampling, scouring and studying the vast volume of non-required literature in search for a more promising framework or point of departure which would help us to understand the causes of the economic misery all around us. I did not invent a new approach but my search for it was not entirely wasted, because it made me learn what mathematics and statistics I know, got me acquainted with the national accounts (of which the faculty were completely innocent), with Marx, Max Weber, Tawney, J.A. Hobson, Schumpeter among many others and it taught me to think hard.

Then Keynes's *General Theory* appeared and seemed to have everything we were looking for. Its effect was overwhelming. I remember staying up all night for sheer inability to put down a book that asked all the right questions and seemed to have all the answers. We turned Keynesian almost overnight, discussed endlessly the new concepts and ideas introduced in the book, and the centre of our existence became our weekly fights in Robbins's seminar against the anti-Keynesian faculty, led by the few Keynesians among the junior faculty, the more vocal among us students and two visitors: Michal Kalecki and Oskar Lange.

We felt at the time that Keynes had resolved all the really important economic issues and were quite ready to devote our careers to filling in gaps, resolving obscurities, and explaining, simplifying, popularizing and gaining converts to Keynes's macroeconomics. That was not a prestigious job but it certainly seemed the most worthwhile and important thing for academic economists to do as long as unemployment and the underutilization of resources remained the main economic problems. That is why my first papers dealt, one with the reasons, the other with the conditions of underemployment equilibrium.

But then fate forced me off the lofty macroeconomic path into a new selfish choice. A fellowship brought me to the United States, World War II kept me here; and as an expatriate newcomer to a none-too-hospitable alien land (The State Department wanted to have me deported for being a 'premature anti-fascist'), I felt under great pressure to gain recognition and ultimately a job by making my mark with publications more eye-catching than the spreading of Keynes's gospel.

That was not easy. In my first flush of enthusiasm for Keynes, I believed that he had pre-empted macroeconomics and left nothing new and important for others to say, so I looked around for lesser problems to solve. Even if I found nothing new to say on how to improve the workings of the economy, there seemed to be plenty of scope for improving economics. Welfare economics provided an especially rich vein, and my early paper, which proved that profit-maximizing businessmen do it not for the money but for show, set the pattern for much future work. While the important problems of macroeconomics remained my main subject for teaching and writing, I also went on with welfare economics, mostly trying to show that neither things nor people are always as simple as economists assume them to be. None of those papers was very important in itself but I hoped that their cumulative effect would be useful. Also, my later writings in that field became more constructive as I tried to import a little psychology into our overly simplistic and axiomatic discipline.

* * *

This volume brings together my recent papers in that vein. They specify, question, go beyond or try to extend the conventional limits of economics. Most of them deal therefore with the borderline between economics and psychology. I always enjoyed trespassing on ground my fellow economists fear to tread, and although I may be no better than they at resolving difficult problems I believe it useful to raise questions even when I have no ready answers for them. Another common element that binds these papers together is their preoccupation with the behaviour and well-being of the individual person.

The papers are divided into groups by subject matter and arranged within each group in the order in which they were written, which is not always the same as the date of publication, which is the one shown at the head of the chapter.

An early paper (Chapter 2) lists and distinguishes the economic and non-economic sources of welfare, the two other papers in the first group (Chapters 1 and 3) discuss their distribution, with the first also specifying the nature of the distribution that the general public seems to consider equitable. As is well known, economists, *qua* economists, are not prepared to say what constitutes an equitable distribution of income and my simple-minded attempt to guess what public opinion regards as such is one instance of my trying to answer an important but seemingly unanswerable question.

The next group of papers (Chapters 4 through 6) focus on the economic problems created by puritanism in the capitalist economy. Max Weber and R.H. Tawney have written on the way in which the puritanism and protestant ethic of workers and businesmen have promoted capitalist development; my papers discuss the not-so-good influence on our economy that the same puritan ethic exerts through its impact on consumers' behaviour.

The next two papers (Chapters 7 and 8) criticize conventional economics but stay within it. The seventh points up the deleterious effects on the functioning of markets of the affluence, high techology and large-scale organization of today's advanced economies; the eighth enumerates and analyses the many amenities and services which monopolistic competition provides under monopoly capitalism to the 'monopolistically exploited', but which in the past have erroneously been lumped together with the benefits of perfect competition.

While the seventh paper discussed the influence of economic progress on the functioning of the economy itself, the next group of five papers deal, partly with its impact (Chapters 10, 11 and 13), and partly with the possibility of changing its impact (Chapters 9 and 12) on people's tastes, ambitions and social behaviour. So much has been written by so many people on the negative effects of economic progress on our environment that I decided against including my rather early papers on that subject. The papers included deal with the impact that better safety, Social Security and medical care had on our tastes (Chapter 10), with the influence of our higher incomes on those elements of the good life whose supply cannot be augmented (Chapter 11), with the effects of technical progress on family and social relations (Chapter 13), and with the scope and justification for swaying the individual's tastes in the community's interests (Chapters 9 and 12).

The last chapter (Chapter 14), which stands by itself, advocates a rather simple reform of the economist's basic model, which would greatly extend its scope and usefulness by including, alongside with productive activities and the satisfactions their products yield, also enjoyable activities and the satisfactions derived from them. The discussion of the advantages of such an extension of the standard model focuses one's attention on man's various, sometimes conflicting, incentives for work, on the dividing line between economic and non-economic activities, on people's desire for distinction, and on the changing nature of fashions.

Many of the papers could be considered companions to my *The Joyless Economy*, though none presupposes previous acquaintance with it. Papers 2, 4 and 5 pose some of the questions which that book later elaborated and tried to answer; 10 and 11 develop further some of the ideas first presented there; 9 and 12 try to make practical use of one of those ideas. The last paper (Chapter 14) proposes to incorporate into a concrete economic model enjoyable stimulation, that important source of ambition and satisfaction whose psychological basis was analysed in *The Joyless Economy*, and which also forms the subject matter of paper 10. All these papers were written to stand alone and require no familiarity with any of the others. That has inevitably led to some duplication, which I hope is slight enough not to be annoying to readers who read the papers in sequence.

Looking back on my earlier writings, I am struck by the fast erosion of America's puritan ethic. Today, my portrait of the American consumer (especially in paper 5) looks somewhat dated, yet it seemed an accurate and up-to-date portrayal when written and first published — a mere fifteen years ago. I am leaving those passages unrevised, because they are a testimony to the great and amazingly rapid transformation of consumer attitudes in the United States, which itself should be of interest to readers who find this book interesting, because it is closely related and easily linked to several topics discussed in the papers.

Let me enlarge on that and so give a foretaste of what is to follow. Fashions seem to come and go faster today than in the past, and especially so in the United States. That naturally raises the question 'why?'. After all, fashion and the changing of fashions are manifestations, the first of man's imitative nature, the second of his desire for the stimulus of novelty. Both imitativeness and the need for stimulation, however, are basic human traits, unlikely to differ from country to country or to change with the passage of time. Why then do fashions change faster today than they used to and why is their sway greater and more ephemeral in America than elsewhere?

Paper 10 answers the first question. It discusses and documents the various ways in which economic advance progressively diminishes such unpleasant sources of stimulation as the dangers and uncertainties of everyday life, which, given people's unchanging *need* for stimulation, causes their demand for the pleasant stimulus of novelty to increase.

To answer the second question, the greater sway of American fashions is partly due to our greater mobility and better communications in this large country and partly to our greater affluence. To keep up with fashion, especially in dress and the ownership of durables, is an expensive source of novelty, which we can better afford than most other people. As to the faster changing of American fashions, that must be attributed not to our being more imitative than others but to the faster changing behaviour and composition of the group of people whom we imitate. As shown in the last section of paper 14, every society imitates the behaviour of its elite, and the elite of most societies is the upper class. The United States, however, is a singularly classless society, whose elite consists largely of its most conspicuously successful members; and they are a younger and faster-changing group, containing a much higher proportion of alert, energetic and creative people, than is usually the case with class elites, which are mostly hereditary. That renders more changeable the fashions America's elite leads and the rest of us follow.

I very much hope that my papers will be as much fun to read as they were to write.

Part I
Welfare and Its Distribution

1 Equity—1964

Equity is a big word and a vague concept, and you may wonder what business have I, as an economist, to speak on such a topic. Economists usually pride themselves on being more down-to-earth, more rigorous, more scientific than most other social scientists; why, then, should an economist choose so nebulous a topic to discuss with his fellow economists?

My reasons are the following. An important part of the economist's task is to find out how well the production and distribution of goods and services conform to the public's wishes. The first thing to ascertain in this connection is what the public's wishes are. In the realm of private goods, economists have succeeded fairly well in doing this. The main function of the theory of consumers' demand is to deduce from consumers' market behaviour what their preferences are; we have even renamed it the theory of revealed preference to remind ourselves and our students of this fact. But while a lot of theoretical speculation and empirical work has been devoted to the private sector of the economy, the public sector is very much neglected. Some economists are ideologically opposed even to the very existence of a public sector; and they, of course, have a fine excuse for not dealing with the subject. The rest of us have no such excuse. Collective goods, provided and paid for through the public sector, are increasing in importance; but economists have done very little work on the subject, although there are plenty of problems, plenty of work to be done. It would be desirable to develop some machinery for ascertaining what the public's preferences are concerning collective goods, machinery for making these preferences known to those who decide on public expenditures, machinery to assure efficiency, adequate resource allocation, and the minimization of costs in the public sector. I believe that some of the most urgent and most important work of the economist lies in this field.

It would be desirable to know something about the public's preferences concerning the distribution of income and wealth—a collective good similar in essentials to such other collective goods as public transportation, state parks and national defence. All collective goods have a common feature that distinguishes them from private goods and consists in their

3

inability to accommodate personal differences in tastes. In the realm of private goods, the market enables one man to drink whisky while another drinks tea, but collective goods do not and cannot cater to personal idiosyncrasies. Your national defence is my national defence; your public transportation is also my public transportation. Existing bus routes and schedules may favour your special needs more than they favour mine; but we share the same transportation system and there is no way of catering simultaneously to my preference and your distaste for buses.

The same way with distribution. Some people are in more fortunate financial circumstances than others; but we share the same degree of inequality of distribution and the same principles on which income and wealth are distributed. If the system of distribution is to conform to the public's preferences, it must conform to a consensus or to a compromise between different preferences. I propose to examine the nature of this consensus, or compromise, or mixture of consensus and compromise, and chose the title equity because it seems to stand for some minimum degree of equality people would like to see realized and on the nature of which they might be able to agree.

It is no accident that the English word equity comes from *equus,* Latin for equal. By equity people mean, if not equality, at least something that approximates it closely enough to satisfy them. The public is satisfied with something short of equality, partly, perhaps, because it is resigned to this being an imperfect world, and partly also because it recognizes the impracticability of perfect equality. The latter is unattainable as long as we need to provide economic incentive to produce the national product. Most of us believe that economic incentives are superior to most other incentives, such as coercion, or social pressure, or the threat of physical punishment; and society needs some incentive as long as the national product it wants is greater than what can be produced with the amount and kind of work the public regards and performs as play. While this has always been so, it need not remain so if automation goes very much further. Karl Marx's motto for Communism: 'From each according to his abilities, to each according to his needs', could describe a future economy of plenty, in which a puritanical limitation and satiability of wants coincides with so great an increase in the productive efficiency of work that the setting-up exercises of society, the tinkering of hobbyists with science, and the social services supplied by the young matrons of the junior league would be the only human inputs needed in an otherwise fully automated economy.

For the time being, we are far removed from such an economy; and with all the effort devoted to the creation of new wants we may never reach it. We still need incentive to get the national product produced, most of us prefer economic to other incentives, and economic inequality is the price of having an economic incentive.

When the economist realizes that inequality is the price of obtaining the national product, he instinctively asks: how much national product for how much inequality? Is there an optimum point at which the marginal increment of national product just equals the marginal increment of inequality? The answer, for the time being, is no. We do not even know as yet whether, and if so by how much, progressive taxation lowers incentive; even less do we know the price of a dollar's worth of national product in terms of inequality; and, as I have argued, we have yet to devise machinery whereby consumers or citizens could express their preferences between a small addition to income and a slight easing of conscience over the inequality of man.

For the time being, all one can do is to guess at the public's feelings concerning equity. Differences of degree are obviously important here. The public will resent inequalities of income and wealth that are too great; and while it is hard to find the dividing line between what is and what is not too great, one can say something about the factors that determine the location of this dividing line. For one thing, society is more likely to tolerate inequalities if these are correlated with merit or people's contribution to society and its values. For another, inequalities are more acceptable to a person who feels that he has equal chances with others of reaching the top. Hence people's strong feeling against discrimination, the provision of free education in our society, and John Stuart Mill's advocacy of confiscatory (100 per cent) inheritance taxes. A third factor is the well being of those at the bottom of the ladder. The public will the more easily tolerate inequalities, the better off are those least favoured, the more nearly they are assured of subsistence and provided with the necessities of life. In the following, I shall concentrate on this last factor and neglect the first two, discussing only the relation between equity and the distribution of the necessities of life. Indeed, to simplify the argument, I shall not only hold constant the first two factors but pretend they are not there. In other words, I shall pretend that equity (that is, the acceptance as equitable of a given distribution of income and wealth) depends solely on the availability and distribution of the necessities of life—admittedly an over-simplification but a useful one.[1]

In this connection it is helpful first of all to ascertain how goods and services are actually distributed under the market mechanism. The distribution of income and wealth determines the consumer's share in the consumable national product; his freedom of choice enables him to obtain his share in that combination of goods and services which gives him the greatest satisfaction. In other words, the market distributes goods and services in accordance partly with people's tastes and needs, partly with the distribution of purchasing power among them. It follows that if everybody's purchasing power were equal, the distribution of each commodity would be egalitarian (by which I mean equal except for differences in tastes and needs); but it does not follow that if people's tastes and needs were identical, each commodity would be distributed uniformly with the distribution of purchasing power. For man's need of necessities is biologically limited and therefore much sooner and more abruptly saturated than his demand for luxuries. An unequal distribution of purchasing power therefore causes different commodities to be distributed very differently, ranging from the egalitarian or near-egalitarian distribution of the cheaper necessities to a distribution of the more expensive luxuries that is likely to be much more unequal than the distribution of income and wealth. The distribution of the cheaper forms of food is virtually egalitarian in a rich country like the United States; and the distribution of most necessities is much less unequal than the distribution of income and wealth. Similarly, the amounts spent on necessities by the rich and by the poor also differ less than the income and wealth available to them; and this implies that what they have left over to save, and to spend on luxuries, must differ by more.

We are now ready to attempt a tentative definition of equity. Public opinion seems to be very much concerned with the distribution of necessities; and the first dictate of people's consciences is that the prime necessities of life should be generally available and distributed in an egalitarian way. Even great inequalities of income and wealth will not be considered oppressive as long as necessities are cheap and plentiful enough to be generally available; whereas slight inequalities of income may be considered unjust if one or more necessities are short—that is, scarce and expensive enough to become the privilege of the well to do. Different people's lists of necessities differ, of course, in both length and composition; but, bearing these differences in mind, one can say that most people consider equitable an economic system or economic organization that leads to an egalitarian or near-egalitarian distribution of the necessities of life.[2] Once this definition is accepted, one can distinguish degrees of equity according to the number of necessities distributed in an egalitarian way; and one can define social progress or progress in equity as an increase in the number of necessities available to all on an egalitarian basis.

These definitions of equity and social progress have a number of interesting implications. To begin with, one must note the absence of any simple one-to-one correspondence between the degree of equity and the inequality of distribution of income and wealth. Given the total income of an economy and given the relative scarcities of different resources and commodities, equity will increase with a lessening of the inequalities of income or wealth; but there are other ways of increasing equity too. For example, given an unchanging distribution of income and wealth, equity will usually increase with a rise in *per capita* income. Indeed, this latter is probably the main source of social progress in our society. Inequalities of income and wealth are probably no greater in the countries of southern Europe than they are in the United States; and if in those countries inequities between the well-fed rich and the starving poor seem greater than in the United States, this is mainly due to the fact that the same inequality of income distribution creates greater inequities when incomes are low than when they are high.

Another peculiarity of our definition of equity is that not only does it depend on the absolute level of income as well as on its distribution, it also depends on yet a third factor, the relative scarcity or cost of production of different goods. Other things being equal, more equity results if necessities are cheap than if it is luxuries whose cost of production is low in relation to that of necessities.

To appreciate the importance of this last factor, it is useful to examine first of all a situation which public opinion regards as inequitable. Such a situation exists when some goods the public would like to see generally accessible are too expensive to become generally accessible, given the inequality of wealth and income. Such a situation can be remedied in either of two ways. One is to reduce the inequality of wealth and income distribution through progressive taxation and death duties. The other is to take the necessities whose unequal distribution through the market mechanism public opinion resents and to distribute them in an egalitarian way outside of the market mechanism.

The first is the obvious, natural and most efficient way; but it is also likely to be the less feasible politically. For a very far-reaching reduction of monetary inequalities may be necessary to assure the egalitarian distribution even of a single necessity if this is expensive and scarce in relation to demand. The second way is by far the less drastic, by far the less revolutionary whenever the number of such necessities is small. Hence the many examples in free enterprise economies of the egalitarian distribution of necessities more or less outside of the market system. Wartime rationing of food, clothing, petrol, etc., is one example.[3] Public education, provided free and paid for out of taxation, is another. Such distribution, however, is often inefficient or administratively cumbersome—problems I shall return to presently.

For the time being, let us look at the subject in the context of secular change and economic development. Development means a rise in incomes; and as incomes rise the public feels that it can afford more equity and usually wants to spend part of its additional income on increased equity. In other words, development increases the *demand* for equity.

At the same time, development may but need not increase also the *supply* of equity. The rise in incomes stems from technological progress, which may lower the cost, improve the quality, or extend the range of the goods and services available. But only when it lowers costs and lowers the costs of necessities, actual or potential, only then does technical progress automatically involve social progress as well.

It so happens that most of America's early contribution to technical progress was precisely of this nature. We made modest contributions to the advance of knowledge—most scientific breakthroughs were of European origin—but we made a large contribution to the simplification of products and improvement of manufacturing methods calculated to make possible mass production at low cost. This, more than anything else, explains why, in the half-century before World War II, America was regarded as the land of the common man and American civilization as the civilization favouring the common man. Our standard of living rose, because more and more necessities, and goods coming to be considered necessities, became cheap and generally available; and this meant social progress hand-in-hand with the rise in incomes.

Such development satisfies more or less the public's wish to obtain part of its additional income in the form of increased equity; but it is not the only form that economic development can take. Indeed, it is likely that since World War II, economic development in most Western countries has taken a different form, involving a rise in incomes with little or no increase in equity.

This latter kind of development results from the cheapening or improvement of luxuries, while some important necessities remain high or even rise in price. An important feature of post-war economic growth in the West has been the reduced cost and increased availability of kitchen appliances and other consumers' durables.[4] Although public opinion is gradually reclassifying many of these from luxuries to necessities, they cater to less urgent and less essential needs than do some personal services whose accessibility to the masses has increased little, if at all. When development takes this form, the public may well be dissatisfied with its course and demand that additional necessities be made available outside the market system on an egalitarian basis. The main example is the demand for free medical care. The growing demand for comprehensive national health service or insurance has been voiced in most advanced countries since the war; and you may well ask why. After all, real *per capita* income has been growing in all these countries at a very fast rate; more people than ever before can afford to *pay* for medical care as a result; why, at such a time, should the public be impatient with the progress already made and demand socialized medicine? There may be many reasons, but one of the most important is the one mentioned above. The public seems impatient that the post-war rise in incomes was accompanied by less social progress than it had hoped for or anticipated on the basis of past experience. As though society would resent the kind of economic progress that puts a second car in every garage sooner than it makes available medical care for all.

Another and similar example of this newly arising demand for the free and egalitarian distribution of necessities not generally available before is the move, in the United States, for establishing the Office of Public Defender. This would provide the funds to finance and the attorneys to conduct the legal defence of those accused of certain crimes, and thereby give the full protection of the law to many who hitherto have not been able to afford that expensive commodity.

Yet another attempt at increasing equity through public action is the campaign of Governor Brown of the State of California to abolish the death penalty. For life is a necessity of life, and one which should be equitably distributed; whereas evidence shows that all inhabitants of death row come from low-income groups, and that the well-to-do can get away with murder—at least to the extent of escaping the death penalty.[5]

One more good that is coming to be considered a necessity that ought to be available to all is the assurance for one's old age of a standard of living commensurate to that achieved during one's active life. For a variety of reasons, this good is not likely to become generally available through the market mechanism and will probably have to be provided collectively. One reason is that its cost is likely to remain high or even rise, partly because life expectancy is on the increase and partly because the aged, often lonely and subject to chronic illness, require more than their proportionate share of personal services, whose price rises with the secular rise in labour productivity. The second reason is that the price of buying, during one's active life, a given standard of living for one's old age is greatly dependent on two unpredictable factors: one's time of death and the cost of living during one's old age. One can insure against the uncertainty of the first by buying a retirement or pension policy, against the uncertainty of the second by putting one's savings into a diversified portfolio of common stock; one can divide one's savings between the two; but one cannot insure against both risks simultaneously. This means that one cannot buy in the market a financially secure old age at a predetermined price; only the State can insure fully against the double hazard of rising prices and a long life.[6]

All the above examples illustrate the same point, which is the following: the secular rise in the standard of living lengthens the list of goods society regards as necessities and wants to have distributed in an egalitarian way; and, as this list becomes longer, it includes an increasing number of goods whose egalitarian distribution cannot be accomplished by the pricing system in the private sector and will therefore have to be effected outside of the market mechanism. Hence my prediction that future social progress (increase in equity) will probably have to be implemented by the public sector to a greater extent than was the case with past social progress. The same point is implied by much of J. K. Galbraith's argument in *The Affluent Society,* and also by the deliberate bias in France's last (fourth) Modernization and Equipment Plan toward increasing investment in collective services rather than in the private sector.

Having discussed the motives for and the likelihood of the future transfer of some services from the private to the public sector of the economy, it may be fitting to end with a reminder of the possibility of shifts also in the opposite direction, prompted by the already mentioned inefficiency and cumbersomeness of distribution outside of the market mechanism. Goods and services paid out of taxes and made available free will be equitably distributed but are also likely to involve inefficient resource allocation. This is so because the demand for free goods is filled to saturation, which necessitates an undue diversion of scarce resources from goods that are not available free. The resulting loss of welfare may be a small price well worth paying for the equitable distribution of services whose social cost is low and the demand for which is quickly saturated. On the other hand, the free availability of services that do not meet these conditions may lead to resource misallocation too costly to be tolerated; and, in such cases, ways must be found of restricting consumption without making distribution inequitable. Demand for free education is restricted (though perhaps not sufficiently) by making access to higher education conditional upon certain minimum achievement at lower levels. In the case of free medical care British experience has shown that, after an initial period of transition, the physician's sensible attitude can restrain his patients from taking up his time and using his services for every trifle. Wartime rationing is another example of circumventing the market for the sake of equity and yet restricting consumption at the same time. This was accomplished partly by the administratively enforced equal distribution of specific commodities, partly by the issuance and equal distribution of a ration currency to circulate side by side with money.[7] The last-mentioned is in many ways the best way of achieving both equity and efficiency but is far too cumbersome to be tolerated except under the stress of war. For peacetime use, no solution has yet been developed (apart from the two examples mentioned), although the need is likely to become more pressing. One reason for this is the increasing density of population.

The increased density of population and its higher standard of living mean that more and more people crowd in upon each other, generating ever larger quantities of noise, exhaust fumes and debris on their way. As a result, many amenities that used to be either naturally free or provided free by government are in the process of being rendered scarce and expensive. Highways, metropolitan thoroughfares, unpolluted water, smogless air, places where man can commune undisturbed with nature are examples. To discuss just one of these, estimates of what city traffic will be twenty-five years from now in this country are totally incompatible not only with the nature but with the very concept of present-day cities. To solve the resulting problem, Professor Vickrey would restrict the use of city streets by charging a price for it—just as he would use prices for solving many similar problems in other areas as well.[8] To reject such proposals as utopian shows a lack of imagination and inability to realize that we are entering a new world in which many of the good things in life we now take for granted and regard as part of nature will become carefully husbanded commodities whose use or consumption must be rationed. The only question is whether rationing them by price would not create problems of equity and whether it would not be preferable therefore to develop other means of rationing free from this objection.

Society is bound to insist on the equitable distribution of goods that were once free; and the larger the number of such goods to be rationed by price, and the greater their scarcity, the smaller the likelihood that the market will distribute them equitably. Indeed, bringing hitherto free goods or amenities into the realm of the pricing system has the opposite effect on the degree of equity from that of a rise in real incomes. To prevent a retrogression in equity therefore, hitherto free goods may have to be rationed through means other and more equitable than the pricing system. I have no new general principle to suggest; and *ad hoc* methods with no overall principle may well be the best solution. An example, additional to those already mentioned, may be worth discussing.

Consider a country or region in which unspoilt nature is getting scarce. As more and more people seek the great outdoors, the time will come when nature cannot both be free and remain unspoilt. The present tendency is for the State to hasten the spoiling of nature by providing better and wider roads, more and faster transportation; for society still believes in man's natural right to the free enjoyment of nature and the State's duty to fill to saturation the public's demand for highway capacity. But should people come to believe that free access to nature is not the better alternative and wish to ration it rather than letting it be spoiled, they would have the choice of either charging an entrance fee to nature or limiting access through narrow, winding or rough roads. The first would be efficient but inequitable if the fee had to be high in order to be effective. The second would limit access to nature to those who value it highly enough to put up with the inconvenience of a long or difficult drive; and while this too can create inequities (e.g. it discriminates in favour of good drivers and people with much time on their hands), these are likely to be less resented than those created by the inequality of income and wealth distribution. More problematic is society's willingness to tolerate unsatisfactory roads as a rationing device. Yet, we may increasingly be forced to accept and learn to live with such *ad hoc* methods of restraint on our freedom to consume if increasing population and its increasing affluence reduce our elbow room much further.

NOTES

1.   The argument of this paragraph owes much to comments of my friends, Professors R. Radner and H. Leibenstein.
2.   This is admittedly a partial and incomplete definition, as pointed out in the last but one paragraph.
3.   Cf. my 'The political economy of consumer rationing', *Review of Economic Statistics,* (1942) Vol. 24, pp 114 – 24, for a detailed discussion of this case.
4.   The effect on farm prices of the even greater increases in agricultural productivity has been largely offset by public policies aimed at protecting the farmer by maintaining farm prices.
5.   Cf. Clinton T. Duffy, *88 Men and 2 Women,* (Garden City, NY: Doubleday, 1962), Ch.23; Edward B. Williams, *One Man's Freedom,* (New York: Atheneum, 1962), Ch.14.
6.   The reason why insurance companies cannot insure against changes in the cost of living should be obvious. At the same time, they ought to be able to sell retirement policies tied, if not to the consumers' price index, at least to some stock index.
7.   Cf. my 'The political economy of consumer rationing' *op. cit.*
8.   Cf. William S. Vickrey, 'Pricing urban and suburban transport', *American Economic Review* (PROCEEDINGS), (1963), Vol 53, pp. 452 – 65.

2 The Place of Economic Welfare in Human Welfare—1973*

Economics deals, or pretends to deal, with that most important and difficult human problem, the satisfaction of man; and the problem is rendered no simpler by our interpreting it to embrace also the satisfaction of woman. In their more modest and sober moments, economists will concede that they deal only with a part of human welfare, known as economic welfare. Strangely enough, this has not simplified the problem as much as might be expected, because economists are still held responsible for drawing the borderline at which economic welfare ends and non-economic or meta-economic welfare begins; and they are also expected to justify the way they draw the borderline and to say something about the relationship between economic welfare and human welfare.

We do have a classic and classically simple definition of economic welfare, which comes from Pigou. According to him, economic welfare is that part of welfare that can be brought into relation with the measuring rod of money. This is a fine definition for the statistician who wants to measure and finds it easiest to measure in terms of money; but it is not very helpful for the economist when he seeks to justify the segmenting of welfare and explain the relation of the segments to the whole. Someone must once have had the grandiose idea of adding together the value of all the products that have been valued. The total was sure to come to an impressively large figure; this was bound to be useful, certain to have something to do with human welfare; and if it had to do only with part of welfare, why not call this part economic welfare?

This may be an oversimplified tale of the origin of GNP; but it is probably quite truthful. To proceed this way had the advantage of imposing on later economists the task of postrationalization, of justifying the distinction between economic and non-economic welfare, of giving it some deeper and economically more relevant meaning, and, if necessary, of shifting the dividing line just a little this way or that in the process.

Once the statistician took the measuring rod of money as the crucial

---

* This article was presented as the David Kinley lecture at the University of Illinois at Urbana-Champaign on 17 May 1973.

13

characteristic, it was natural for the economist to take scarcity as his differentia specifica; but this guess, that economic welfare is that part of total welfare which depends on scarce resources, will not quite do, I am afraid. Scarcity is certainly a necessary but not a sufficient condition. A simple example will show this. Companionship is an important part of human welfare; but it is not considered part of economic welfare, although it is definitely scarce. Witness the loneliness of the aged, which is one of the major unsolved problems of our society, clearly a problem of scarcity but one which seems to persists or even get worse despite our increasing affluence. It seems then that we must look further for the defining characteristics and the true nature of economic welfare.

The subject was widely debated in the nineteenth century, but in an unfortunate form, which generated much bitterness and rather obscured the issue. Some economists on the outer fringe of the profession accused those at the centre, the establishment economists, of dealing only with man's lower instincts and those of his actions motivated by lower instincts, to the exclusion of everything that is noble in man. Unfortunately they did this in a tone that drew blood rather than reasoned counterargument.

Let me quote on this Henry Carey, the early American protectionist. According to him, 'The British School of Economists recognizes not the real man of society but the artificial man of their own system. Their Theory, occupied with the lowest instincts of humanity, treats its noblest interests as mere interpolations of the System'. The economist's '. . . science was that of material wealth alone, to the entire exclusion of the wealth of affection and of intellect . . . the subject of political economy was not really a man, but an imaginary being moved to action by the blindest passion . . .' For a definition of this 'blindest passion', let us turn for a change to Carey's pupil, Robert Thompson. He defines homo oeconomicus, economic man, as 'a covetous machine inspired to action only by avarice and the desire of progress . . . they (by which he means the classical economists) cut away or stole away the better half of the real being, and persisted in treating the remaining human fragment (if we can call it human) as a living reality'.[1]

Needless to say, establishment economists did not take this lying down, which is all right. But neither did they take it calmly, which is a pity. To argue that such accusations were based on a complete misunderstanding of their theory was all right, I suppose; but one cannot help feeling that urged on by such attacks they tended to claim more generality, more all-inclusiveness for their models than they might have claimed otherwise. Whether for this or other reasons, they finally ended up by attributing to the consumer a preference function which was completely general and which would accommodate man's loftiest aspirations and basest desires with equal ease.

This seems to have been victory and the end of the battle, because those early accusations can be heard no more. But then, in mid twentieth century, the attack came from the opposite side. In 1955 Herbert A. Simon attacked the supreme generality of the individual preference function, on the ground that it attributes to the consumer perfect knowledge and infinite and instantaneous computational ability over a wide range of potential decisions—both of them unrealistic and untenable assumptions.

Now I would like to put to you—to you as establishment economists—that you cannot defend the theory against both accusations at the same time. If you insist that the preference function is or must be general enough to embrace all of man's desires, then you make it vulnerable to Simon's criticism. On the other hand, you can protect it from such criticism by lowering your sights and restricting the preference function to a narrow definition of economic welfare which only embraces man's lower desires. Our computational ability seems pretty good when it comes to satisfying those lower desires, because with respect to them, most of us know on which side our bread is buttered. Also as to information, a little more truth-in-lending, truth-in-merchandising, with some assist from Ralph Nader, can do a great deal. But if you do not like either of these alternatives, there is a way out, which is to develop a new and better theory of consumer behaviour. That, obviously, was in Simon's mind; and it is also in my mind. What I would like to do here, however, is merely to indicate the lines along which such a new theory might develop, because it will throw considerable light on where a dividing line might best be drawn between what economists, with their present tools, can deal with and measure, and what seems to be beyond their reach.

I

In this connection, it will be helpful to look for guidance at the psychologist's work on welfare and motivation. After all, he too is concerned with what motivates man's behaviour; and he definitely aims at completeness and tries to provide a theory to explain all behaviour. What is more, the psychologist's approach to human welfare is very much like the economist's, in the sense that he, too, observes behaviour, makes inferences from observed behaviour, and builds up his theory from these inferences. Let me give you therefore a short account of the physiological psychologist's theory of the motivation of behaviour—just enough to relate it to the economist's theory.

The most general such theory, and the one that seems most pertinent to economics, is the one that explains behaviour in terms of arousal. Virtually all needs and desires, biological as well as other needs, are arousing. They raise the arousal level of the nervous system, its alertness, tension, and anxiety. This is a useful and functional reaction, because to satisfy a need or eliminate a discomfort, action is required; and higher arousal usually increases the organism's speed and efficiency in responding to stimuli, deciding on the requisite action, and carrying it out. At the same time, heightened arousal is also the immediate motivation for doing what will satisfy the need, eliminate the cause of heightened arousal, and so bring the arousal level down again. In other words, heightened arousal is unpleasant; and to eliminate it is the proximate cause of action aimed at satisfying needs and desires.

This is about as far as the psychology of behaviour went at the beginning of the century. Even as late as 1915, Sigmund Freud (1925) wrote that:

The nervous system is an apparatus having the function of abolishing stimuli which reach it or of reducing excitation to the lowest possible level; an apparatus which would even, if this were feasible, maintain itself in an altogether unstimulated condition.

This 'unstimulated condition' used to be considered the height of bliss, the perfect satisfaction of all needs and desires. In my mind, it conjures up the picture of a pampered, neutered cat, spending its life yawning or sleeping on the living room sofa. Or if you prefer a human context, it reminds me of a delightful painting in the Kunsthistorisches Museum in Vienna titled *Schlaraffenland* or *Land of Cockaigne* by Brueghel the Younger. This shows a number of full-bellied men sprawling on their backs, too lazy and satiated to move, with roast chickens picking their way among them within easy reach, a knife and fork stuck in their backs for the greater convenience of the men, should a base desire seize them to catch and to eat the chickens.

Psychologists realized long ago that this was only half the story; and only a part of the state of perfect bliss. At the time, however, they believed it to be a complete theory of motivation; and unfortunately, it is this lopsided psychological theory that seems to have been at the origin of the economist's theorizing. For the notion that specific needs raise arousal and that this motivates people to satisfy such needs and so lower arousal fits in very well with the economist's utility function. In contrast, the missing part of the psychologist's theory does not fit in with the economist's utility function at all.

What is this missing part? It gradually became apparent that just as too high an arousal seems unpleasant and motivates action designed to lower it, so too low arousal and too little stimulation are also unpleasant and motivate the seeking of stimulation that will raise arousal and bring it up to some optimal intermediate level. From the psychologist's point of view, this desire for stimulation is a very different kind of thing from the desire to lower too high arousal; and over the past twenty-five years or so, a vast and fascinating literature has emerged, and a wealth of empirical evidence has been collected on the nature, the urgency, and the generality of this need, and on the nature of the sensory inputs that can provide stimulation which is pleasant and desired. There is no time to go into any of this here; but I shall argue that, also from the economist's point of view, the two types of needs and their satisfactions are very different.

To start off, let me point out that the distinction coincides pretty much with the distinction between man's higher and lower desires. After all, the list of sources of stimulation includes the arts, literature, sports, seeing the world, as well as work, artistic creation, exploration, and discovery. Now I shall argue, first, that economists tend to ignore or exclude from consideration some of the main sources of stimulation and stimulus satisfaction, even when it would be natural to include them among the sources of economic welfare. Second, I shall argue that although economists do take into account sources of stimulus satisfaction when these are a by-product of or a package deal with some other need satisfaction, in such cases they would usually be wiser to exclude them because they can lead to some misleading results. Finally, I shall argue that by and large those nineteenth-century critics were more right than wrong and that economics and economists would be better off by acknowledging this.

One source of stimulus satisfaction that is not considered part of economic welfare is one I mentioned right at the beginning: companionship. Economists wash their hands of it, because usually no money changes hands; and the reason for that is that the satisfaction I give my companion pays, so to speak, for the satisfaction she gives me. There is mutual stimulation, mutual satisfaction, and no need for an economic contract.

Take next a slightly, but only very slightly, different example: work. I am going to be paid for this lecture, because it gives satisfaction to the audience but frankly, I enjoy lecturing and would not have accepted the invitation to come here if I did not. Now what is the satisfaction I get out of my lecturing? It is part of my payment for services rendered; it is satisfaction derived from an economic activity, yet it is not included in economic welfare. It does not enter into the national product accounts; the economist's customary models of individual behaviour make no provision for it. Yet I am not that exceptional. There are many people who get satisfaction out of their work.

I might mention one economist who did not ignore this satisfaction but included it in economic welfare, and that was Karl Marx. As you know, he was very much concerned about alienation, which to him meant primarily those changes in the nature and conditions of work that took the enjoyment out of it and turned it into a chore, performed only for the sake of pay. Was it Marx's stress on the subject that made modern economics ignore it so completely? There is a great quantity and variety of statistical evidence to show that the marginal satisfaction from work is very different for different professions and groups of people; some of the evidence suggests a difference not only in quantity but also in sign—a positive marginal utility from work for some, a marginal disutility for others. The evidence also shows that these differences are positively correlated with income differences, which suggests that inequalities in our society may be much greater than we think they are. Our statistics of the unequal distribution of income may be only the visible tip of the iceberg.

So much for the sources of stimulus satisfaction customarily ignored by the economist. How about my next topic, stimulus satisfaction that is a joint product with some other need satisfaction and therefore included by the economist in economic welfare? As you know, we infer the shape of the consumer's utility function from his preferences as revealed in the market place. This is known as the theory of revealed preference. For example, I understand that over the past few weeks, there has been a great rise in the sales of *Newsweek, Time,* and the *Washington Post,* and a lesser but still noticeable rise in the circulation of almost every newspaper in the country. It takes no sophisticated econometric study to find out why.[2] On the basis of the theory of revealed preference, we must infer that the American public wants, and gets satisfaction from, criminal activity and suspicion of criminal activity by members of the White House—the more satisfaction presumably, the more criminal the activity and the greater the number of people involved.

You may be revolted by the very idea and may think that I am mixing up a desire for the reporting of acts with a desire for the acts themselves, or a desire for sensational news with a desire for the contents of that news—and of course you will be quite right. But note that you are able to make these distinctions only because I chose a political and not an economic example, and in politics you have, or think you have, additional and independent knowledge of the public's desires and standards. In the realm of economics, we usually have no information other than what revealed preference reveals; and even if we have non-market information, we are not supposed to use it lest we violate consumers' sovereignty.

Another example, this time an economic one, has to do with consumers' durables, which as you know are mainly automobiles. They are thought of as providing a flow of services, a flow of comfort and convenience, if you like. But they also provide something else. Thanks to constant model changes and style changes, the latest models also provide the pleasant stimulation of novelty. They are new gadgets to play with, to show off, and to enjoy. This aspect of durable goods, of course, is definitely non-durable, because the attraction and stimulation of novelty wears off rather quickly. On the basis of the Fisher − Griliches − Kaysen study (1962) of the cost of model changes in the automobile industry, one can estimate the economic cost of such stimulus satisfaction. It comes to almost two-thirds of our total expenditure on recreation and to about 30 per cent of the imputed service flow from our stock of consumers' durables.

This is very costly entertainment, however you look at it; and it raises all sorts of questions. Orthodox economics is no help at all in dealing with these questions; it closes its eyes to the whole issue and pretends it does not exist. Radical economists at least acknowledge its existence; but they blame advertisers or the capitalist system for squandering society's resources on the expensive frivolity of model changes and tricking consumers into footing the bill—not realizing that the consumer is a quite willing victim and that his demand for frivolity, novelty, or stimulus satisfaction is no less urgent and no less legitimate than is his demand for automobile transportation. The issue is not that consumers get and have to pay for something they do not want; it is rather, that various pressures push them into filling one of their needs in a very expensive way.

These two very different examples show the same thing, which is that our customary, uncritical, and unanalytic acceptance of revealed preference in the interests of defending consumers' sovereignty can lead us into all sorts of troubles and leave unresolved problems, which are definitely economic problems, but which the economist cannot deal with, because he lacks the tools to deal with them.

My examples were also meant to show how unsuited traditional economics is for dealing with man's desire for stimulation and with the satisfaction he gets from stimulation. Two of the examples, the satisfaction of work and the pleasures of having a new car or appliance for a toy, do seem to have something to do with economic welfare—one should certainly like to put a value on them, to include them if possible, and to include them separately in our national product estimates, and at the very least to deal with them analytically in our models. But somehow they are very elusive; and you may well wonder why.

I have already mentioned one reason: the fact that much, perhaps most, stimulation is mutual. Conversation, argument, making love, playing games, and all the many other forms of personal interaction are probably the main sources of human satisfaction; and it is their mutuality that keeps them out of the market, away from the measuring rod of money, and so beyond the economist's reach. When the mutuality is very lopsided and one person gets much less out of it than the other or the others combined, then they may be forced and willing to pay and he may be willing to prostitute himself and play partly for pay, partly for fun.

Economics clearly enters in this case but in a very unsatisfactory way, because the economist still cannot deal with the mutual part of the transaction, since he cannot put a price on the satisfaction of the person who, in addition to getting paid, also gets satisfaction. Perhaps the newly fashionable awareness of work satisfaction will stimulate attempts to put numerical estimates on its value—but no market valuations, that is, no prices emerge from market transactions.

The second reason has to do with a dimensional difference between stimulus satisfaction on the one hand and all other satisfactions on the other hand. Psychologists have done a lot of experimental work on the sources of stimulation and have found that it is novelty, variety, change, surprisingness, and unexpectedness that is stimulating. This is a very inadequate and crude way of putting it. Let me assure you that their work is much more scientific and above all more quantitative than you may gather from this one-sentence account.

Now the peculiarity of novelty as a source of stimulation lies in its being a one-shot affair. This is obvious when you think of it. After all, novelty wears off and ceases to be new with repetition. I have mentioned already that a car yields a steady flow of comfort but only a short-lived, one-shot dose of stimulus satisfaction. To secure a steady flow of 'automotive stimulus enjoyment' it would be necessary to have a steady rate of growth of our per capita stock of motor vehicles or its continuous rejuvenation with newer and newer models, or both. You seem to get the same dimensional difference, the difference between a stock and a flow, whenever comfort and stimulation are joint products—and they very often are joint products. One important reason that they so often are joint products is that any addition to one's comforts, any rise in one's standard of living provides a pleasant feeling of change and novelty, which soon wears off, of course, and probably leaves one bored as soon as the new increment to one's comfort has become routine.

This dimensional difference between the novelty and the convenience, or the stimulus and the comfort aspects of many of the goods and services we consume, coupled with the fact that the two aspects usually come in a package deal, makes it impossible to identify or separate them in our national product estimates. Yet the dimensional difference makes it essential to keep them separate. For if my argument is right, it means that part of welfare depends on the rate of flow of the economic output and another part of welfare depends of the rate of growth of that flow and the rate of qualitative change in that flow.

II

These are some of the problems with the national income accounts if we want to use them as an index of welfare. Before continuing with this subject, let me also point out what kind of problems stimulus satisfaction creates for our theory of consumer behaviour and our customary individual preference function.

This is very much a static concept. We usually assume unchanged tastes over time and set great store by the consistency and transitivity of the individual's preference function. One of the only two experiments economists ever perform is perpetrated on graduate students and is designed to prove the transitivity of their preferences. They are exposed to a number of pairwise choice situations, are asked to make a choice in each, and so reveal their preferences; and then their successive choices are compared to see whether they are consistent. If he prefers A over B and B over C, then a well-behaved graduate student, or rather a well-behaved preference function, is supposed to have preference also for A over C. Why anyone should want or expect consumers' preferences to be consistent and transitive has always been a puzzle to me. Perhaps it seemed the only test of consumer rationality, or the only proof that consumers' behaviour is not random; but this surely is wrong. For this static, transitive preference function is at complete loggerheads with man's desire for stimulation. To show this, let me tell you about one of the psychologist's most frequently performed experiments (Dember, 1961), the so-called alternation experiment. This has been used, and is still being used, to demonstrate that the desire for stimulation, for novelty, and for variety is a basic desire not only of man but of every organism that is endowed with a central nervous system. The experiment consists in introducing an animal a large number of times into a T-shaped maze at the foot of the T and observing which way it goes or crawls in successive runs. It has been performed with every conceivable animal you might name, down to the cockroach and even the earthworm; and all of them alternate between the left and the right arm of the maze significantly more often than they would if their behaviour were random. The experiment has many variants, including one designed to test whether such alternating behaviour might not be due to the temporary fatigue of the nerve cells involved in turning one way. The result of that experiment was negative; and now, one of the most firmly established results of psychology is that what all the animals seek, and what they reveal a preference for, is variety and novelty, if only the very limited and short-term novelty the situation offers. I bring this up, because it goes so utterly and completely counter to the economist's very static notions of revealed preference.

III

Now it should be possible to reform our theory of consumer behaviour—make it more dynamic, able to deal with the kind and variety of satisfactions I have discussed. But where does all this leave the relationship between human welfare and economic welfare, or more pertinently perhaps, the relationship between human welfare and the economic indicators of welfare? I have already mentioned some problems in the use of national product estimates; are there any others and how can one deal with them? National account statisticians have long been aware, of course, of some of these problems and have always warned against the use of national product or income estimates as an index of welfare. But since mankind is desperately anxious to have an index of welfare, such warnings have always fallen on deaf ears. There is no choice therefore but to try to improve these estimates and make them more suitable for a welfare index, or to make very explicit what kind of limited welfare the estimates do measure, or to do both.

The job of trying to fix up the national product estimates and convert them into a reasonable index of welfare has been attempted by William D. Nordhaus and James Tobin (1972). They excluded most of the goods which on closer inspection turn our to be bads, and which they call 'regrettables'; they excluded from the government account some intermediate services and tried to make the concept more nearly *net;* they made a very ingenious correction for the disamenities of pollution and urban life; and they also subtracted the part of net investment necessary to keep unchanged the standard of living despite the growth in population. They then proceeded to add a couple of items: the value of services that do not go through the market but resemble those that do and therefore are measurable though not actually measured; and they also added in leisure, though valued, in my opinion, the wrong way. They also make a few other minor changes. The series so obtained they called MEW, for measure of economic welfare. Paul A. Samuelson, reporting on the operation in *Newsweek,* rechristened it NEW, for net economic welfare.

This new index is a great improvement over the uncorrected national product estimates and has certainly become a much better index of the volume of creature comforts our economy provides; but it does not and cannot meet any of the objections I have raised. For example, the new welfare index shows a faster rise in welfare than the per capita national product statistics show, mainly because the inclusion of an estimate of leisure enables it to capture the benefits from the secular reduction in the burden of work as the workweek gets shorter. But the index cannot capture reductions in the burden of work through the now so-much-talked-about changes in the nature of work, which aim at making it more challenging, more interesting, more enjoyable. Yet such lightening of the work burden might well turn out to be no less or even more important for people's welfare than the reduction in working hours.

Again, the new measure of economic welfare includes an estimate of the flow of services emanating from the public's stock of consumers' durables, such as TV sets; but it does not and cannot estimate, of course, the flow of the novelty and stimulus content of the programmes offered. Yet this is again every bit as important for human welfare as the convenience of being able to watch from one's own best armchair.

I am pointing all this out, not at all as a criticism of the fine and imaginative job Nordhaus and Tobin have done, but to make you aware of the inevitable limitations of even the economist's best available yardstick of economic welfare. And please bear in mind that these limitations resemble quite closely those that the nineteenth-century critics of establishment economics were talking about. The new index does a much better job capturing the volume of all the things that contribute to comfort, convenience, safety, and freedom from want; and it has become more nearly 'net' than the net national income and product estimates. But it is still a measure of 'gross' economic welfare, because it does not and cannot net out from the value of output the disutility of the work producing it. (Remember that the disutility of work can no more easily be estimated than its satisfactions). Also, it is still just as incomplete and haphazard as national product estimates are in capturing stimulus satisfaction.

IV

To see where all this leaves us, let us compare the Nordhaus – Tobin index, our best available measure of economic welfare, with our best available measure of human welfare. By this last I refer to the many questionnaire surveys of self-rated happiness, which have been conducted both in the United States and abroad. (Easterlin, 1974).

In the United States, ten surveys were made at fairly regular intervals, the first in April 1946, the most recent in December 1970. People were asked to rate their satisfaction with their own lives on a three-point scale, describing themselves as 'very happy', 'fairly happy', or 'not very happy'. In addition they were also asked to give their demographic data including their income.

Not surprisingly, people's self-rated happiness is positively correlated with their income in each of the ten surveys. The samples are large enough; they are carefully randomized; and one's confidence in the data and the significance of the findings is strengthened by the fact that the distributions in the different surveys, conducted by different people and at different dates, are fairly similar. In fact, they are too similar. Over this period of almost twenty-five years, per capita real income rose by 62 per cent, by the Nordhaus – Tobin index, which does not cover the whole period, probably by a little more. Yet the percentage of people who consider themselves very happy, fairly happy, and not too happy has hardly changed at all. Our economic welfare seems to be going up and up but we seem to be no happier as a result. How is one to reconcile this?

Fortunately we economists have a lot of practice in dealing with this kind of seeming contradiction, because saving and spending behaviour in this country shows exactly the same relation between the cross-section and the time-series data; and there is a vast literature and a number of theories to explain it. Let me try, leaning heavily on this spending-behaviour literature, to suggest a few possible explanations of the peculiar behaviour of people's self-rated happiness.

The most obvious explanation would be that one's happiness depends not so much on one's absolute standard of living as on where one stands in the income distribution and how one does in relation to the Joneses next door.

A second explanation might be that much of happiness depends not on income but on a variety of other factors whose availability is correlated with people's *relative* income. If you think of social status and self-respect, then this explanation is not very different, really, from the first explanation. But there are some other factors in addition correlated with relative income. One of these is the amount of satisfaction or dissatisfaction people get out of their work. I mentioned earlier that there is much empirical evidence to show that the marginal satisfaction or dissatisfaction of work is positively correlated with people's standing in the income scale. People with more independence, who are expected to take more initiative and to assume more responsibility, are also better paid; perhaps it is the greater challenge of their work and their greater discretion in doing things their own way that explains also their greater satisfaction. I suspect this may be a very important factor; it certainly would contribute to explaining the peculiar behaviour of the self-rated happiness data.

The third explanation brings us back to what I started out with, the distinction between comfort and stimulus satisfaction. You will remember the stress I put on the dimensional difference between the two—on the fact that the level of comfort satisfaction depends on the level of output, whereas the level of stimulus satisfaction depends on the rate of growth of output and on changes in its nature and quality. I gave you a somewhat primitive example to illustrate this difference; but there is a great deal of evidence of very different types and in many different fields that also bears this out.

Now how can such a difference explain the fact that people's happiness rises with their income as you go across the population from low- to high-income groups, whereas there is no increase in happiness over time? Bear in mind that the high-income groups contain a high proportion of people whose incomes have recently risen, whereas the low-income groups contain a high proportion of those people whose incomes have not risen or even fallen. This means that a preponderance of the people who enjoy much stimulus satisfaction will always be in the higher-income groups, whereas a preponderance of those with little stimulus satisfaction will always be in the lower-income groups—and this quite independently of their absolute levels of income.

I hardly have to point out how speculative all this is. All the explanations are tentative. I can think of a few others not worth mentioning here; there may well be others I know nothing about or that no one has thought of yet; and it is quite impossible at this stage to judge their relative importance. All this merely shows how much work remains to be done in this area; and to me it also indicates the promise of pursuing some of this work along the lines I have suggested, exploring further the psychologists' findings and looking into the economic differences between the production of comfort and the production of stimulus satisfaction. Most of all, however, I hope that this discussion has served to give you perhaps not an answer to the question implied in my title, but at least a better understanding of the issues involved, the difficulties encountered, and of the state of flux in which the subject still finds itself.

NOTES

1.   All these quotes come from Machlup (1972).
2.   The lecture was given at the time of the Senate Committee hearings on Watergate.

REFERENCES

Dember, W.N. 'Alternation behaviour', in Fiske, D.W. and Maddi, S.R., eds., *Functions of Varied Experience* (Homewood: Dorsey Press, 1961), pp. 227-52.
Easterlin, Richard A. 'Does economic growth improve the human lot?' in David, Paul A. and Reder, W.M., eds., *Nations and Households in Economic Growth: Essays in Honor of Moses Abramovitz* (New York: Academic Press, 1974).
Fisher, F.M., Griliches, Zvi and Kaysen, Carl 'The costs of automobile changes since 1949', *Journal of Political Economy,* Vol. 70 (October 1962), pp. 433-51.
Freud, S. *Collected Papers* (London: Hogarth Press, 1925), Vol. 4, p. 63.
Machlup, Fritz 'The universal bogey', in Peston, Maurice and Corry, Bernard, eds., *Essays in Honour of Lord Robbins* (London: Weindenfeld and Nicholson, 1972), pp. 99-117.
Nordhaus, William D. and Tobin, James A. 'Is growth obsolete?, in National Bureau of Economic Research, *Economic Growth,* 50th Anniversary Colloquium V., 1972.
Simon, H.A., 'A behavioral model of rational choice', *Quarterly Journal of Economics,* Vol. 69 (February 1955), pp. 99-118.

3 Inequalities: Open and Hidden, Measured and Unmeasurable—1973

Concern over the inequality of man naturally leads to a desire for a measure or index of inequality; there are only too many of these. In this paper, I will not be concerned with the great array of statistical indicators of varying degrees of sophistication; I will be concerned with the proper choice among a variety of existing statistical data which measure different causes, attributes or consequences of inequality. For example, it is clear that some inequalities are avoidable while others are not; one should focus on those inequalities about which something can be done. Hence, our preoccupation with economic inequalities. But even in the realm of economics, there are many variables. Wealth, income and consumption—to mention merely three—are all unequally distributed; the first much more so than the second; the second, more so than the third. Which of these is the most meaningful?

INEQUALITIES OF INCOME AND CONSUMPTION

Both the man in the street and the economist seem most concerned with inequalities of income, which they usually explain by the unequal distribution of wealth, ability, drive, educational opportunity and luck. If the distributions of these contributing factors overlap only partially, the explanation for the lesser inequalities of income in comparison with the greater inequalities in the distribution of such a causal factor as wealth becomes apparent.[1] The American dream of free and equal educational opportunity for all is an important leveller, as would have been John Stuart Mill's dream of confiscatory inheritance taxes. Therefore, inequalities of wealth and educational opportunity are worth watching, if only to explain inequalities of income.

The difference between inequalities of income and the somewhat lesser inequalities of consumption is explained by some economists as fluctuations in the same person's income—over both his life cycle and short-run changes in luck and employment—for which prudent people are expected to compensate by saving in fat and dissaving in lean, years, thus maintaining a more stable flow of consumption. If this were indeed the explanation, one would opt for the distribution of consumption as the more meaningful and relevant measure of economic inequalities. Why should one worry about differences in income that merely reflect fluctuations over time in the same person's income if such a person can average these out and maintain a steady level of consumption in the face of fluctuating incomes?

Unfortunately, further study and more detailed information are beginning to discredit this explanation. For example, it is contradicted by the finding that many more of the old are poor, and many more of the poor are old, than would be expected if these two conditions were not causally related.[2] We are beginning to realize that maintaining steady consumption, in the face of variations in income and lack of it during old age, is a luxury of the rich alone—and the reason for their high saving out of high income. The poor and the not so rich seem to be spending most of what they can earn throughout their active years even at the height of their prosperity; thus, they are forced to pull in their belts during retirement and times of unemployment. Such improvidence on the part of people who are rather prosperous by most standards—both by those of other countries and by our own earlier standards—is an interesting and puzzling phenomenon which lies outside the scope of this paper.

A high income provides not only high consumption but the assurance of continuing a comparable level of consumption into retirement as well. Lower incomes do not carry a corresponding assurance of a comfortable old age. If this is so, then income distribution does seem more relevant than consumption distribution as an index of economic inequalities. Also, people's great concern about their position on the income scale seems quite independent of the standard of living their income buys. Whether this is so because they consider income a status symbol or a token of society's appreciation of their services is immaterial. As long as income is valued not only for the consumption it yields but for other reasons as well, it is that much better as an index of satisfaction.

Public services
So far, the discussion has dealt with only money incomes received and market goods and services consumed. Welfare, however, even economic welfare, has many other components as well. One of these is public services, available free or below cost and paid by taxation. As a rule, these services are fairly equally distributed; therefore, the greater their importance in total output, the lesser the inequalities of economic welfare. This is an important argument for the public and free provision of services which formerly were private; it is also the reason for believing that

inequalities of welfare are smaller in countries with large public sectors, because inequalities of income are of less consequence. Such thinking also lies behind the heavy subsidies many European countries pay to public transportation, communications, the performing arts and the production of bread. The poor may be deprived of comfort, but should have access to at least the basic nourishments of body and spirit.

In the United States, 45 per cent of total—federal, state and local—public expenditures on goods and services is estimated to provide present or future benefits to the general public. The rest is expenditure on 'regrettables', such as defence, prestige and diplomacy, which make no direct contribution to the welfare of households. These expenditures add 12 per cent to the disposable money income of households—a relatively small addition and a very small mitigating influence on inequalities of income distribution.[3]

While the equal distribution of public amenities may be the rule, there are exceptions, some bad and some good. For example, one of the more depressing aspects of poverty in Harlem is the dirtiness of its streets and the sights and smells of uncollected garbage. The blame lies not so much with the low income or dirty habits of the inhabitants as with the sanitation department of New York City. Although one can hardly accuse the city of discrimination in the distribution of its favours, it does seem that services are provided in proportion to geographical area rather then population density.

Another, and very different, example is the distribution of eligibility for subsidized low-rent housing under the federal housing programme. A recent study shows that those with higher incomes among the eligible groups are clearly favoured, in the sense that they have a better chance of becoming tenants. Once in the programme, however, the poor receive a greater average subsidy.[4]

The opposite type of exception to the rule of equal shares is distribution according to need. From the point of view of social justice, this is clearly preferable to equal distribution. Yet, it is usually impracticable in view of the difficulty of objectively and fairly ascertaining individual differences of need. However, where differences in need are self-evident or ascertainable by objective tests—as in the case of education, medical care and legal representation—distribution of free public services according to need is quite practicable. Indeed, this is one of the strongest arguments in favour of bringing such services into the public sector. Economists tend to be hostile to the provision of free public services as a means of mitigating inequalities on the ground that it is an inefficient means—compared, say, to progressive taxation—because it imposes on the individual a consumption pattern that is generally different from the one which he, himself, would have chosen. The objection is valid, but surely outweighed when the aim is not equality but distribution according to need—which is best accomplished by free distribution on the basis of a separate criterion of need for each of the services so distributed.[5]

Private services
Another, and much more important, component of economic welfare is the unpaid services people perform for each other and themselves. These mitigate inequalities because their distribution typically goes counter to the distribution of bought goods and services. Empirical data show that people in the higher-income groups spend less time doing work around the house and favours for friends and relatives than do those at the lower end of the income scale. The value of such services is estimated to add about one-half to disposable income after taxes.[6] As to their impact on inequality, a 1964 questionnaire study shows that while the poorest and the richest 25 per cent of families earned 6 and 52 per cent of society's money income, respectively, their shares in the sum of money income and the value of non-market services were 10 and 46 per cent, respectively.[7] This indicates a substantial lessening of inequality.

If public services are equally distributed, their value can be added to obtain a further correction of the estimate of inequality. This correction will be very slight, since the value of public services is only about a quarter of the estimated value of non-market services. The estimate is that the poorest quartile of families receives 11 per cent and the richest quartile 44 per cent of the sum of private, public, market and non-market goods and services.

Leisure
Some economists go one step further and add another component, leisure, which is valued at the income given up to enjoy it. Typically, such computations show leisure to be worth one and a half times the disposable money income; its inclusion in the total is believed to reduce inequalities further—although only slightly, because the amount of leisure enjoyed by rich and poor is just about the same, if the involuntary 'leisure' of unemployment is not included. It would appear that some higher providence compensated the poor for their low money income with more generous rations of both non-market services and the enjoyment of leisure.

Government policies
So far, the effects of government policies directly aimed at mitigating inequalities by progressive taxation and by transfer payments such as old age and disability insurance and public assistance—have been ignored. Economists disagree on whether the cumulative effect of all taxes in this country—federal and state income, Social Security, real estate, excise and

sales taxes—is progressive or regressive. The Council of Economic Advisers, in their 1963 Report to the President, estimated it to be regressive; many other economists believe it to be progressive. Excise and sales taxes and Social Security contributions are so regressive that they more than offset the progressivity of income taxes—especially because income taxes contain major loopholes for the very rich. Differences of opinion centre on who ultimately pays real estate and profit taxes. If these really taxed wealth as they were meant to, then the entire tax system would tend to be progressive and to mitigate inequalities. A detailed, careful appraisal of the system and its effects is now in progress at the Brookings Institution. So far, no results are available, and no guesses will be offered here.[8]

Less controversial, and probably more important, are the redistributive effects of transfer payments. It has been estimated that without them the poor would constitute not a fifth, but a quarter, of the total population and not one-third, but two-thirds, of the aged population.[9]

Unfortunately, it is too early to rejoice over the increasingly favourable picture of our economy that these estimates give. First, there is a flaw in the estimation of the value of leisure. Furthermore, this list of items, comprising disposable income, public services, non-market services, leisure and transfer payments, is still incomplete; for, it omits an item which could be as important as all the others combined, but which tends to be overlooked and has defied measurement: the impact of work on satisfaction.

WORK SATISFACTION

Work, the meeting of its challenge and the sense of accomplishment which arises from it are considered the main sources of human satisfaction by at least two philosophical schools: (1) the puritan ethic, to which we are heirs and (2) Marxism, to which much of the rest of the world is heir. Marx's main objection to modern capitalism and the factory system was not that they led to inequalities of income, but that they tended to change the nature, conditions and organization of work in a way which destroyed satisfaction derived from work; thus, it became an unpleasant chore performed only for income and valued only for the product it yielded. This seems to be the original meaning of that fashionable word, alienation.[10] Modern economics seems tacitly to have accepted Marx's view—at least, to judge by its always implying that work is unpleasant and its avoiding the subject.

Work, however, is economic activity; therefore, its direct effect on man's well-being—whose incidence must be considered in a discussion of inequalities—is part of economic welfare, the more so because it is increasingly evident that much can be done to mitigate the unpleasantness of work. There is a wealth of evidence of great differences in different people's attitude to, and satisfaction from, work: less absenteeism among functionaries than among production workers; more unpaid voluntary work performed by the higher, than by the lower, income groups; the failure of near-confiscatory tax rates to dampen the work incentive of professionals; the much longer workweek of independent businessmen, the free professions and higher civil servants than of lowly wage and salary earners; the great secular shrinkage of the latter's workweek in contrast to the complete absence of any such trend among independents and professionals. All such evidence shows (1) that those with more initiative, ◄ more responsibility and more control over what they do and how they do it also find their work more enjoyable and (2) that these are usually the people with the bigger incomes. Such economic data are amply corroborated by questionnaire surveys. Not only are quantitative differences great between different people's marginal satisfaction, or dissatisfaction, from work, there seem to be differences even in sign.

Inequalities of work satisfaction

Such inequalities in the satisfaction, positive and negative, generated by work are quite distinct from the inequalities so far considered; since they are, by and large, positively correlated with inequalities of income, they aggravate measured inequalities. To make matters worse, they also call for a correction of the valuation of leisure and its distribution; for a rational person will so divide his time between work and leisure as to make the satisfaction of the last hour of leisure equal to the sum of satisfactions from the last hour of work performed and income earned. This means that ◄ people who like their work also get more satisfaction out of their leisure than do those for whom work is a chore. Lucky are those who enjoy their work, because they enjoy leisure even more; leisure, for those who consider work a burden, is quite often merely a lesser burden.[11] Since work satisfaction is positively correlated with income—and the amount of leisure available to rich and poor is about the same—one may conclude that the rich are likely to be favoured even in the enjoyment of their free time.

It is now time to take stock and see where we stand. I listed and measured, in very simple terms, the inequality of distribution of the measured and unmeasured but measurable sources of satisfaction. The effects of monetary redistribution on inequality ought also to be measurable; however, one could quote estimates only of the effects of transfer payments—and even of these, not in a form comparable to the other measures of inequality. I then discussed the unmeasurable factors and listed the indirect evidence of inequalities in their distribution, noting that they go the same way as inequalities in the measurable differences. The question is, how great are these unmeasurable inequalities and how important are they compared with the measured and measurable inequalities? On this subject, one can only hazard a guess; I am offering mine with due warning of its subjective personal nature.

Importance of work satisfaction

There seems to be no doubt that differences in different people's work satisfaction can be very great, ranging from the person who hates his job and finds it completely boring and monotonous to the person who enjoys every minute of it. Of course, many people are somewhere in-between, enjoying part of their work but chafing under the dull routine of some of its aspects. What percentage of the labour force constitutes this middle mass and what are the bordering percentages on each side we do not yet know, but the answer may be forthcoming on the basis of the many sample survey studies of work satisfaction and work attitudes now in progress.[12]

More important perhaps, as well as more difficult to answer, is the question of the weight which should be attached to differences in work satisfaction compared with differences in income and in the distribution of the things that money will buy. The puritan tradition of American society stressed work satisfaction and disapproved and discouraged just about all other sources of worldly satisfaction. To what extent are our lives in present-day America still dominated by the puritan ethic and its scale of values? There are many signs that the puritan influence is still strong. We take fewer vacations, spend less time at active sports, seek less entertainment and spend a significantly smaller percentage of our income on recreation than do Europeans; we even pay less heed to the pleasures of food—to judge by the much shorter time we devote to both the eating, and the preparing, of it.[13] Yet, our real income is much higher than theirs, and they often accuse us of being excessively fond of money. A tempting resolution of this seeming contradiction is that we are interested in money income more as a symbol of society's appreciation of our work than for the goods it will buy. The great importance of do-it-yourself activities among our pastimes—the one pastime that most resembles work—and the amount of time we devote to adult education—two thirds of which is aimed at vocational training and imparting production skills[14]—are further evidence of the great importance we attach to our work, its satisfactions and its appreciation by others.

A second piece of evidence is much more direct and to the point. Appendix table A, in Sheppard and Herrick's *Where Have All the Robot's Gone?* (cited in Note 9), shows—for thirty-two different groups, classified by age, sex, marital status, colour, education, income group and occupation—the percentage of workers with negative attitudes toward work and the percentage with negative attitudes toward life. The two percentages are so very close for all thirty-two groups that one cannot help feeling that those who dislike their work are the same people as those who dislike their lives. The text discussion bears this out, but the data to clinch the matter are missing. Also, this is only one of many such studies still in progress; one has to wait and see how the others will confirm, modify or contradict the results of this one.

To conclude, let me mention one more piece of evidence. Over the past twenty-five years, ten sample surveys were conducted in the United States at fairly regular intervals in which the respondents were asked, among other things, to state their income and to rate their satisfaction with their own lives on a three-point scale. As could be expected, the highest proportion of the 'not very happy' were to be found among the poor and the highest proportion of the 'very happy' among the rich. Of the entire population, slightly less than 50 per cent were in the middle group; slightly less than 10 per cent were 'very happy'; and slightly more than 40 per cent were 'not very happy'. Surprising, however, was the finding that this distribution of the population remained amazingly stable over the entire period between 1946 and 1970, although per capita income in real terms rose by 62 per cent.[15]

There are at least three possible explanations of this puzzle. One is that concurrently with the measured rise in our real income, the unmeasurable quality of our lives worsened to an extent that offset that rise. The second explanation is that we are so competitive, so much concerned with matching or outdoing the Joneses, that out happiness depends on our relative position in the income scale rather than on our absolute standard of living. The third explanation is that correlated with the distribution of income there also exist inequalities in some other source of satisfaction, such as the enjoyment of work, inequalities in whose distribution have persisted over time and whose contribution to happiness is much more important than that of income. Needless to add, nothing is ever so simple that a single explanation will adequately explain it.

NOTES

1. Note that Taiwan and South Korea, two developing countries with exceptionally favourable income distributions, almost certainly owe that to the drastic levelling of inequalities in their *wealth* distributions by the expropriation of Japanese colonists and the thorough land reforms carried out at the end of World War II. *See* my 'Economic Development in Taiwan and South Korea: 1965-81'. *Food Research Institute Studies,* Vol. XIX, 1985, pp. 215-64.

2. Almost half the old are poor, although the poor are only one-fifth of the total population; one-third of the poor belong to families whose head is sixty-five or older, although such families constitute only one-sixth of the total population. Compare the chapter on poverty in *The Annual Report of the Council of Economic Advisers* (1964).

3. Compare W. Nordhaus and J. Tobin 'Is growth obsolete?' in National Bureau of Economic Research, *Economic Growth, Fiftieth Anniversary Colloquium V* (New York: Columbia University Press, 1972), Tables A.1 and A.15.

4. Compare E. Smolensky and J.D. Gomery 'Efficiency and equity effects in the benefits from the Federal Housing Program in 1965', in *Benefit Cost Analyses of Federal Programs,* A Joint Economic Committee Print, 92nd Cong., 2nd sess. (Washington DC: Government Printing Office, 2 January 1973).

5. An alternative means of distributing a specific service according to need is insurance. For a rigorous theoretical argument in favour of the free public provision of such services, see the discussion of national health insurance in K.J. Arrow 'Uncertainty and the welfare economics of medical care', *American Economic Review,* Vol. 53 (1963), pp. 941-973.

6. W. Nordhaus and J. Tobin 'Is growth obsolete?' Table 1 gives estimates closer to two-thirds of disposable income; for a probably more reliable estimate, which puts the value of non-market services at 48 per cent of disposable income, see I.A.H. Sirageldin, *Non-Market Components of National Income* (Ann Arbor, Mich.: Institute for Social Research, The University of Michigan, 1969), Tables 4 and 5.

7. Compare Sirageldin *Non-Market Components,* Ch. 4.

8. Since the above was written, the Brookings study has been completed and suggests that the net effect of all taxes combined was slightly, but only slightly progressive in 1966 and has become even less progressive since then. *See* Joseph A. Pechman, Who Paid the Taxes, 1966-85, The Brookings Institute, 1985, Washington DC.

9. Compare B.A. Okner 'Transfer payments: their distribution and role in reducing poverty', *Brookings Institute Reprint 24.* These figures refer to 1966; they show no change from the 1964 data cited in Note 1.

10. Compare E. Fromm *Marx's Concept of Man* (New York: Ungar, 1961); and E.J. West 'The political economy of alienation: Karl Marx and Adam Smith', in *Oxford Economic Papers* (Oxford: Oxford University Press, 1969).

11. That this is a correct inference is strongly suggested by a recent questionnaire survey of work satisfaction which shows a high correlation between workers' negative attitude to work and their negative attitude to life. Compare H.L. Sheppard and N.Q. Herrick *Where Have All The Robots Gone? Worker Dissatisfaction in the 1970s* (New York: Macmillan, 1972), p. 193, appendix table A.

12. The work cited in the last note gives 14 per cent as the proportion of employees with negative attitudes toward work.

13. See Chapter 4 for these and similar data and their sources.

14. Compare the report of the Commission on Nontraditional Study, as reviewed in *Saturday Review of Education* (April 1973), p. 56.

15. Compare R.A. Easterlin 'Does economic growth improve the human lot?' in *Nations and Households in Economic Growth: Essays in Honor of Moses Abramovitz,* ed. P.A. David and M.W. Reder (Palo Alto, Cal.: Stanford University Press, 1974).

Part II
Irrationality in Puritanism

4 What's Wrong with the Arts Is What's Wrong with Society—1972

I believe the arts to be in a bad way in this country. Measured by admissions to live performances of legitimate theatre and music, our art consumption per head is a quarter of Austria's, less than half of West Germany's, little better than a half of Norway's and Switzerland's, and less than a third of such East European countries as Hungary, Czechoslovakia and East Germany (see Table 4. 1). In a cultural centre like San Francisco, the past season's more than 1.8 million admissions are very impressive when related to her 700,000 population—they probably exceed those in any city of comparable size anywhere in the world (see Table 4. 2). But when one remembers our suburban way of life and the fact that San Francisco is the downtown of 4½ million Bay Area residents, then this turns out to be not quite so high a figure, more in keeping with our low national average. The American national average used in these comparisons is very approximate and subject to a wide margin of error; but other indices show much the same disparity. For example, the sale in this country of recorded serious music, at 4 per cent of total record sales, is about a third of the corresponding European ratios: 12 per cent in England and 14 per cent in France and West Germany.[1]

Attempts to blame this situation on the economy have not been too successful. We have many serious economic problems in this country, but failure of the pattern of consumption to conform to consumers' preferences is not among them. If the arts get insufficient attention and insufficient funds, consumers' preferences are mainly to blame and changing them the best remedy.

It is true that our mass production society is biased against minority needs and tastes and that the enjoyment of the arts has usually been the privilege of a small elite. But rather than ask if this small minority gets its due or how it could be made to get it, I propose to raise the larger question of why this minority has remained quite so small in our affluent society; indeed, why it has remained a minority at all.

After all, our standard of living has been rising pretty fast. We have long ago caught up with and left behind Western Europe in affluence. Why aren't we, all of us, members of the elite? The real income of the average

American equals the average real income of the richest two-fifths of Frenchmen, the wealthiest one-fifth of Italians and of the top 3 or 4 per cent of Japanese.[2] If statistics of income distribution were available for the world's 3½ billion population, I daresay that the top decile would contain the vast majority of Americans, perhaps all but the twenty-five million who are on welfare or below the poverty line.

Table 4.1: Annual admissions to theatres and concerts per 100 of population

	Theatres	*Concerts*	*Total*
Austria (1967-8)	66	(22)[a]	(88)
Czechoslovakia (1967)	70	17	87
East Germany (1967-8)	72[b]	12	84
Hungary (1968)	57	15	72
West Germany (1967-8)	44	14	58
Norway (1968)	30	?	?
Switzerland (1968)	28	(13)[a]	(41)
Netherlands (1965)	17[c]	14[c]	31
United States (1970-1)	(16)	(6)[d]	(22)

[a] Concert admissions estimated on the assumption that the ratio of concert to theatre admissions is the same for the country as it is for its largest city for which complete data are available. Probably an underestimate.
[b] Admissions to workers' theatres, not included here, would add another 5 points.
[c] Admissions only to subsidized events and those subject to entertainment tax. Probably an underestimate.
[d] Excludes chamber music groups and solo performers.

Sources: The Statistical Yearbooks of Austria, Czechoslovakia, East Germany, Hungary, Switzerland, the Netherlands; also those of Vienna and Zurich. For West Germany, B. Mewes, "Theater und Orchester 1967/68", in *Statistisches Jahrbuch Deutscher Gemeinden 1969* and F. Harlan, "Konzertstatistik 1968", to be published in the 1972 volume. For Norway, "Innstilling Nr. 40 1970 til Stortinget om Teatervirksomheten i Norge".

The US ratios are based on data for nonprofit performing arts, Broadway, Off Broadway, "the Road", and summer stock, contained in *Economic Aspects of the Performing Arts* (National Endowment of the Arts), *Variety,* June 9, 1971, and T.G. Moore, *The Economics of the American Theatre.*

Money alone does not, of course, make an elite; it also takes education. But in years of schooling received we are again on top of the world—perhaps by an even wider margin.[3] We are, the great majority of us, the world's elite in terms of both income and education; why then don't we have the tastes of an elite? The answer to this question is all the more important because our tastes, as reflected in our consumption and production patterns, are being followed the world over. The fear of Americanization, voiced by so many other countries' elites, is well founded. What then shapes the American taste, how and why is it different from that of other elites?

Table 4.2: Total annual admissions to theatres and concerts in San Fransisco and the average of total annual admissions in Munich and Hamburg

	San Francisco pop. 716,000 Bay Area pop. 4,628,000	Munich-Hamburg av. pop. 1,538,000
Opera	203,500	514,000
Light Opera, Operetta	332,400	226,500
Concerts	457,800[a]	399,000
Theatre, non-profit	308,000	743,000
Theatre, commercial	298,700	810,900
Other[b]	224,700	54,100
Total	1,825,100	2,747,500

[a] Excludes solo performers and visiting chamber music groups.
[b] The S.F. figure is more inclusive and comprises ballet, folk-dance groups. rock concerts, the British Grenadier Band, etc. The M.-H. figure refers exclusively to dance.

Sources: The San Fransisco estimates are my own. I am grateful to the business managers of the Opera, the Symphony, the Northern California Ticketron agency, the several theatres and dance and music groups of San Francisco and to Mr John Kornfeld for supplying the data; and to Mr Martin Snipper for advice. For the Munich-Hamburg data, see German sources cited in Table 4.1. These cities' similar populations and almost identical per capita art admissions render the use of averages meaningful. Unlike San Fransisco, neither is surrounded by separately incorporated bedroom communities.

Our modest interest in the arts can hardly be blamed on a sparing distribution of aesthetic sensibility by providence. It probably has to do instead with the nature of our education and the direction it has taken. From classical Greece to eighteenth century Europe, work and leisure were specialized functions, specialized along class lines. Education was largely the privilege of the leisure class; and this was logical enough, considering that the successful pursuit of leisure and pleasure requires far more learning and a far greater variety of skills than does work. The development of the arts and their appreciation was one result of education mainly aimed at developing the skills and providing the background necessary for the enjoyment of life.

Beginning with the eighteenth century, progress has greatly accelerated and taken a new turn; and in this we had a great share—so much so that America has for long symbolized progress and been called the land of progress. Work and leisure have come to be distributed more equally among men; and we in America laid the economic basis for the better distribution of leisure by developing most of the products and appliances that provide domestic service without domestic servants. Education, too, has ceased to be a privilege and become available to all, but its nature and aims have changed and are still changing. It is increasingly aimed at providing professional training in production skills rather than the general liberal arts education, which provides training in the consumption skills necessary for getting the most out of life. The changing aims of education are responsible for our increased productivity. They also explain the paradox that, as progress frees more and more of our time and energies from work, we are less and less well prepared to employ this free time and energy in the pursuit of an interesting and enjoyable life. Our social engineers are much concerned, and rightly so, that America is acquiring leisure faster than the preparation for using it.[4] What is even more distressing is that we should need to be trained and told what to do with our leisure because our many years of schooling have failed to develop our taste and awaken our interest in the many pleasures that life can offer.

The schools of education are not so much to blame as society at large and its puritan attitude. Our founding fathers did not want to abolish the leisure class, to which most of them belonged, but they did change its attitudes and aspirations. They wanted man to get his main earthly satisfaction from work, with consumption providing merely the necessities and comforts of life. This may have been a workable proposition in the craft society of the eighteenth century; since then, technical and economic progress have rendered most work far too mechanical and fragmented to be enjoyable.[5] Today, only the manual and intellectual arts and crafts and businessman's profession (his profit-maximizing activity) remain challenging and rewarding. For the majority of us, work has ceased to give pleasure and meaning to life and our puritan tradition and education also prevent our seeking them in consumption. We smile condescendingly over the prejudices of eighteenth-century America, which morally disapproved of the theatre and frowned on wasting time and money on sports and the arts. But this is no smiling matter, because our behaviour is still governed by those prejudices. The average American devotes to active sports and exercise one-third of the time the average European does,[6] his visits to theatre and concert hall stand in about the same ratio. Even our relative money expenditure on recreation and amusement is one-third lower than Western Europe's.[7] The arts have become respectable in the United States, but the enjoyment of life has not. We are for Culture, because it is spelled with a capital *C*, not because we derive or know how to derive pleasure from it. The resulting ambivalence is what's wrong with the arts.

We have inherited a deep-seated conviction that the serious business of life is production and the making of money. Consumption, and especially the spending of money, time and effort on the enjoyment of life, we regard as a frivolous and not quite respectable occupation. This is why we eat, not what is good, but what is good for us; go on holidays, not for enjoyment, but to keep the kids busy or give the wife a rest; and buy extra chrome and accessories with our cars, not for the fun of it, but for better resale value.

Keynes rescued the respectability of spending money, if not as a source of enjoyment, at least as a means of stimulating production, employment and profit; but we have never overcome our moral embarrassment over spending time and effort on enjoyment or acquiring the skills of enjoyment. The American consumer has relinquished to the producer all initiative, expertise, even discernment, concerning the taste and quality of most consumers' goods, from the food he eats and clothes he wears to the furnishings around him. He takes a passive attitude to consumption, relying on the seller to supply the know-how and relieve him of the bother. He even takes pride in being an unskilled consumer, above the trifling cares of consumption and able to pay others to supply the skills and do the caring.

The result has been, not a mere transference of tasks from one side of the market to the other, but a complete change in the very nature and content of consumption. For one thing, when the consumer is unskilled and unwilling to exert himself to enjoy and enrich his life, the satisfactions accessible to him become pretty restricted. For another, the producer's intitiative has inevitably led to the stressing of satisfactions whose production yields the greatest economies of scale and to the extension of producer technology into the consumption sphere. Hence the largely defensive nature of our consumption, its focusing on the avoidance of pain, effort, discomfort, boredom, the unknown, and the uncertain. Such seeking of comfort and safety is very different from the active pursuit of pleasure the leisure classes of the past engaged in. Nor is the choice between comfort and pleasure a simple matter of economics imposed by budgetary constraints, except to a limited extent. We shall never be affluent enough to afford both pleasure and comfort, because pleasure depends on the assimilation of novelty, the relief of strain, the resolution of conflict, the understanding of complexity; and one cannot have the pleasure without accepting into the bargain the facing up first to the initial shock. A predictable happy ending or too simple a piece of music is that much the less enjoyable; too great ease or explicitness turns much potential pleasure into mere defence against boredom. The old leisure classes fully understood this and were adventurous enough to take the risks and make that investment of time and effort in the development of mind and body, senses and spirit, so essential for the enjoyment of the good things of life. By contrast, our increasing reluctance to accept discomfort and face the uncertain and the unexpected is increasingly in the way of our obtaining pleasure; and technical progress has completely failed so far to resolve the dilemma. It seems a strange irony of fate that our puritanical rejection of pleasure as the ultimate aim of life should have led to a preference system in which the making of money is the main challenge and effortless, pleasureless comfort the main reward. Adopting such a preference system on the selfish plane can also bedevil one's unselfish actions: our efforts to help the poor among us and in the Third World are bound to be marked by the way in which we help ourselves.

This bias in our preferences is best illustrated by a comparison of our living patterns with Western Europe's, but I can only quote a tiny sample from the wealth of available data. Time budgets, consumer spending surveys, a miscellany of statistics and other information all show that we typically spend less on pleasure and more on safety and comfort than they do; that we usually trade quality of life to save effort or obtain extra safety; and that often we are forced into such tradeoffs by restrictions our authorities impose, supposedly to protect people from their own folly and with never a thought of the pleasure they force people to sacrifice for what often are insignificant increments of safety.

We save half an hour a day on cooking, housecleaning and errands; it is they who spend half an hour more over their meals, presumably because they enjoy them that much the more, while our skimping on the time, effort, and skill needed for good cooking is the secret of the dullness of our food.[8] We have twice as many operations and hold twice the number of life insurance policies than inhabitants of the more affluent countries of Europe;[9] but we go on vacations not even half as often as they do.[10] This latter is especially significant because vacationing depends very much on income. US data show a high income elasticity of demand for vacations; European data show a high rank correlation between countries' standards of living and percentages of adults vacationing. Yet when the United States is compared with Europe, we rank among the poorest European countries, with Portugal and Italy—as though our high standard of comfort and safety were an irreducible minimum, absorbing so much of our income that, measured by what's left over for the enjoyment of life, we seem worse off than many others poorer than we.

Other reasons for our fewer vacationers are our lesser tolerance for the hazards of life away from home and our less good vacation amenities, partly explained in turn by our authorities' lesser tolerance for citizens' taking risks for pleasure. For example, one of the more unreasonable reasons why swimming is so seldom accessible in this country is the extremely high bacterial standards of water purity most states require before they authorize swimming. This is approximately as high as the standard the Public Health Service sets for the milk we drink; a few states set much higher standards than this for swimming and bathing.[11]

I mention these matters, seemingly unrelated to our subject, because the hazards of vacationing and tourism are not so different from the hazard of art and art appreciation and because government's cheerful sacrifice of the citizen's access to nature for the sake of illusory or insignificant increments of safety is part of the same philosophy that lies behind its neglect of the

Table 4.3: Public subsidies to the performing arts and to medical research (current operating expenditures only) in national currencies and as percentages of the GNP

	Performing arts		Medical research	
	in millions	%	in millions	%
United States (1969-70)	$30[a]	0.003	$1,695	0.17
United States (public subsidies plus private contributions from foundations, business and individuals) (1969-70)	$80[b]	0.008	$1,890[d]	0.19
United Kingdom (1970)	£ 6.6[c]	0.015	£ 41	0.09
West Germany (1968)	DM 505.5	0.09	DM 490	0.09
France (1968)	Fr 83.5	0.013	Fr 457.3	0.07
Sweden (1969-70, 1965-6)	Kr 222.6	0.15	Kr 91	0.09
Norway (1968, 1970)	Kr 29.2[e]	0.04	Kr 53.2	0.08

[a] Federal subsidies of $5.5 million were brought to $10.3 million by assuming that the performing arts received half of the $9.6 million grants the States' Arts Council dispensed out of state and federal funds. No data exists on grants from the cities. I assumed these to be twice the combined federal and states' grants.

[b] The income of the 187 major non-profit companies from sources other than ticket sales was $58.7 million. My rounding to $80 million to account for the minor ones may be overgenerous.

[c] Does not include local government support to music.

[d] Does not include drug research by pharmaceutical firms.

[e] Does not include the substantial support from municipalities.

Sources: For medical research expenditures: US, D.P. Rice and B.S. Cooper, 'National Health Expenditure, 1929-70', *Social Security Bulletin,* (Jan. 1971), Table 2, p.6; UK, private communication from Professor B. Abel-Smith, School of Economics, London; West Germany and France, 'Le financement public de la recherche et du développement dans les pays de la communauté' in Office Statistique des Communautés Européennes, *Etudes et Enquêtes Statistiques,* Vol. 2, (1970); Sweden, TCO, *Forskning o Framsteg (1970),* Table 4, p.38; Norway, English Summary of the 1968 report (published in 1970) of the Norwegian Technical Scientific Research Foundation, (1970), p.53.

For subsidies to theatre and music: US, National Endowment for the Arts, *Economic Aspects of the Performing Arts;* UK, The Arts Council of Great Britain, *25th Annual Report, 1969-70;* France, 'Le budget des affaires culturelles depuis 1960', in Ministère des Affaires Culturelles, *Notes d'Information,* (April 1967), p.5; West Germany, B. Mewes, 'Theater und Orchester 1967/68', in *Statistiches Jahrbuch Deutscher Gemeinden 1969,* D. Linkmann, 'Gemeindliche Kulturausgaben 1968', in the 1970 volume and personal correspondence with Dr. Mewes; Sweden, Swedish National Council of Cultural Affairs, *Some Preliminary Facts About the Cultural Expenditures in Sweden,* mimeo 3 May, 1971, Table 1, 8, and Table 4, 22; Norway, see source given in Table 4.1.

arts. The same government, whose $30 million subsidy to the performing arts is a tiny fraction of Western European public subsidies, spends on medical research almost $1.7 billion, which is twice the proportion of the GNP that Britain, France, and West Germany spend on it (see Table 4.3).

I was trying, with these few examples, to establish that the economic difficulties of the arts have more to do with our preferences than with our economy; that our very modest appreciation of the arts is part and parcel of our very modest enjoyment of life; and that our government's miserly attitude towards the arts is again an integral part of a larger collective preference system, which is fully in keeping with consumers' individual preferences as revealed in the market place.

I presented a diagnosis which, if correct, calls for action. If you deplore the neglect of the arts in our midst, you can help matters by whatever means will influence the public's taste. Those of us who would like to see government more generous toward the arts would do well to consider on what basis this can be justified. None of the standard arguments in favour of government financing is really applicable to the arts.[12] They are not a collective good, which could be more cheaply or efficiently provided by government; their subsidizing is not a suitable means for mitigating income inequalities; nor can it be justified on grounds of protecting the interests of future generations. A subsidy to the arts favours the art-loving minority of the present generation; and while something can be said for offsetting the tendency of our economy to discriminate against minority tastes, the argument loses much of its force when one remembers how well-heeled most members of this minority are.

The only valid argument for government aid to the arts is that it is a means of educating the public's taste and that the public would benefit from a more educated taste. It is fashionable to deprecate this argument on the ground that it has often been tried and never with success.[13] Such reasoning, however, is dimensionally false and unduly pessimistic. One cannot expect society to share mortal man's ability to learn once and be the wiser for life. Society, being immortal, must acquire every bit of wisdom at the cost of continuing education. But once one gets the dimensions right and realizes that art education is not a matter of pump priming but a continuous process, then there is plenty of cause for optimism. The arts may be badly off today, but they used to be much worse off in the past. Progress has been enormous and there is no reason why it should not continue. Today's youth is highly critical of its parents' values, probably including those I talked about. They may well be against our putting comfort and safety ahead of pleasure—and not only when this takes the form of young musicians being hauled off the streets for obstructing the sidewalk with baroque music. On the other hand, whether subsidies to the arts will influence their or anybody's tastes depends on how and on what they are spent. The Arts Council of Great Britain has justly been criticised for spending too much on Covent Garden, thus subsidizing the cost of living of high society but gaining few recruits to music. We too tend to favour the safe and comfortable arts and neglect both the experimental and the middlebrow, although all these need equal treatment if we aim not at national prestige but at helping the public to learn to enjoy the arts.

Spreading subsidies broadly is desirable also as a means of maintaining competition and consumers' market pressure to keep prices and costs from skyrocketing. The financing of the arts bears many similarities to the financing of medical care; we must be careful lest the cost of the arts follows the course that the cost of medical care has taken. This, however, having to do with the spending of money not yet available, is one of the problems of the future. For the present, I have made my point. If anything is wrong with the arts, we should seek the cause in ourselves, not in our economy. I am asking you to think about it, and to think about it as consumers rather then economists.

NOTES

1. The US percentage is based on 1970 totals of the dollar value of factory shipments of phonograph records as collected and released by the Recording Industry Association of America in New York. The European percentages were obtained by private communication from the Musical Heritage Society. cf. *Stereo Rev.* for a good discussion.
2. I am grateful to Mr S. Kohlhagen for these estimates, which he based on W. Beckerman and R. Bacon (1966) and on national estimates of personal income distribution by size.
3. The ratio of students enrolled in institutions of higher education to total population was, in 1967, four times as high in the United States as in Western Europe. cf. *UNESCO Statistical Yearbook 1969,* Table 2.12, pp. 257-73.
4. cf. J.C. Charlesworth (1964), ed.
5. For the best, and best-known discussion of this subject, cf. Georges Friedmann, (1964).
6. INSEE's *Etudes et Conjoncture* (1966).
7. In 1968, US expenditures on 'Recreation and entertainment' were 5.6 per cent of total private consumers' expenditures; the corresponding percentage for the *EEC* countries, the UK, Norway, and Sweden combined was 8.0 per cent. cf. *United Nations Yearbook of National Accounts Statistics, 1969,* Table 7 of each country's tables.
8. cf. the items 'Ménage' and 'Repas' in the table cited in note 6 above. The comparison is between the US and the average of the three Western European countries cited.
9. cf. J.P. Bunker, Institute of Life *Insurance,* and *A Survey of Europe Today,* (1970), Tables 12, pp. 70-1.
10. In Western Europe, the proportion of the adult population taking holidays of six days or more in 1967 was 66 per cent in Sweden, 64 per cent in Great Britain, 62 per cent in Switzerland, 49 per cent in France, 28 per cent in Italy; 44 per cent in Western Europe as a whole. In the United States, the proportion of the total population taking trips of six nights or more for reasons other than business, family affairs and attending conventions was, in 1967, 28 per cent. By assuming that half of those giving business, etc., as the main purpose of their trip combined this with a holiday, one raises the proportion of holiday takers to almost 32 per cent. The fact that the European data refer to adults only renders the disparity even greater, since a higher proportion of children than of

adults can be assumed to take vacations. cf. *A Survey of Europe Today,* (1970), Table 42, pp.138-9 and *National Travel Survey,* (1967), Table 8, pp.24.

11. The US Public Health Service sets the greatest permissible number of coliform organisms in pasteurized milk at 1,000 per 100 millilitres. Most states set the same standard, as a monthly average, for water declared suitable for swimming and bathing, although some require much higher standards of water purity. In Utah and Washington, 50, in Maine, 100, in Montana and New Hampshire, 240 coliforms per 100 millilitres on a monthly average are the permissible maxima for water to swim and bathe in. cf. California State Water Quality Control Board (1970).

12. cf. Alan Peacock (1969), where the conflict between the music lover and the good economist strikingly illustrates the truth of my statement.

13. cf. A. Hilton (1971)

REFERENCES

Beckerman, W. and Bacon, R. 'International comparisons of income levels: a suggested new measure', *Economic Journal,* (1966), Vol. 76, pp.519-34.

Bunker, J.P. 'Surgical manpower—a comparison of operations and surgeons in the United States and in England and Wales', *New England Journal of Medicine,* (1970), Vol. 282, pp.135-44.

Charlesworth, J.C., ed., *Leisure in America: Blessing or Curse?,* (Philadelphia, 1964).

Friedmann, G. *Le Travail en Miettes,* (Paris, 1964).

Hilton, A. 'The economics of the theatre', *Lloyds Bank Review,* (July 1971), 26. National Travel Survey, US Bureau of Census, 1967 Census of Transportation.

Peacock, A. 'Welfare economics and public subsidies to the arts', *The Manchester School,* (1969), Vol. 37, pp.323-35.

Stereo Review, 'The crisis of classical records in America', (Feb. 1971), pp.57-84.

A Survey of Europe Today, (London, 1970).

California State Water Quality Control Board Resources Agency, *Water Quality Criteria,* California State Report, 2nd edn., (1970).

Institute of Life Insurance, *Life Insurance Fact Book,* (1970).

INSEE's *Etudes et Conjoncture,* 'Recherche Comparative Internationale sur les Budgets Temps', (Spet. 1966), Table III. 1, p.155.

5 Notes on the Producer Society—1972

Economists have long been considered the apologists and defenders of capitalism, and not without reason. They are concerned with how well the economy delivers the goods consumers want; and, justly proud of the great gains they have made in the understanding and management of our economy, they feel that it performs well enough despite its many shortcomings. If the main trouble with our economy, its failure to provide a satisfactory life, escapes the economist's notice, it is not his method of approach nor his intellectual honesty that is wanting but the basic assumptions of his discipline that are at fault.

Modern economics rests on the assumption that consumers know what they want, want what they buy, and their purchases can be trusted therefore to reflect society's preferences. The consumer is king in the economist's world, which is a noble conception but somewhat at variance with the realities of our society. In today's America, the consumer lacks the < strength and assurance it takes to be king. He is a shy and oppressed figure, the ignorant layman lectured by experts on what is and what is not good for him, the small man squeezed between big business and big government, the defenceless target of incessant assaults by loud advertisers and aggressive salesmen, and heir to a moral tradition that considered suspect the very act of consumption, the satisfaction of one's desires. Perhaps at the bottom of his heart, in the privacy of his insomnia, the consumer does know what life he would like to lead and what goods he would need to attain it, if so, he lacks the guts to stand up in the market place, face its pressures and reveal publicly what he glimpsed secretly in a moment of truth.

Economists, when they observe the high correlation between what consumers want and what producers provide, take that for evidence that the economy conforms to consumers' preferences, because they assume consumers' sovereignty to begin with. The same evidence, however, could equally well be taken as proof of the consumers' weakness of character and willingness to buy the bill of goods producers offer him. Economic data can never show whether the first or the second interpretation is nearer the truth; nor can we hope to fathom the consumers' innermost desires beneath the complex motivation of his market purchases. We shall try instead to analyse the pressures that influence his behaviour and the direction in which they push him. Many of the ills of our society can be explained this way, they appear as the symptoms of a producer society, obsessed with production, dominated by producers and their view of the world, and not always aware of the consumer's proper interests. Much of this may coincide with some of the things today's student generation is revolting against, even if they blame it on the consumer society and its materialism. This seeming difference in diagnosis is probably just a difference in terminology, although to blame the consumer for the wrongs the producer society inflicts upon him is to add insult to injury.

I. THE MORAL SUPERIORITY OF PRODUCTION

When one divides man's many activities and problems into those connected with production and those concerned with consumption, one finds that the former are almost always considered more important, more serious, than the latter. This higher prestige of things having to do with production is probably a legacy of the same puritan ethic, which also explains so many other aspects of modern capitalism. The frugality and wordly asceticism of the puritan ethic, its disapproval of spending on superfluities, cultural goods, and just about everything beyond the necessities of a plain and sober life, could not have been better calculated to deprive of prestige not only the task of householding, the spending of money to obtain the good things of life, but virtually all concern with man's welfare, his pursuit of pleasure, cultural interests and aesthetic values, whether selfish or unselfish, personal or general. The main force of protestant asceticism has been spent long ago, of course, but it still governs the Anglo-Saxon and especially the American hierarchy of values to the extent of making these concerns appear as the less serious side of life.

The more serious side of life is production, the creation of market value, one's contribution to production, and the earning of income in the process. Originally, the puritan ethic stressed the virtues of hard work and the diligent pursuit of one's calling; but these were more appropriate to the craft society of an earlier age, which seems also to have derived considerable satisfaction from the rewards appropriate to those virtues: pride of craftsmanship and the recognition due to a man who excels in his calling. Capitalist development has rendered meaningless some of these virtues and eroded most of their satisfaction—at least in this form. The very concept of calling has lost its meaning for most people in our age of great mobility and extreme specialization. Only artists, writers, professional people, and members of a few remaining craft occupations still get satisfaction out of their work, feel responsible for what they produce and are proud of it. The great majority of mankind has been alienated from its product. Just about every innovation that raised productivity and contributed to economic development did so by removing one more need to exercise human skill—and one more opportunity of deriving satisfaction from its exercise.

We retain some of the values of the craft society but do so in a much attenuated and symbolic form. When profits or earnings are all a man has to show for his work, he transfers to them his pride of achievement and regards them as the symbol and measure of society's appreciation of what he does for society. That was the interpretation the puritan ethic put on money income and we still cling to it. We use money not only as a medium of exchange but also as the measuring rod of man's worth; we value income not only for the goods it will buy but also as the proof of our usefulness to society.

Here, then, is the moral basis of the higher place accorded to production than to consumption. To produce goods or contribute to their production is to cater to market demand and so to perform services to others. Services to others are services to society, it is natural to place a higher ethical value on these than on selfish preoccupation with one's own welfare. It is also worth noting that, since services to others usually pass through the market on their way to the person they finally benefit, they acquire a monetary value in the process; whereas services rendered to oneself or one's family are seldom valued in terms of money. That probably explains the higher value customarily attributed to values expressed in money than to those not so expressed. Indeed, the primacy of production over consumption and of monetary over non-monetary values are both manifestations of the moral judgement that sets service to others ahead of concern for oneself.

Respect for the high moral principle that was at the origin of this hierarchy of values must not blind one, however, to the absurdities and errors of judgement it can lead to. To begin with, our society has, for many generations, ignored or belittled the nuisance value of the dirt, soot, fumes, sewage and ugliness generated in the process of creating wealth and marketable products, on the ground that a little encroachment on the beauties of nature, the purity of the air, or the freshness of a creek is too vague, even too frivolous a side-effect of production to be worth bothering about, let alone weighing against the cash value of its output. We waited for the secular accumulation of these side-effects to endanger human life and the ecological balance of nature before even acknowledging the existence of a problem that requires attention.

Second, and more generally, it is nonsense to attach more value to production than to consumption when the latter is, after all, the sole purpose and justification of the former. Whatever the individual's scale of values, from society's point of view, all economic activity aims at providing, assuring, or facilitating consumer satisfaction, present or future. One must not let that important truth be obscured by the customary separation, for reasons of convenience, of the tasks that have to do with production from those that have to do with consumption. Producing to earn income and spending the income so earned are complementary acts with the same consumer satisfaction as their ultimate aim: they are links in a chain, whose strength is that of its weakest link and whose weakest link, in the market economy, is almost always on the demand side. The market economy produces no more output than what its consumers and users are willing to buy, and the quality and composition of that output conforms to consumers' preferences only to the extent that they know their preferences and are willing to assert them.

Those two statements are just two facets, the quantitative and qualitative facets of the same problem, which is that for consumers' sovereignty to become reality, they must actively exercise and assert it. The ◀ volume of output produced is limited by consumers' effective demand, made effective by their ability and willingness to pay for it; the quality and composition of output is governed by consumers' tastes and needs, which again must be made effective by their ability and willingness to stand up for them.

I am stressing the similarity between those two problems (or facets of the same problem) because, thanks to the Keynesian revolution, knowledge of the first has become part of every economist's standard equipment; but the truth of the similar and closely related second problem escapes him still.

Yet, for a given productive effort to yield the greatest consumer satisfaction, economic decisions would have to be made with the same care and attention in the spending of money as in the earning of it—a condition clearly *not* fulfilled in our society. Wesley Mitchell, the grand old man of American economics, deplored 'the backward art of spending money', and complained about the 'poor cooking' and 'slipshod shopping' that went with it.[1]

We saw that the distinction between production and consumption has a large overlap with that between earning and spending—activities traditionally divided between husband and wife, perhaps because in the old days earning money used to require strength and its spending shrewdness. Mitchell raised the question whether such division of labour between the sexes explained the backwardness of the art of spending, but the causality could also run the other way round. Because puritanical society deprecated spending, it also looked down upon women, its main practitioners, and then left them to look after also such other lesser matters as art, culture, welfare—all of them aspects of consumption. Women shared, of course, their men's hierarchy of values, which explains why the fight for the emancipation of women began in the protestant countries, which most looked down upon women's traditional functions; and it may also explain why emancipation was so largely a fight for women's rights to enter man's domain: production and training for production. The success of that fight led, naturally enough, to an even greater neglect of the arts and crafts of consumption, since it diverted some of the ablest women from caring to learn and practice them.

To make matters worse, one aspect of consumption, careful spending and householding, has acquired a *negative* value, for reasons which again have to do with the protestant ethic. While a person's income has become the measure of his value to society, it seldom secures outside recognition such as an artist's or a craftsman's fame secures, because knowledge of it is seldom in the public domain. To get recognition, therefore, one must make known one's income through appropriate spending behaviour. A large income is best advertised by largesse in spending, by not counting too finely the cost of consumption and by buying conspicuous objects for their high cost rather than despite of it. Such behaviour, however, undermines yet further what little rationality the producer society brings to the problem of consumption.

II. PRODUCERS' DOMINATION

The problem of consumption is how best to employ one's income and leisure time to obtain the greatest satisfaction from them. The leisure classes of most past societies, from ancient Greece to the courts of eighteenth-century Europe, made a full-time occupation out of solving this problem, and our repugnance at the extreme inequalities such specialization usually implied must not blind us to the value of what they achieved. We owe to them most of our heritage of art, architecture, literature, philosophy and sports, all of which testify to the high level that the arts and skills of consumption attained in the past. The great achievements of Greek civilization were mostly the result of the leisurely leisure activities of a full-time leisure class,[2] and later full-time leisure classes were largely responsible for the rest of what is generally called culture, but what, in the economist's jargon, would be called the skills, means and techniques of consumption. Leisure, for most of those leisure classes, was a pretty strenuous activity, no less highly skilled than production, and requiring rather more training, practice and general education. The great investment of time and effort into acquiring the skills of consumption was generally considerd worth while, because it made consumption yield a much higher level of satisfaction than that enjoyed by the unskilled consumer.

All this may be obvious but is nevertheless worth stressing, because it tends to be forgotten. Europeans seem to have stopped thinking of consumption as a skilled occupation, perhaps because the spread of general education appeared to resolve the problem by promising to render the consumer's skill a part of everybody's cultural heritage. General education provides much of the necessary training and background for leisure; most Western Europeans who receive a good secondary education become skilled consumers. Unfortunately, this is becoming less true as the demands of technical progress for more vocational training encroach more upon the general, cultural parts of the school curriculum. It is paradoxical that this should happen at the very time when the same technical progress makes available more leisure and so would call for more, rather than less, preparation for its enjoyment. This is why the trend towards more specialized and vocational training is so strongly resisted in those countries where the tradition of an old leisure class still lingers and still serves as an example to follow for that ever-increasing part of the population that is able to partake of leisure.

In the United States, the historical development was somewhat different, because a leisure class with an established pattern of leisure activities never developed. For one thing, the country was too large and its population too heterogeneous to follow a single pattern; for another, the rich of the revolutionary period were too puritanical to form a leisure class and set an example—indeed, the very idea of investing time and effort into making consumption yield more satisfaction must have seemed repulsive to their way of thinking. By the nineteenth century, mass immigration and economic development led to so fast an increase in affluence that the newly rich soon outnumbered the old rich and would hardly have followed their example, even if they had set one. There was plenty of newly earned money in the hands of people willing to spend, but with little knowledge or guidance on how to spend. The puritan spirit was eroding, no longer able to enjoin frugality and prevent spending, but still strong enough to keep serious-minded men and women from devoting time and effort to the unserious business of organizing (let alone preparing themselves for) their leisure.

The vacuum so created was filled by the producer. He seized the initiative and took it upon himself to develop new products, design them, and, through advertising, let the consumer know about their availability and educate him in their use. That is known as producers' domination and ＜ to appreciate its significance one must cast a quick look at its predecessors and alternatives.

In a craft society, the consumer often had direct contact with craftsmen and could prescribe exactly what he wanted and how he wanted it done. Presumably every consumer had his own special desires; and, in an economy not yet subject to economies of scale, there was no obstacle to everybody's having his particular tastes catered to. Such consumers' domination was brought to an end by the industrial revolution and the emergence of economies of scale. This created a conflict between catering to every consumer's different requirements and lowering costs through a reduction in the variety of styles produced, and the conflict, in most countries, was resolved by merchants' domination. The merchant was not a mere middleman between producer and consumer but the person who took the initiative to ascertain consumers' tastes, to place orders with producers according to what he felt consumers wanted, and to 'strike a balance between following consumers' requirements more closely by offering wider assortment and obtaining things more cheaply by ordering larger volumes on the same pattern'.[3] In short, merchants' domination made for compromise between catering to consumers' preferences and exploiting economies of scale, and it still exists and flourishes in those many countries where a large part of the consuming public has strong ideas on what it wants and is willing to pay more if necessary to get exactly what it wants.

Producers' domination, by contrast, goes a long way towards sacrificing conformity to consumers' tastes for the sake of lowering costs and exploiting the advantages of mass production. The producer is the most aware of the saving in cost made possible by designing or adapting products in a way to make them suitable for mass production; he also has the greatest inducement to exploit such possibilities. He cannot sell, of course, what the consumer does not want, but advertising has given him the means to free himself from too slavish dependence on consumers' tastes and to try, instead, to mould consumers' tastes to fit his product.

From all that we said on consumer behaviour before, it is obvious that the United States was destined to be the country in which producers' domination would first and best succeed. It was here that consumers' preferences were least pronounced and therefore the most malleable, often the consumer did not know on what to spend the high income he earned and was willing to accept guidance on how to spend from whoever offered it. This attitude, especially when coupled with the general unwillingness to devote too much attention to the not-quite-important-enough business of consumption, and with the cavalier attitude of the rich that their status demanded (although they could best afford to insist on exact conformity to their tastes), created the ideal conditions for producers' domination. No wonder that the profitability of advertising was first discovered in the United States; and that it is still the greatest here, to judge by the proportion of the national income spent on it.[4] That presumably means that advertising in America was and is the most effective in moulding the consumers' tastes and making him accept products designed by the producer.

That was essential for the development and exploitation of mass production; and it explains America's economic lead over the past 100 years and her continuing superiority in terms of labour productivity. One must also remember that American producers used their dominating market position for introducing innumerable domestic appliances, ranging from vacuum cleaners to dishwashers, from automobiles to hi-fi systems, all of which have added greatly to our comforts and made them more generally available. Those very substantial benefits are the background against which one must view the other side of the coin: the American consumers' passivity and unchoosiness, which both facilitated the establishment of producers' domination and was encouraged by it.

III. THE CONSUMER'S ABIDCATION OF SOVEREIGNTY

The idea of consumers' tastes being moulded to fit the product rather than the other way around sounds more ominous than it is. After all, products are designed to please consumers, and the moulding of tastes mostly aims merely at making them more uniform and so render cheap mass production possible. Nevertheless, it is worth looking into the causes and consequences of the American consumer's passivity.

In the modern world, the individual cannot escape conducting most of his dealings with others from a position of weakness, because expertise counts for much and, in our highly specialized society, the other person can much more often claim to be (or to represent) the expert than one can oneself. All the more precious therefore are those few remaining personal contacts and areas of decision making where one is not at a disadvantage but can deal as an equal and exercise fully one's initiative and freedom of choice. Into this realm belong the consumption decisions of how to arrange one's life and get the most out of one's income, because these are among the problems whose solution requires not only specialized expertise but also general education and culture, common sense and ordinary care. It is one of the few areas therefore where the average layman occasionally has more competence than the specialized expert—if only he cares to exercise and assert his competence.

In most Continental countries of Western Europe, consumers still exercise this prerogative. They are demanding, choosy, fussy, aggressive in the market place, have strong ideas on what they want and seem willing to devote time, effort and money to asserting their individuality, making their tastes prevail, and getting the most for their money. They are anxious and proud to become and to be considered experts on the value and quality of what they buy and will go out of their way to assert such expertise. To American eyes, the typical French or German or Italian shopper often seems cantankerous; but her or his behaviour keeps open a channel of communication from consumers to producers, which indirectly benefits also those who make no direct use of it.

Such consumer behaviour in those countries gives the appearance more of a sport pursued for its own sake, than of rational behaviour aimed at getting a better bargain, because the time and energy expended and shoe-leather worn out in its pursuit seem out of proportion with the saving of money or gain in quality achieved. It could be a holdover from a feudal age when the nobility went out of their way to be extra fussy and fastidious in their shopping partly as a means of upholding their social position and reminding the merchants and artisans living off them that it was they who called the shots.

Such finicky behaviour, however, while often irrational from the individual's point of view, is likely to be socially beneficial. For, while the effect of an individual consumers' extra careful choosiness on the terms of his own market transactions may not be worth the time and effort expended, it does improve the market position of other consumers as well, and when the benefits to the whole consuming public are taken into account, then such choosiness may appear worth its cost. In other words, the Continental European consumer's shopping behaviour resembles a crusade to defend the consuming public's interests by enforcing shopkeepers' honesty, reliability and efficiency, which is likely to be more effective than either competition or Government regulation unaided by consumers' vigilance.

The behaviour just described is a good example of 'the prisoners' dilemma', in which the shoppers knowingly and deliberately depart from individually rational behaviour for the good of the general consuming public. That they know what they are doing and why they are doing it is suggested by the oft-heard complaint of some Frenchmen—and not only anti-American Frenchmen—that good resturants are often ruined by too many American customers, because they are too lavish and indiscriminate with their praise.

While the European shoppers' hypercritical behaviour seems to go beyond individual rationality, the American consumer's easy-going attitude seems to depart from rationality in the opposite direction. It is as though he or she would consider it undignified to show an active interest in getting the best quality or the lowest price, let alone display skill at doing it. The most striking evidence, perhaps, of this passivity is the consumer's utter inability or refusal to bargain and his reluctance even to shop for the lowest price. This cannot simply be explained by our tradition of set prices, which came to the United States half a century later than to France and is nevertheless more firmly established and more universally accepted here.[5]

Many books have been written on how the consumer gets exploited in the

United States;[6] and many legislative attempts have been made to protect him by facilitating comparison shopping, requiring the posting of prices, the stating of true interest rates, etc. Yet, it is obvious that the consumer is partly to blame and needs protection against his own carelessness as much as against the sellers' unscrupulousness. For one thing, much information is available to consumers if only they would make use of it; for another, we know that in markets where the majority of buyers shop carefully, the sellers themselves facilitate comparison shopping and find it profitable to do so. Finally, the American tourist's handicap when abroad, evident to himself in his feeling of being cheated and exploited and evident to writers of American tourist guides (to judge by their ever-recurring advice to bargain and shop around before buying), indicates a difference in this respect between American and other consumers.

What accounts for the American consumers' passivity in the market place? Among possible explanations are his reluctance to seem penny-pinching and overly concerned with consumption, his enjoyment of a high standard of living in the form, partly, of not bothering to 'cheapen goods', and his tendency to look upon the seller, not as his opponent against whom he must be on guard and defend his interests, but as an impartial expert whose advice he can seek and trust.[7] That attitude inevitably weakens his market position and perhaps explains his vulnerability to aggressive salesmanship.

A second manifestation of the American consumer's passivity is his unchoosiness. He seldom gets to know the full range of available alternatives before making a purchase, because he seldom takes the trouble of making the round of stores in quest of better price, better quality, or of the model, styling, shade of colour or cut of clothes exactly to his liking. In keeping with this apparent unconcern with what he gets, the American consumer is also more given than most to accepting good-naturedly and without fuss a badly cooked dish at a restaurant.

The consumer's passivity not only weakens his bargaining strength but worsens his market position in other ways as well. One of these is the loss in variety of the goods available, another is his loss of influence over the nature of those made available to him, both due to the decline and disappearance of the small retail outlets where he used to be king. Having abandoned comparison shopping in order to save time, bother and effort, the consumer, in effect, opted for large-scale distribution and must accept the consequences.

Economies of scale in distribution lower costs; but they also impede the distribution of products for which there is only a limited demand. It is easy to get anything destined for nationwide mass consumption but hard to satisfy a need that is different. Books on the bestseller list and popular paperbacks are available in every drugstore; but to get others is often a major undertaking. Hardly any bookstores remain in the United States that aim, as many used to, at stocking a full range of available titles in a particular subject; and few will oblige a customer by ordering for him a book they do not stock. Fortunately for the intellectual, with patience and extra effort he can still get the books he wants by ordering from the publisher or foreign booksellers. The non-intellectual individualist is not so well off, because he cannot order from the manufacturer items that his local chain stores, department stores or supermarkets find unprofitable to stock. Worse still, by not stocking the less popular items, the distributor chokes off some of the demand for those items and may thus prevent their production altogether.[8]

In short, scale economies in production restrict the range of goods produced, scale economies in distribution restrict even further the range of goods widely distributed—and goods not distributed widely enough cease to be produced sooner or later. All this limits the economy's ability to cater to the variety of consumers' tastes and discriminates against the minority consumer who finds it difficult, costly and occasionally impossible to satisfy some of his tastes. The loss is not only his but the whole community's, because the minority consumer is often the person who could lead the majority towards the new and the better.

That brings us to the question of how the majority consumer fares. The factors just discussed need not frustrate his taste for variety,[9] and economics of scale clearly redound to his advantage; but what price does he pay for that advantage? Is he free to make known his wishes and rewarded when those coincide with the majority's, or are no consumers' wishes heard and heeded in the producer society, rendering passive acceptance of what is available the condition of benefiting from the saving in costs that scale economies make possible? We shall argue that this latter comes nearer to being the truth, and that the difference therefore between majority and minority consumers is a difference not so much in tastes as in temperament. While the minority consumer fights a difficult, costly and often losing fight to get what he wants and lead a life of his own choosing, the majority consumer accepts what is available, on the principle that even if the goods he gets are not exactly of his own choosing, they are still pretty good and at least within his grasp.

We saw how channels of communication from consumer to producer are progressively narrowed as the economy moves from consumers' to merchants' and from merchants' to producers' domination; but a few channels remain open nevertheless as long as small businesses in direct contact with the consumer manage to survive side-by-side with large firms. In the American economy, where this last channel is also being closed off, market research is supposed to take its place. Ideally, this could be a perfect substitute for the spontaneous expression of consumers' wishes; but how well or how badly it performs in practice can almost never be ascertained.

In the realm of politics, opinion polls of voter sentiment regularly get tested against election results and improved in the light of such tests; but if (God forbid) they were to take the place of elections, there would be no test; and one never would know and never could learn how truly or falsely the rulers so 'elected' represent the ruled. Yet, this is the way in which the producer society designs and decides upon its new products. We have no way of telling to what extent products are made to conform to majority tastes and to what extent majority tastes are moulded to conform to the products marketed, except in those very rare cases where a test is possible.

One such case is provided by the automobile industry. In its annual model changes, Detroit always made its cars longer, bigger, more impressive looking, allegedly in response to the American consumers' well-researched wishes. The cheapest and shortest standard models grew about a foot a decade, their average length going from 185 inches in 1938 to 197 inches in 1948 and 208 inches in 1960; and we had the industry's assurance that the public no longer wanted to buy yesterday's shorter and lighter cars. Fortunately, the existence of imported cars, a full 4 feet shorter on average (160 inches long) enabled the American consumer to show his preferences not only within but also beyond the range provided by domestic producers. Sales of imports rose from half a per cent of new-car sales in 1948 to 10 per cent in 1958 and 15½ per cent in 1969, which suggests quite a discrepancy between what the industry's market researchers surmized about consumer preferences and what consumers' actual market behaviour revealed about the preferences of a part of the buying public, which, though a minority, was large enough (1,620,000 buyers) for Detroit not to want to lose. This is why the compacts were launched in 1960, 181 inches long on average, almost 2½ feet shorter than the cheapest standards if still quite a bit longer and heavier than the imports and growing more so. (They reached 186 inches by 1969). No wonder if their introduction failed to arrest the growth of imports.[10]

Another and very similar case is that of the American film industry. Hollywood, for many years, aimed all its films at the maximum audience of every member of every family; and this naturally made it necessary to gear subjects, language, and their whole approach to a very low mental age. Without the great and growing popularity of foreign films neither Hollywood nor the rest of us would ever have suspected the existence in the United States of a sizeable adult population with grown-up interests and sophisticated tastes.

It may be objected that these cases are not representative, because neither industry is known for its competitiveness. Competition, however, assures a large number of brands and models but not, by itself, a wide range of choices in any meaningful sense.[11] Beer brewing, for example, is a highly competitive industry in the United States; but almost all the breweries aim, with varying success, to produce essentially the same kind of beer. There is lacking in this country that great variety of light and dark, bitter and malty brews produced by other, much smaller beer-producing countries, although it is unlikely that the American beer-drinking public, if given a chance, should have a lesser variety of tastes and a lesser taste for variety than the Dutch or the Mexican, let alone the German or the British.

All these are illustrations of the narrowing of consumer's choice in the producer society; but the consumer's freedom is confined even further by various pressures that make him conform to other people's tastes rather than his own. To begin with, in a society where man is judged by his income and his income by his way of living, he must (if willing to play the game) live in a way others consider appropriate to his income and station. Accordingly, he will spend not for enjoyment but to show off, buy not what he would like but what he thinks or is told the world likes. Second, consumers' durables loom large in the consumer's budget, and many of them are bought partly as an investment or at least with an eye to their resale value, which again means that they are bought by the standards not only of one's own but of other people's tastes as well. Third, the neighbourhood one lives in and its appearance are important status symbols in the producer society; and the man who chose his neighbourhood for the status it confers is not averse to putting pressure on his neighbours to make them, if necessary, conform to what he judges to be the neighbourhood's standards.[12]

Such and similar factors weaken the consumer's ability and determination to follow the dictates of his own taste; they also make him depend more on the seller's advice. For the one thing on which sellers can claim to be expert is other people's purchases and what these reveal of their preferences and style of living. The consumer's concern therefore with resale value, social status, keeping up with the Joneses, and the like, tends yet further to confine his freedom of action and yet further to weaken his (and strengthen the seller's) bargaining position in the market place.

The consumer's subordinate position in the market place carries over into many of his other personal contacts as well. Organized society and the expert are more protective and paternalistic towards the individual in the United States than in most other Western countries. The list of 'don'ts' in our public parks is longer than in most other nations', although nature here is neither more dangerous nor more precious than elsewhere. In parks where there is a pond and swimming in the pond, lifeguards watch over children and adults alike; and when there is no guard, there is no swimming. This is only one of many instances of our lack of faith in the citizen's common sense and ability to act responsibly. Other instances are the greater precautions than elsewhere against people falling or jumping off high places; the much longer list of drugs requiring doctor's prescription; and the druggists' practice of keeping the prescription and not showing the name on the label of drugs bought on prescription. Patients in the United States are not trusted to medicate themselves—not even for recurring ailments—with anything more potent than an aspirin. The same tendency to treat them like children is reflected also in doctor-patient relations: the American physician tends much more than his European colleagues to wear the expert's mantle and prescribe tests, drugs, treatment, hardly ever mentioning their names and purpose, mostly without taking the patient into his confidence, and seldom discussing with him the nature of his trouble, alternative courses of action, their costs or chances of success.

IV. THE DISTINCTION BETWEEN DEFENSIVE AND CREATIVE CONSUMPTION

Consumer satisfaction begins with the satisfaction of man's needs. To satisfy one's needs requires effort, which has a duration and intensity; anything that diminishes its duration or intensity is supposed to add further to one's satisfaction. But man has few needs and all can be filled in relatively simple ways. By adding sophistication to the way in which they are filled, one's satisfaction can again be enhanced, although it usually takes training to acquire such sophistication and effort to practice it. Finally, satisfaction can also be derived, quite apart from the filling of needs, by catering to one's senses and exercising one's faculties; and this, too, is an acquired taste, which takes time and effort to learn to appreciate.

All these satisfactions can be classified into defensive and creative consumption, catered to by defensive and creative products respectively. Defensive consumption serves to ward off hunger and thirst, protect against wet, cold, and heat, prevent fatigue and sickness, as well as bother and boredom. In addition, it includes everything that diminishes the time and effort required to obtain these and other satisfactions.

Creative consumption consists in the delectation of the senses, the exercise of one's faculties, and in the sophistication added to the simple satisfactions of life to enhance their enjoyment. The enjoyment of extending or deepening one's experience and knowledge of the world in any of its aspects, from taste sensations to literature and intellectual constructs, is creative consumption. Much of this is a process of learning: learning to know or to know better for the sake of enjoyment.

The distinction is far from clear cut. Many products (such as a well-cooked, sophisticated meal) have both defensive and creative aspects; some activities can be creative consumption for one person, defensive for another; and the same activity becomes less creative for the same person as its novelty wears off with repetition and its enjoyment becomes routine. Nevertheless, the distinction is meaningful and in most cases easy to make.[13]

Defensive consumption is instinctive and has an immediate appeal; much of creative consumption caters to acquired tastes and must be learned to be enjoyed. Defensive consumption maintains life and makes it < easier; creative consumption provides most of its pleasures. Some defensive consumption is a necessary condition of enjoying life, because it frees time, conserves energy, maintains health, and provides freedom from the discomforts of hunger, thirst, heat, cold, etc.; and a modicum of all these is needed to enable one to enjoy the good things of life. At the same time, however, these are not, in themselves, what makes life worth living. Defensive consumption. however far it may be pushed, seldom carries one beyond the dividing line between the avoidance of pain and the experience of pleasure. Something positive must usually be added to bring one into the realm of pleasure; it is here that creative consumption plays its role.

Not that creative consumption is needed to provide pleasure. Many pleasures have nothing to do with the consumption of marketable products but consist in the enjoyment of nature and, even more, of human contact in its many forms. Creative products, however, can and do make important additions to the enjoyment of life. Most people's consumption includes both defensive and creative products, just as many of the products they consume contain both defensive and creative elements. The proportions in which the two are combined vary, according to people's incomes, tastes, and cultural conditioning; but they must stay within limits. Defensive consumption must not fall below that absolute minimum which is a necessary condition for the enjoyment of anything in life; neither must it be carried too far and crowd out creative consumption, lest it lead to boredom, a feeling of emptiness, and consequent dissatisfaction with life. This last is the danger of the producer society.

V. THE PREPONDERANCE OF DEFENSIVE CONSUMPTION

The protestant ethic aspired to the pleasures of the next world, not of this one, which explains its suspicious, even hostile attitude to all forms of creative consumption, all of which yield and are meant to yield worldly pleasures. The founding fathers of the Constitution were suspicious even of cultural activities and opposed to spending money on them;[14] and, as already mentioned, there was a similar disapproval also of education in the skills of consumption, which are always the skills of creative consumption.

This probably explains America's initial bias in favour of defensive and against creative consumption; but we need much more of an explanation to account for our continued and perhaps even greater concentration on defensive consumption today, when the puritan ethic seems so very much a matter of the past.

A part of the additional explanation is producers' domination. Producers have prime responsibility for developing and launching new products and compelling reasons for favouring defensive products. For one thing, development in the realm of production usually means reducing the labour time and effort needed to produce a given output; this makes it natural for producers to apply the same principles and strive for the same results also in the development of consumer's goods. Most of the many consumers' goods and appliances America has given the world aim at reducing the time and effort spent in housekeeping, transportation, communication, even recreation; this is also what makes them defensive products. For another, in contrast to creative products whose enjoyment is an acquired taste, defensive products have an immediate appeal for the consumer. This makes them easy to sell, which is, in its turn, another important reason for producers to prefer them.

The producer's preference, however, for producing and selling defensive products is fully matched by the consumer's preference for buying them. One reason, their instinctive and immediate appeal, was just mentioned; but this can hardly explain by itself the great, almost automatic popularity of all products that save time and effort or render simple what once required skill. As if the main aim of life were to save time, effort and skill, not only in production but in consumption as well. Such behaviour is puzzling, because man has a fair amount of time for which he prefers (or cannot help) staying awake, and a certain fund of energy and potential skill which to exercise gives him satisfaction. It makes sense not to overexpend one's time and energy, or to save them in unplesant pursuits in order to have more left over for pleasant ones; but it makes no sense to save them indiscriminately, in consumption and production, in pleasant and unpleasant pursuits alike.

Eating habits, sports and driving provide the most striking illustrations of the American desire to avoid effort, because in their case, the activity itself constitutes, by most people's standards, part of the enjoyment. Many of America's most popular foods are processed to be consumed in a minimum of time and with almost no muscular effort. We eat most of our fruit juiced or diced, much of our meat ground;[15] and the effortless speed with which milk, milk shakes, ice cream and cereals can be used to refuel our bodies probably explains much also of their appeal.[16] American technology developed a bread with 'the resiliency of a rubber sponge, (which) . . . is half masticated, as it were, before reaching the mouth'.[17] Combined with the ground or chopped substance of sandwich-spread or hamburger, it too can be swallowed almost without chewing. That this is precisely what happens is also suggested by time-budget studies, which show Americans spending one-third less time over meals than Western Europeans (1.1 against 1.6 hours daily).[18]

To take the effort out of sports is much more difficult, [19] which may be why active sports seem so much sooner relinquished by youths in the United States than elsewhere. Most undergraduates in college chafe under the burden of compulsory physical education; the participation of native whites, the dominant group, is relatively small in US olympic teams; and the average male in the United States devotes to active sports approximately one-third of the time Europeans devote to them.[20]

The third illustration is the American way of driving. Most Americans drive in a relaxed, leisurely way, as though out for a stroll, in strong contrast to Europeans and others to whom driving, including daily commuting, is a competitive sport and an occasion to prove their skill. In keeping with this difference in attitudes, Americans prefer a maximum of automatic equipment to minimize the effort and attention required; whereas Europeans welcome the additional control, challenge, and chance of showing off their skill that many gears, instruments and controls provide. The more generous speed limits in European countries and their larger market for sports cars also testify to the same difference in attitude. Indeed, Americans often comment on what, by their standards, is the hair-raising attitude to driving of most other nationals, usually attributing this to the automobile's still being a new toy to foreigners. But this, surely, is a wrong interpretation, at least as far as Western Europeans are concerned, who after all were (and still are) in the forefront of the development of the automobile. The contrasting attitudes are unmistakable; but since they are also found in so many other areas of behaviour, a more general explanation for the American avoidance of effort is clearly called for.

The American consumer's desire to avoid effort is certainly not due to laziness. Americans in all walks of life are well known to put no less and often more effort into their work than other people. That the American worker works if not always harder, at least more continuously and concentratedly was well attested by the many foreign productivity teams that came to the United States to learn the secret of America's superior labour productivity;[21] and the same seems to be true also of businessmen, the liberal professions, and university students. Only in their leisure are Americans anxious to avoid effort; and this may well be the typical attitude of a people used to hard work. One can well imagine the hard-working members of the producer society to equate leisure with idleness and to want their time free from work to be kept free also from exertion; moreover, these mental habits are quite likely to persist even after technical progress removes the necessity to work quite so hard.

This seems like a plausible explanation; but it explains neither a desire to save effort so great as to lead to a sacrifice in the quality of consumption, nor the concomitant desire to save time. The most striking evidence of the willingness to sacrifice quality for the sake of saving time and effort is the great and growing popularity in the United States of that large array of highly processed, frozen, ready-mixed, pre-ground, pre-cooked, pre-sliced, pre-prepared foods all of which save time in preparation and shopping, but also involve a sacrifice in flavour and freshness. This again is in strong contrast to the European consumer's quality consciousness and insistence on the freshness and impeccable quality of the raw materials of the housewife's art. Most of America's food technology is available in the markets of Western Europe; but few of our processed and ready-prepared foods and imitation flavours found favour there. Europeans seem reluctant to sacrifice for their or their wife's greater comfort the more delicate flavour of fresh fish, freshly-ground coffee, and freshly-baked bread—to mention just three of the items that most Americans have given up long ago. At the same time, the acceptance of mechanical kitchen appliances has gone further in Europe. Instead of our pre-sliced. pre-ground, pre-grated foods, Europeans seem to go in for many more cooking aids than we, ranging from slicing machines to electric graters, grinders, choppers, mills, etc., revealing a great desire to ease and speed the housewife's task but not at the cost of losing freshness and flavour.

There is a clear and amply documented difference in consumers' preferences between the United States and Continental Western Europe, the former preferring to save time and effort, the latter to enhance the enjoyment of consumption by improving its quality. Much can be said, of course, for saving time and effort if these are then put to better use; but are they? Information on the way in which people budget their time is available and will be discussed; at this stage, let us merely point to America's great and ever-increasing consumption of do-it-yourself equipment, which suggests a correspondingly great and increasing role of do-it-yourself activities in people's lives.[22] Here is the world's richest nation, too much in a hurry to make sure it gets its money's worth in the market, eating also in a hurry[23]—food judged inferior by most other people's, as well as its own earlier standards [24] for the sake of saving a few steps in shopping and in the kitchen; yet the same people spend much of the time and energy so saved on doing their own plumbing, papering, carpentering and furniture finishing, all of which professionals would do better.

To reconcile these seemingly contradictory aspects of the American consumer's behaviour one must go back once again to the puritan ethic. Its disapproval of frivolous consumption once instilled a reluctance to spend money, which has long since been eroded by the battering of aggressive salemen against weak consumer resistance, by the desire to gain status through conspicuous spending, and perhaps also by the economist's praise of spending as the means to create prosperity and employment. However, the puritan disapproval of frivolous consumption seems to persist if in a changed and attenuated form. The approved but narrow category of 'necessary consumption' seems to have broadened into 'consumption that is good for you' and the reluctance to spend money has turned into a reluctance to spend time and effort. In this modern form, the puritan ethic, or what remains of it, is buttressed by the rise in productivity, which, by raising wages, has raised the value of time and effort and so the apparent need to conserve them; it also has the support of salesmen, who peddle the equipment needed to conserve time and effort and have long known how to exploit the consumer's desire for what is good for him.

This explanation makes many seemingly puzzling features of the producer society fall into place. To begin with, it explains the consumer's willing acceptance of a worse quality of life for the sake of saving time and effort, especially when this is a gradual, step-by-step process. The sober, hard-working forebears of present-day Americans are known to have abhorred the luxury consumption of the aristocratic leisure classes; and they must have found especially odious the latter's obsession with fine differences in quality and willingness to go to much trouble and expense for a touch of additional sophistication, to judge by the fact that this judgement of theirs has survived and is still with us today. Modern Americans feel an almost moral compulsion to make use of the shortcuts with which modern technology simplifies life and to use the many prepared and processed foods, each of which saves so many minutes of preparation and only detracts ever so little from the quality of the outcome. The saving in time and effort always seems worth more than the loss in quality, not only because time has a market value whereas differences in quality do not; but also because merely to notice, or to notice too much a loss in quality on which a great saving in time depends can seem snobbish, overrefined, even morally repugnant.

This same puritanical valuing of time and fear of wasting it also helps to explain the average American's tendency to save time on social contacts. The foreigner's impression that Americans always hurry seems largely based on the observation that we seldom linger over meals, drinks or a friendly chat. Time budgets show that Americans spend half an hour a day less over meals than Western Europeans;[25] American men also spend almost half an hour a day less than European men in the company of friends, neighbours, relatives not of their household, or sitting alone in a cafe or other public place.[26] These are all signs of hurrying, which saves a lot of the time others spend gossiping, discussing, or watching the world go by. That it is a deliberate saving of time and not just a matter of temperament or metabolic rate is suggested by the same Americans' admirable, even exceptional patience when they wait their turn in a queue or wait for blocked traffic to start moving.

Having explored some of the motives of our preference for defensive over creative consumption, we must now look at the way in which, for these and perhaps also other motives, we choose to consume our high income. The gross national product of the United States per head of population is, in real terms, between 25 and 100 per cent higher than that of the more prosperous nations of Western Europe. This means a much greater productive potential than theirs, which would also mean a correspondingly higher standard of living if we knew as well as they how to use it. We have not used it to take better care of our poor;[27] have we used it to secure a better life for the not-so-poor?

We spend less of our time at work than we used to but no less than Western Europeans with their much lower production potential. Our working week is a little shorter than theirs but so are our holidays and vacations, while we have the highest percentage of wives working and probably also the highest percentage of moonlighters.[28] On balance, we spend just about the same time at work.

Neither do we enjoy more than others the time spent at work. Our high productivity as well as the testimony of the Europeans productivity teams already quoted show that we work no less hard; and if our work is rendered more convenient and requires less physical effort, it is also more continuous and concentrated. Most people consider their job dull and regard work as drudgery, life as what begins when work ends. The days are long past when work was a part of life to enjoy and take pride in. American workers today seldom even take the trouble to make their workplace more cozy with a personal touch—as if they disliked it too much to bother, even though they do spend much of their lives there.

The exception to this rule are professional people and independent businessmen, who work longer hours and take shorter holidays than anyone else, and for whom the main satisfaction and meaning of life clearly lies in their work.[29] Whether they are better or worse off in the producer society is hard to say; one can say, however, that the need for them and their like has been greatly reduced. Technical progress continues to reduce the proportion of people who find satisfaction in their work. This makes it all the more important to find out how much and what kind of consumer satisfaction people derive from the high production potential of the producer society.

The above notes have raised more questions than they have answered; it may be quite fitting therefore to end them with a question unanswered. Hawtrey's twofold classification of consumption seems a good framework for clarifying and documenting the nature of our preferences; and we hope to have taken a few steps and pointed the way towards explaining them in terms of a few cultural and economic factors. Much, however, remains unexplained.

Economists have shied away for too long from analysing consumers' preferences, probably for fear of being found guilty of judging other people's way of life and pattern of expenditure by standards other than their own. Such fears seem grossly exaggerated. For one thing, one can usefully seek and explain the sources of behaviour without judging it. This was the aim of these notes. For another thing, many aspects of consumer behaviour resemble closely the producer's behaviour and are amenable to the same or similar tests of rationality. Much consumption involves both positive and negative satisfactions, which occur at different points of time and involve different degrees of uncertainty: decisions with respect to such consumption can usually be judged by the test of rationality. Indeed, the legal obstacles to the use of opiates and hallucinogen drugs are based on such a judgement. Another and different example, typical of many forms of creative consumption, is the necessity of acquiring a musical education for the sake of musical enjoyment. This amounts to an investment of present time and effort for the sake of future, uncertain benefits; and it is amenable to the same type of cost-benefit analysis as an investment in productive skills or productive equipment. Looking into the nature and motives of such decisions may well be the next step that needs to be taken for our better understanding of the consumer's behaviour in the producer society.

NOTES

1. cf. Wesley C. Mitchell, 'The backward art of spending money', *American Economic Review,* (1911), Vol. II pp. 269-81. It must be noted, however, that Mitchell's explanation of why this art is backward is very different from the one advanced here.
2. Remember that the citizens of many of the city states in ancient Greece, whose culture and achievements we justly admire, constituted a full-time leisure class if one includes politics and warfare among leisure activities, because they lived on the surplus labour of their working class: the slaves, helots, freedmen, and resident but non-citizen aliens, who made up the bulk of the population.
3. cf. N. Kaldor 'The economic aspects of advertising', *Review of Economic Studies,* (1951) Vol XVIII, pp. 1-27, for this and the following argument.
4. Advertising expenditure, in relation to the gross domestic product, is 2.2% in the United States (early 1960s), 1.8% in Great Britain (1960), 1.5% in Canada (1964), 0.9% in West Germany and the Netherlands (1957), and 0.7% or slightly less in France, Belgium and Italy (1957). Source: *Statistical Abstract of the United States, 1968;* B. B. Elliott, *A History of English Advertising, (London: Business Publications, 1962),* p. 207; Dominion Bureau of Statistics, *Advertising Expenditures in Canada,* (1964), p. 6; H.A. Münster, *Werben und Verkaufen im Gemeinsamen Europäischen Markt,* (Darmstadt: Leske, 1960, pp. 107-20).
5. On the origin of set prices, *see* R. M. Hower *History of Macy's of New York, 1858-1919,* (Cambridge, Mass: Harvard University Press, 1942), Ch. 4.

6.   cf. H. Black, *Buy Now, Pay Later,* (New York: Morrow, 1961); D. Caplovitz, *The Poor Pay More,* (Glencoe, Ill: Free Press, 1963); S. K. Margolius, *The Innocent Consumer Vs. the Exploiters,* (New York: Trident Press, 1967).

7.   The same point is also discussed, but from an entirely different angle, in Chapter 8.

8.   Imagine a commodity profitable to produce in a quantity of 100,000 or more units at a price at which consumers' demands in the US would be 200,000, that is, 1 unit per 1,000 inhabitants. Clearly, if all consumers could make their demand effective, their demand would be catered to. But if they were evenly spread over the country, then the demand in communities with less than 100,000 inhabitants would be less than 100 units, probably insufficient for local retailers to stock the commodity. With 71.3% of the US population living in such communities, their potential demand would be rendered ineffective, thereby reducing national sales to below the 100,000 minimum required to render any production profitable. Only if a third or more of the potential buyers from the small towns had the persistence and initiative to make their demand effective by shopping through mail-order houses or in neighbouring large towns would production become profitable.

9.   A taste for variety—as distinguished from a variety of tastes—can often be satisfied by minor differences in the product or its design, which can be provided without sacrificing economies of scale.

10.   The data on sales come from *Automobile Facts and Figures,* 1949, 1959 and 1969 editions; those on car lengths are unweighted averages based on data from *Consumer Reports,* February 1938, May 1948, September 1958, April 1960, January, April and July 1969.

11.   cf. P. O. Steiner, 'Program patterns and preferences, and the workability of competition in radio broadcasting', *Quarterly Journal of Economics,* Vol. LXVI, (1952), pp. 194-223, for a rigorous analysis of the question whether competition caters to a variety of tastes or merely duplicates the same product.

12.   Even more important is the pressure firms put on their executive staffs and salesmen to help support the image the firm wants to create with their personal appearance and way of living.

13.   These concepts were introduced by Sir Ralph Hawtrey, in his *The Economic Problem,* (London: Longmans, 1925). *See* especially Chs. 17 and 18.

14.   cf. G. S. Morgan, 'The puritan ethic and the American Revolution', *William and Mary Quarterly,* 3rd Ser. Vol. XXIV (1967), pp. 3-43.

15.   Approximately one-half of the beef consumed in the United States is in the form of hamburger. Frankfurters would add another sizeable proportion but they take some chewing.

16.   cf. S. Giedion, *Mechanization Takes Command,* (New York: Oxford University Press, 1948), p. 204.

17.   *ibid.* p. 198.

18.   cf. 'Recherche comparative internationale sur les budgets temps', *Etudes et Conjoncture,* (September 1966), Table III.1.

19.   A promising beginning has been made, however, by ski lifts, snowmobiles, electric golf carts, all-electric bowling alleys, power driven exercycles, and battery-powered effortless exercisors.

20.   Active sports, which include hiking and walking, average six minutes a day in the United States, over nineteen minutes in Europe. cf. 'Recherche comparative internationale sur les budgets temps, Table III.1.

21.   cf. G. Hutton, *We Too Can Prosper,* (London: Allen & Unwin, 1953), for an account of the experience of the British productivity teams in America.

22. Sales of do-it-yourself equipment and materials were 2 per cent of the US national income and equal to almost one-half of non-farm residential construction already by 1953. cf. 'Summary of information on the do-it-yourself market', *Business Service Bulletin,* Vol. LXXXIV (1954), US Department of Commerce.
23. *See* p. 63 above for the time we spend over meals.
24. cf. R. O. Cummings, *The American and His Food,* (University of Chicago Press, 1940), for plenty of evidence on this.
25. cf. 'Recherche comparative internationale sur les budgets temps', Table III.1
26. cf. *ibid.* Table V. 1.
27. The poorest 10 per cent of our population get a smaller share of our larger total than do the poorest 10 per cent of most Western European nations—the data are not good and detailed enough to show how the standards of living of the poorest 10 per cent rank.
28. cf. Juanita M. Kreps, *Lifetime Allocation of Work and Income,* (Durham, N.C.: Duke University Press, 1971), Ch. 5.
29. They are also more prone to premature heart attacks; but this is beside the point. It merely indicates that consciously or subconsciously they set the enjoyment of life ahead of its mere prolongation, which is a legitimate and not irrational preference.

6 Are Men Rational or Economists Wrong?—1974

Economics, having originated in the age of reason, has adopted the rationality of man as one of its basic postulates. Today, in the age of unreason, psychologists and psychoanalysts have gained a lot of understanding of the dark, irrational forces that motivate men; but while the general public has readily accepted their interpretation of human motivation, the economist—perhaps alone among social scientists—still clings to the assumption of human rationality. His reasons for this are understandable enough. The assumption of human rationality is a powerful simplification of the economist's model of reality; and this is not the first nor the last time that economists sacrifice realism for simplicity. Moreover, economists can proudly point to seeming confirmations of their rationality hypothesis. Many implications of several of the economist's theories of individual behaviour are based on this hypothesis; and every time empirical data fail to contradict it, the economist's belief in human rationality is understandably strengthened, whatever psychoanalysts may say to the contrary.

Yet there is a flaw in this logic, if it is true, as it seems to be, that man is neither wholly rational nor wholly irrational. From the proven rationality of a limited aspect of his behaviour one cannot deduce that he is rational in everything—just as one cannot generalize from the manifest irrationality of some of his behaviour characteristics either. The insane are so regarded, because a part of their behaviour is irrational to the degree of creating a serious conflict between what they need or want and what they seem to seek or be asking for—yet, the mad behaviour and reasoning of a madman is often impeccably logical and maddeningly rational, almost as if to compensate for the irrationality of the one fatal flaw in his mental makeup. This alone should be a warning against regarding man's rational behaviour in one respect as proof of anything beyond his rational behaviour in that particular respect.

Having sounded a warning against a too easy assumption of man's rationality, one may well ask if economists have ever come across proof of man's irrationality. Not surprisingly, perhaps, economists are human. They sometimes do and sometimes do not find what they are looking for;

but very seldom do they find what they are *not* looking for.[1] Their faith in man's rationality is almost absolute: perhaps the only generally accepted exception to it is a minor one, known as the money illusion.[2]

I. MONEY ILLUSION

A person is said to be suffering from money illusion if his market behaviour remains unaffected when rising prices reduce the real purchasing power of his unchanged money income and money wealth, or if, seeking more income, he is content with more *money* income although a simultaneous rise in prices keeps his *real* income unchanged. Economists consider such behaviour irrational—and it is (or would be) irrational in people who acquire money solely for the purpose of spending it and value it solely for what it will buy. These are indeed the people who inhabit the economist's world; but what about those whose attitude toward money is different? Money is sought and valued, not only for its purchasing power but also as a symbol of achievement, of success, of society's appreciation of one's services; and this other function of money does not quite fit into the economist's model of rationality.[3] Economists define man's preference function broadly enough to accommodate plenty of variety and aberrations in taste in everything except matters of money. As far as money is concerned, the budgetary constraint in the theory of the consumer's behaviour seems to imply that the desire to hold money as anything other than a medium of exchange and a store of value is irrational—just as irrational as money illusion seems to be in those who hold money for these purposes only. Accordingly, we propose to extend the concept of money illusion to embrace all attitudes to money that must be considerd irrational in the sense of being excluded from the economist's narrow definition of money rationality.

Unfortunately, the conflict between man's actual behaviour and the economist's theory of his behaviour, and with it the dividing line between rational and irrational behaviour by the economist's standard, are often hard to find, because the economist's theory of rational behaviour is far from complete. In this particular instance, the theory of consumer's choice and the theory of choice between work and leisure (and hence also between income and leisure) have been long and well established; but missing, until quite recently, was any connecting link between them, leaving unexplained the interdependence of the threefold choice that determines earning, spending and saving. Modigliani was the first to fill the gap and provide the missing link with his theory of the consumption function based on the life cycle hypothesis.[4] Not only was this the first theory of rational choice between spending and saving; but it extended the economist's theory of human rationality and so rendered explicit and empirically testable the implications of the assumption of rationality in a crucially important area.

Modigliani's theory visualizes people as making a deliberate choice between spending and saving, wishing to save just enough to provide for contingencies and their old age, and to some extent also to leave something to their surviving children and relatives. His model assumes away this last, to him lesser, motive; and its failure to fit the statistical facts better than it does he attributes to the desire of many also to leave an inheritance. It is not irrational, of course, to accumulate a fortune to leave behind, provided one has someone to leave it to and wishes to leave it to him or her. Unfortunately, Modigliani had no interest in ascertaining the extent to which this condition of rationality is fulfilled—after all, he was concerned with establishing the microfoundations of the aggregate consumption function and could, for this purpose, concentrate on central tendencies and neglect minor eccentricities and deviant behaviour. The question is whether these are really negligible.

It seems plausible that there should be other reasons for saving beyond the rational ones advanced by Modigliani. For one thing, some people have a desire to accumulate a fortune for its own sake, with never a thought, or even a horrified rejection of the thought, of ever spending it. The miser has been much discussed in literature, from Plautus to Molière and beyond, and his behaviour was usually regarded as a mild (though far from innocuous) form of insanity until the protestant ethic and the rise of capitalism placed the stamp of respectability on saving for its own sake. Today, to make money just for the heck of it and greatly in excess of one's spending habits has become not only respectable but respected, and society has fully adjusted its notions of normal psychology and rational man to accommodate such behaviour. It is something of a paradox that, of all people, the economist alone should have failed to make room in his world for the likes of Anselm Rothschild and John D. Rockefeller.

For another thing, saving is often the unintended result of separate and uncoordinated decisions to earn money and to spend it. When a person is better at spending than at earning money, the tightness of the market for consumer credit soon forces upon him a more rational division of his energies between the two occupations; the reverse disparity between the two, however, though no more rational, generates no inducement to make one mend one's ways. On the contrary, our society puts strong pressures on the individual to make him concentrate on production to the neglect of consumption; this often gives rise to savings in excess of what Modigliani's rational motives would account for. Money is power over so many things that most of us unquestioningly assume its general usefulness while we are busy making it, without ever pausing to ask if an increment of earnings will really be useful to us or our families. This may well be the main reason if savings are, indeed, beyond what is rational.

Modigliani's life cycle hypothesis makes no allowance for people's inability to predict their day of death and consequent tendency to play safe by overestimating their life expectancy; this explains why so many people leave more inheritance than they wish to bequeath to their loved ones. This would account for at least part of the $1.5 billion philanthropic bequests, the $0.5 billion bequests left to federal state and municipal governments; and those unknown amounts left by people who die intestate without known relatives.[5] It does not explain, however, philanthropic contributions individuals make during their lifetime, which in 1970 amounted to $14.3 billion, more than a quarter as large as personal savings at $50.2 billion. There is nothing irrational, of course, in philanthropy, but the public is not likely to have deliberately decided to make the extra effort to earn the extra $14.3 billion just in order to make them available to philanthropy—except perhaps for the $2 – $2.5 billion they contribute to church collections, United Fund campaigns (which grossed $800 million), and the like. As concerns the remaining $12 billion, it is likely that people made their earning decisions first; and only afterward, on finding themselves with more accumulated savings than they needed and wanted for their own and their families' use, did they decide to contribute to philanthropy.[6] To propose this argument is not to deprecate the generosity of the American public; although it is to deny that economic rationality, as commonly interpreted in the marginalist neoclassical tradition, is the governing principle of what may be the most important area of economic choice. The part of income given away to charity is far too large, both absolutely and in relation to personal saving, to be dismissed as exceptional or deviant behaviour. At the same time, it is by no means the only sign of our tendency to make more money than we know how to spend or what to save for. Money can be squandered as well as given away; and this, while difficult to qualify, is easy enough to illustrate. The billboards and daily press announcements in which Mr. O. L. Nelms thanks people in and around Dallas for having helped him make another million are as good an illustration as any, and not too extreme by Texas standards.[7] Nor is it necessary to go to Texas for examples.

The rich are generally believed to spend more carelessly than the poor, and the lesser attention they devote to minimizing the money cost of their desired level of consumption is considered an integral part of their high standard of living. Not having to pinch pennies is a good in itself. Economists rationalize this by saying that the rich are better off in terms of money than in terms of time, so that it is rational for them to spend money on saving time. This is what carefree spending accomplishes. The crucial question is whether they really are short of time and in need of saving it. We shall argue that this is not so.

II. TIME ILLUSION

A close parallel to the desire for money for its own sake and without reference to how and when it will be spent is the desire for leisure time, without reference to how it will be enjoyed. Just as money is general purchasing power over whatever one wants to possess, so leisure is general command over time to spend in whatever way one wishes. Just as the many possible ways of spending money make it seem worth having before one has decided how to spend it, so the many uses of time make leisure seem desirable before one knows what to do with it. The important difference between money and time is that, while money not spent today can be saved up for tomorrow, time saved today on one thing must be spent today on another thing or be lost forever. One can postpone the spending of money day after day and continue until death to believe that there is yet time to make use of it; no such self-deception is possible with the budgeting of time. If one saves more time than one knows how to spend agreeably or usefully, one is bound to be reminded daily of one's irrationality. One would expect therefore less illusion to prevail in the budgeting of time than in the budgeting of money.

Here again, the implications of economic rationality in the allocation of time have only recently been made explicit in a formal and rigorous theory of the subject.[8] It appears that the higher the productivity and hence the value of a person's labour, the higher his income and the higher the price to him of leisure; and since the former will raise, and the latter lower, his demand for leisure, this may, on balance, move either way. Most people seem, with rising incomes, to free more of their time for leisure, but the proportionate increase in their leisure is usually less than the proportionate increase in their spendable income. It would be rational, therefore, for them to change their consumption activities so as to make them less time-intensive and more goods-intensive. In other words, faced with a rising cost of time relatively to the cost of goods, the rational person ought to consume more goods per hour of consumption, just as he produces more goods per hour of work. This is the economist's expectation, based on his faith in human rationality; how does it compare to man's actual behaviour?

The 1934 and 1965-6 questionnaire surveys of household time budgets are not fully comparable, but one's confidence in the trend they show is strengthened by its similarity to the difference the 1965-6 international comparison shown between the high-income United States and the low-income European countries.[9] There has been a great reduction in the time spent in preparing and consuming meals, a reduction in time spent on public entertainment, active sports, in reading, club activity, walking for pleasure, and listening to the radio; and most of the time so saved was spent on watching television, shopping, and running errands. All of these changes are matched by a corresponding and very similar difference between the time budgets of Europeans and Americans.

There need be nothing irrational, of course, about such an allocation (or reallocation) of time; still there are other, independent indications that there is. For one thing, the increase in the time spent in shopping probably has much to do with the introduction of the supermarket and other self-service-type retail distributors. The rising price of labour has prompted retailers to save on costs by making the customer perform much of the work clerks used to do and making him wait in line at the check-out desk rather than having more clerks wait on him. Part of the resulting savings are passed on to the customer, who—to judge by the popularity of these stores—seems quite willing to spend the additional time if he can thereby save money. Indeed, the thing is so popular that even manufacturers can save on the cost of final assembly by letting the customer do the assembling of certain toys, furniture, hi-fi equipment, etc. Closely related to this is the great success and large sales of do-it-yourself equipment and materials. Time budget studies are not detailed enough to show, as a separate category, the time spent on do-it-yourself activities; if they were, they would almost certainly show an increase.

There is something of a paradox here. We know that the rise in labour productivity, or rather the technical and economic progress which results in a rise in labour productivity, causes earnings to rise faster than prices, and the price of time to rise faster than the purchasing power of income and the price of goods. This was the reason why it seemed rational for people to become (and for the rich to be) more careless in shopping, thereby spending money to save time. How can there be a simultaneous tendency of spending time to save money? Also, can sellers respond to rising wages by shifting onto customers' shoulders some of the work previously done by their employees if, as seems likely, the cost of customers' time is also rising, and presumably rising just as fast as their employees' wages?

There would be no paradox if the people who spent money to save time and those who spent time to save money belonged to different income groups, and if the average customer's earnings rose more slowly than the average employee's, owing to the rise in the standard of living causing the customers for each commodity to be recruited from an ever-larger segment of the population, thus including an ever-increasing proportion of the lower-income groups. But this explanation, however logical, is at best a partial one. The serve-yourself and do-it-yourself movement cuts across all income groups—one of its more absurd and inefficient manifestations, mothers (instead of the school bus) driving children to and from school, is concentrated in upper middle-class suburbs. Also, the argument concerning the lesser rise in customers' than employees' valuation of time hardly applies to necessities, whose market already includes the bulk of the population; yet it is precisely in the realm of necessities, such as the basic foods and the more essential articles of clothing, that self-service distribution is making the greatest headway.

It seems therefore that the paradox must be accepted and explained by irrationality in the way people budget their time—the more so, because this is not the only paradox that needs explaining. It is not unreasonable that time spent in shopping or painting one's own house or apartment should seem less burdensome than the same amount of time spent in the routine of factory or office work; surprising is only that such a difference in people's evaluation of the two activities should be increasing at the very time when the workweek is getting shorter, presumably rendering the tedium of work lesser too. A tentative explanation is that higher earnings create a feeling that time is getting more precious, and that this feeling in turn causes people to save more time than they know how to spend. If this is so, it will manifest itself in people's hurrying through some activities only to be left with more than enough time to waste on others. The question is where and how the dividing line between the two kinds of activities is drawn. One would expect deliberate decisions, structured and planned activities to economize time, residual activities to squander it; the conscious valuation of time to be high, its unconscious or implied valuation to be low; and one would also expect a lavish expenditure of time on activities that provide a tradeoff. There is evidence to confirm all these expectations.

The 2.1 hours the average adult American watches television on an average day[10] is the obvious and main example of such a residual activity—and not only because it comes at the end of the day. People might, of course, value the one hundred and twenty-sixth minute of the day's TV viewing as highly as they value the sixty-sixth minute spent over meals or the eighteenth minute of public entertainment; but this supposition, implied by the rationality hypothesis, is hard to reconcile with the public's rejection of pay television. If people's enjoyment of television were really great enough to make them cut down for its sake on income earned by work and time spent over meals, at sports, and a variety of other amusements, then they ought, one should think, be equally anxious to reduce or eliminate the many interruptions of television programmes. which now take up ten minutes of each hour of television. Some people grow eloquent in complaining how these interruptions not only waste time but break up the thread of the programme's story or argument; yet the general public has clearly revealed the very low nuisance value it attributes to them.

The Hartford experiment with subscription television clearly shows this. The programmes, while no more highbrow than commercial television, with movies constituting 86.5 and sports another 4.5 per cent of the total, were better in the sense that the films were newer and the sports events more important. Their average hourly cost was $0.59, so that even if one valued the advantage of better programmes at zero, the cost of avoiding interruptions would still be only $0.6 per minute or $3.50 per hour and below the average subscriber's rate of earnings and marginal valuation of time.[11] Yet a two-year promotional drive persuaded less than 1 per cent of all viewers to subscribe, and those who did watched subscription programmes only 5.5 per cent of their viewing time, mostly for the sake of especially attractive programmes and seldom if ever to avoid interruptions.[12] The fact that the proportion (and absolute number) of high-income subscribers declined and of low-income subscribers rose substantially throughout the experiment is another indication that to utilize television time better was *not* an important aim of subscribers.[13]

These findings are confirmed by various sociological questionnaire studies of television viewers. According to one of these, of the people watching television, 24 per cent 'occasionally feel like doing something else', another 12.5 per cent 'often' felt that way, and a further 6.5 per cent 'almost always' have that feeling. Yet, all of them continue watching![14] Other studies, while phrasing their questions differently, found much the same attitude (cf. Steiner, 1963).

All this is hard to fit into a theory of rational time allocation, which would have people respond to the ever-rising value of time by its more effective use through crowding more goods or more action into each hour of consumption time. American television habits look much more like the relaxed, lazy attitude of people with plenty of time on their hands, or their attitude to residual time, left over when the day's hustle and bustle is done, to be spent or wasted, wisely or foolishly, but without the deliberate planning, choosing, and decision-making economists associate with rational behaviour.

Differences in people's valuation of different bits of their time point in much the same direction. Econometric studies of passenger transportation show that commuters value the time they spend in commuting at something between one-fifth and one-half of their wage rate, typically around one-quarter (cf. Beesley, 1965; Lisco, 1967; Quarmby, 1967; Stopher, 1969; Traffic Research Corporation, 1965). This is surprising, because one would not expect people to regard commuting as significantly more pleasant (or less unpleasant) than work except conceivably on the margin, as a result of a steep rise in the marginal disutility of work at the end of a long workday. However, we have statistical evidence that our present 40-to 42-hour workweek is well within the range of constant marginal productivity, which is *prima facie* evidence that it is also within the range where the marginal disutility of work is also fairly constant (cf. Owen, 1970). In addition, the wage rate is a good measure of the average worker's valuation of the marginal disutility of his work if the length of the working week is, as most labour economists believe it to be, just about as long as he wants it.[15] Hence, with the wage rate a faithful reflection of the average person's valuation of the marginal disutility of labour, and the latter's marginal disutility not very different from its average disutility, the so much lower value people attribute to time spent in commuting is very hard to explain in terms of the narrow rationality the economist attributes to man.

Becker (1965, p. 510, footnote 5), one of those to estimate empirically people's implied valuation of their commuting time and the first to formulate a rigorous theory of rational time allocation, was clearly puzzled by his finding that people value commuting time at a mere 40 per cent of their wage rate; and he hesitated whether to attribute this to errors in assumptions or 'to severe kinks in supply and demand functions for hours of work'. Now that at least five other estimates, derived by different people from different data and in different ways, show much the same result, it is much harder to escape the conclusion that perhaps the assumption of human rationality is at fault.

For the data fit in very well with our tentative explanation that people overdo the saving of time under the social pressures of a society that puts a high premium on minimizing costs and saving resources irrespective of whether alternative uses for the resources so saved are available. Is it not plausible that these pressures should have the greatest impact on plans and decisions that involve an explicit valuation of time, and a much lesser one on those in which such valuation is merely implied by a choice between one mode of transportation and another? A further and even more striking confirmation is the finding of an air-travel study, according to which the implied valuation of time spent by people in personal (as distinguished from business) air travel was not significantly different from zero (cf. Gronau, 1970). Since long-distance air travel for personal reasons (e.g. vacations) is bound mostly to occur in what we called residual time, this is very much what we would expect. However, this being the only study of long-distance travel so far in which personal and business trips were separated, too much significance should not be attached to its findings.[16]

Coming now to time lavishly spent on activities with a tradeoff, we are back at the paradox we started with on p. 75 above. If it is true that the public is caught between its desire to save time and its inability to make good use of the time so saved, then any activity that can save money must appear as a resolution of the dilemma. If a person has more than he can rationally spend of both money and time, then devoting each to an activity that saves the other becomes an excuse for a more relaxed budgeting of both than he would dare to engage in without excuse. Moreover, the saving of time or money is not the only excuse for spending the other; to save effort may be yet another reason for spending time, or money, or both—a legitimate reason if effort were in short supply, merely another excuse if the budgeting of effort turns out to be at all similar to the budgeting of time.

III. EFFORT ILLUSION

To economize human skill and physical effort is the principal aim of all technical and economic progress. Most innovations of methods of production reduce the skill and effort needed in work; invention and improvement of the final products themselves diminish the skill and effort required in householding and living in general. These being known as the main aims and achievements of economic development, most people gladly and unquestioningly accept and use whatever private and public amenities, vehicles, appliances, and goods become available for easing and simplifying their lives. This is only natural in a world at whose creation man was condemned to gain his bread by the sweat of his brow. The question arises, however, whether to ease the effort and skill requirements of life remains desirable indefinitely, however much they have been eased already; and. should the answer be no, whether the critical point of optimal effort reduction has not been reached and passed already.

Every organism has innate energies and capacities, the exercise of which seems to give it satisfaction. Experiments with animals have shown that even in captivity they try, if at all possible, to engage in about the same amount of physical activity as they would in their natural habitat: smaller animals by running in activity wheels; larger ones by pacing or moving around in their cages. Children also manifest a spontaneous desire to expend muscular energy and develop and exercise their bodily and mental skills. In adult man, these natural tastes seem, in some societies, to be suppressed by cultural influences—presumably his belief or the belief of society around him in ease and comfort as the supreme aim in life.

Where this is so—and there is plenty of evidence that in the United States it is so[17]—the question arises whether to accept these acquired tastes as rational or whether to regard them as a subversion of man's natural tastes, which impedes rational choice. The basis for the latter view is the well-established fact that the exercise of one's senses, faculties and muscles is essential for the health of one's limbs and organs, and that the prevalence of obesity and premature heart disease in the United States population has mainly to do with lack of physical exercise. This is why millions of middle-aged, middle-class Americans, following doctors' orders, ride exercycles in their bathrooms or jog around the block in the evenings trying to spend the muscular energy they so carefully saved during the rest of the day. Such uneven budgeting of effort is strongly reminiscent of the uneven budgeting of time discussed earlier; and we question its rationality, because people seem to take exercycle rides as bitter medicine, and not for fun.[18] It is true that people choose this behaviour pattern out of their own free will, but to accept this as proof of rational behaviour is to ignore its genesis. We first ◄ learn to appreciate the saving of effort, the wonderful technology that makes it possible, and the social status it imparts; only many years later, when we are fully addicted to it as a way of life, do we realize its drawbacks; and by then, remedial therapy is often the only recourse left.

The static nature of the economist's theory of human rationality explains its inability to deal with this particular problem, the problem of habit formation and its implications; yet this is not its only shortcoming.[19] We tried to point up some others as well, hoping to hasten the infusion of a little empirical content into the economic theory of man and his behaviour.

NOTES

1. Sparked by Arrow's work (1951) on the social preference function, there were experiments to test the transivity of individual preferences, which yielded some unexpected results; these were, however, quickly forgotten.
2. Professor Peter Temin reminded me that, however minor, this one exception to the assumption of consumer rationality had become one of the cornerstones of the microfoundations of macroeconomics.
3. Marx was well aware of this and made it an integral part of his theory of accumulation, but it never found its way into bourgeois economics; my own attempt (Scitovsky, 1943) to introduce it into the theory of the firm was a failure.
4. The best published statement perhaps is by Ando and Modigliano (1963).
5. The firms that specialize in tracking down their unknown and long-forgotten relatives for a share (usually a third) of the spoils form quite a large industry.
6. All the data in this paragraph refer to 1970 and come from the 1971 *Statistical Abstract of the United States,* except for the estimate of bequests to government, which comes from publications of the Internal Revenue Service.
7. These announcements, continued over the past twenty years, are not advertisements, because they do not state Mr. Nelms's form of business. (In any case, this is real estate speculation).
8. cf. Becker (1965), and Linder (1970).
9. cf. Lundberg *et al.* (1934, 1966).
10. Averaged over weekdays *and* weekends, and including TV watching engaged in simultaneously with other activities.
11. cf. United States Congress. House of Representatives (1967).

12. This is evident from audience ratings.
13. Time being more precious to high-income earners, one would expect them to be more willing to spend money on avoiding interruptions.
14. These data have been obtained for, but not published, in this form by Wilensky (1964). I am indebted to Professor Wilensky for making available these percentages.
15. According to labour economists, there would be much greater disparity between rates of absenteeism and rates on moonlighting if the representative worker were not fairly well satisfied with the length of the workweek.
16. In another study, Institute of Defense Analyses (1966), it was assumed but not tested that there is no difference between business and personal travellers with respect to their valuation of travel time.
17. cf. Scitovsky (1972) for a small sample of the evidence.
18. Note the development of motorized exercycles. What once was a wishdream—the effortless exerciser—has become a marketable and widely marketed product. Has it ceased to be a wishdream?
19. cf. von Weizsacker (1971) for an interesting theoretical attempt at a dynamic theory of consumers' preferences.

REFERENCES

Ando, A. and Modigliano, F. The life-cycle hypothesis of saving: aggregate implications and tests. *American Economic Review,* Vol. 53 (1963), pp. 55-84.

Arrow, K. (1951) *Social Choice and Individual Values,* (New York: Wiley, 1951).

Becker, G. S. A theory of the allocation of time. *Economic Journal,* Vol. 75, (1965), pp. 493-517.

Beesley, M. E. The value of time spent in travelling. *Economica,* Vol. 32, (1965), pp. 174-185.

Gronau, R. The value of time in passenger transportation. Occasional Paper No. 109, pp. 52-53. (New York: National Bureau of Economic Research, 1970.)

Institute of Defense Analyses Demand analysis for air travel by supersonic transport, Washington, DC, 1966, 7 ff.

Linder, S. B. *The Harried Leisure Class,* (New York: Columbia University Press, 1970).

Lisco, T. E. The value of commuters travel time: a study in urban transportation. (Ph.D. dissertation, Chicago, 1967, unpublished.)

Lundberg, G., Komarovski, M. and McInerny, M. *Leisure: A Suburban Study,* (New York: Columbia University Press, 1934).

Lundberg, G., Komarovski, M. and McInerny, M. Recherche comparative internationale sur les budgets temps. *INSEE Etudes et Conjonctures,* (Sept. 1966), pp. 103-88.

Owen, J. D. *The price of Leisure, an Economic Analysis of the Demand for Leisure Time.* (Montreal: McGill Univ. Press, 1970), pp. 32.

Quarmby, D. A. Choice of travel mode for the journey to work: some findings. *Journal of Transportation Economics and Policy,* Vol. 1, (1967), pp. 273-314.

Scitovsky, T. A note on profit maximization and its implications. *Review of Economic Studies,* Vol. II, (1943), pp. 57-60.

Scitovsky, T. What's wrong with the arts is what's wrong with society. *American Economic Review,* Vol. 62, (1972), Papers and Proceedings. Chapter 4 above.

Steiner, E. A. *The People Look at Television: A Study of Audience Attitudes* (New York: Knopf, 1963), Ch.3.

Stopher, R. R. A probability model of travel mode choice for the work journey. *Highway Research Record,* No. 283 (1969), pp. 57-65.

Traffic Research Corporation Model split analysis: Metropolitan Toronto and region transportation study. (Toronto: Traffic Research Corporation, 1965.)

United States Congress, House of Representatives Subscription television—especially Joint comments of Zenith Radio Corporation, and Teco, Inc. *Hearing before Committee on Interstate and Foreign Commerce, Subcommittee on Communications and Power, 90th Congress, 1st Session, 1967.* (Washington, DC, 1967.)

von Weizsäcker, C. C. Notes on endogenous change of tastes. *Journal of Economic Theory,* Vol. 3, (1971), pp. 345-72.

Wilensky, H. L. Mass society and mass culture; Interdependence or independence? *American Sociological Review,* Vol. 29, (1964), pp. 173-97.

Part III
Faces of Capitalism

7 Can Capitalism Survive?—An Old Question in a New Setting*—1980

Can capitalism survive?—that was the question raised a generation ago by Josef Schumpeter and answered in the negative. We have accumulated a lot more hindsight since then—even so, you would hardly expect me, a senior-citizen economist from California, the retirement State, to be so bold and bright as to try to improve upon the most celebrated performance of America's most brilliant economist. Nor, for that matter, would I wish to do so even if I could—certainly not here, where I am addressing an audience of professional forecasters and would-be forecasters, and not at this time, when the sheer volume and variety of economic forecasts are depreciating the product. I propose instead merely to change the venue: not to reconsider Schumpeter's argument and conclusions but to approach the question differently and see what additional light that throws upon it.

Capitalism, when you think of it, is not an attractive form of social organization; but it is, or at any rate has been, redeemed by two great merits: the impersonal nature of its constraints, and its unequalled flexibility—flexibility in exploiting opportunities, absorbing shocks, adapting to changed circumstances. I shall focus on this last feature and ask whether that flexibility still exists and still redeems.

To come back to the variety of forecasts for a moment, the remarkable thing about them is not the variety itself but the fact that those many different forecasts all have the same basis. We economists proudly consider our discipline the queen of the social sciences, on the ground that unlike other social scientists, we subscribe to the same paradigm and use the same concepts, approach and tools of analysis. All the more surprising therefore is the contrast between the monolithic solidity of the base we start from and the great variety of predictions, diagnoses and policy recommendations we end up with. That, I dare say, has many reasons; but

* The Richard T. Ely Lecture delivered at the 1979 Christmas meeting of the American Economic Association in Atlanta, Georgia. I am grateful to Moses Abramovitz, Nathan Rosenberg, Stanley Sheinbaum and Lorie Tarshis for many useful suggestions and corrections, but the neck I am sticking out is entirely my own.

85

there is one which to my mind is more important than the rest, and which is well exemplified in the field of international money.

In the good old days, when there still were believers along with the unbelievers in the functioning of the international financial system, balance-of-payments theorists used to be divided into elasticity optimists and elasticity pessimists. They shared the same theory of balance-of-payments adjustment, which said that a system of variable exchange rates would be self-equilibrating if the Marshall-Lerner conditions were satisfied, but disequilibrating if the demand and supply elasticities of imports and exports were too low to satisfy those conditions. The optimists and the pessimists differed merely in attributing different values to those elasticities, whose actual values no one knew nor had means of finding out.

Another example of a similar division of opinion comes from the theory of growth. There used to be a distinguished group of economists whom you might have dubbed the growth pessimists. Alvin Hansen and other believers in his stagnation thesis were in that group; and so were Sir Roy Harrod and Hansen's pupil, Evsey Domar, who in a classic case of tacit collusion propounded the Harrod-Domar growth model, so elegant in its simplicity and so disturbing in the instability of its knife-edge equilibrium. Fortunately, there was also a no-less-distinguished group of growth optimists, led by Robert Solow and Trevor Swann, who gave us the equally elegant but reassuringly stable Solow-Swann model of economic growth. Here, too, the difference between optimists and pessimists lay in the differing assumptions thay made about elasticities. Indeed, we could again call the pessimists elasticity pessimists, since their dire conclusions hinged on their assuming fixed coefficients and zero elasticities.

That similarity between the two examples is not accidental, of course. On the contrary, they are both variations on the same simple theme, which is that capitalism works when it's flexible but self-destructs when it's not. The great merit of capitalism and the secret of its past successes was its great flexibility, imparted to it by the automatic forces of the market.

What then is that flexibility and how does it come about? In general, there are two kinds of economic flexibility. The first is the flexibility of the economy's individual members: the flexibility of consumers in adapting their expenditure patterns, of producers modifying methods of production and utilizing the most available outputs, and of the owners of productive services in providing the services most in demand. The second and more drastic kind is the ability of the system as a whole to adjust its reliance on its individual members: increasing its reliance on those best adapted or able to adapt to changed circumstances and jettisoning those unadapted and unable to adapt.

Capitalism owed its unrivalled flexibility to the fact that market prices and earnings were an excellent means of assuring both kinds of flexibility.

Price signals proved to be a quick, reliable and accurate system of communication; the incentives they provided seemed to spur individuals to the utmost flexibility of which they were capable; and the distributive function of prices added flexibility of the second kind, because every redistribution brought about by market forces shifted the economy's centre of gravity away from non-adaptors towards adaptors and the already adapted.

With the passage of time, however, the joints of that once wondrously flexible structure are becoming more and more calcified and rigid; and the process seems hard to reverse, because it stems from so many different and diverse causes. Growing affluence, improved technology, the greater role of government, and the increased bureaucratization and expanding size of firms are among factors that explain why individual buyers and sellers have become less responsive to market signals and tend increasingly to ignore the gains and losses with which the market rewards adaptation and punishes failure to adapt. Such a decline in people's and firms' responses to price signals would normally cause the price signals to become stronger and flexibility of the second kind to take over. However, the price signals themselves have their own rigidities, which are also on the increase owing to oligopolistic and bureaucratic price fixing; and besides, the second kind of flexibility, acting through a redistribution of income, grates on our sense of distributive justice, which is why we are forever tempted to impede its action. All those factors, of course, the failure of people and firms to heed changing prices, and the failure of prices to reflect changing conditions, contribute to rendering the economy less flexible.

Let me give just a few illustrations. The most obvious example is the growth of goverment as a buyer of goods and services. Government usually considers itself above petty cost considerations and seldom revises its shopping list in response to changing prices. Its growing economic role therefore increases the weight of its own inflexibility.

Private firms, once so flexible and quick to exploit new opportunities and adapt to price fluctuations, have also become less responsive to changes in market conditions. One reason, probably, is the increasing complexity and size of the most efficient producing unit, due to ever more mechanized and automated productive processes; another perhaps is the increasingly bureaucratic way in which those ever larger units are administered; and both of those factors make it harder, dearer and slower to innovate, revise production methods and change input coefficients. A third reason is the great importance of government contracts, which encourage the firms that receive those contracts to become just as inflexible as their main customer. Yet another reason is the ever more pervasive regulatory powers of government, prompted by concerns over health, environment, job safety, product safety, equity and similar considerations. That last is generally considered the main impediment to the firm's flexibility, and one gets an idea of its importance from estimates of the costs it imposes on the economy. The static cost of administering and complying with government regulation is put at 5 per cent of the national income. More important for us is the dynamic cost, in the sense of the slowing of innovation, adaptation, introduction of new products; and the part of that cost imposed merely by environmental and job-safety regulation is estimated at a quarter of the potential rise in labour productivity.[1]

A striking illustration of what has happened to flexibility is our economy's failure to date, six long years after OPEC had started flexing its muscles, to have taken even a first step towards substituting coal for oil in response to rising oil and falling coal prices, although idle capacity, unemployed miners, and coal deposits are all plentiful. The California Energy Commission is said to need between two and a half and three years to approve the siting and construction of a coal-fired thermo-electric generating plant; the Environmental Protection Agency took six years to grant a permit for such a plant in Montana.[2] If those cases are typical, they explain much of the inflexibility of production coefficients.

Government and business firms are, of course, complex organizations; perhaps it is inevitable that their inflexibility should increase with sheer size alone. But what about the consumer, whose market behaviour is a no less important part of the behaviour of the economy? Surely, human nature is unchanging; how can one reconcile that fact with evidence that the consumer too has become less adaptable and less responsive to changing market prices? The obvious explanation is his increased affluence. To change one's behaviour in response to worsened circumstances is, in a sense, an acceptance and admission of defeat. Not to change one's behaviour is like keeping a stiff upper lip in adversity: it is manly, dignified, impressive and costly. Affluent consumers are quite able and willing to bear the private cost of such behaviour; they are unaware and unheeding of the social cost, which includes the diminished flexibility and viability of the system.

One illustration is the Amercian consumer's response, or rather lack of response, to the rising price of imports. We are fortunate enough to be able to produce at home most of the things we need and want. That is why most of our imports of consumer goods are like icing on a cake: small additions to the much larger volume of domestically produced versions of the same product, prized just for being more fancy or just for being foreign. It should have been all the easier therefore to dispense with many of them as the depreciation of the dollar raised their prices. Yet, nothing of the sort happened. As if the dollar had not depreciated, or as if price were no object, we continue to import wines, beer, shoes, automobiles and much else besides in undiminished quantities, sometimes in undiminished proportions of our increasing total consumption of those commodities. The public seems ready to pay through the nose for the maintenance of its living standards and status symbols; but its uppety behaviour robs the balance of payments of its ability to right itself, causes the dollar to depreciate further and further, and adds to our inflationary woes. When consumers don't respond to the rising cost of imports, domestic prices do; and that, of course, is the worst kind of response.

Another example of that same stiff-upper-lipmanship is the behaviour of workers both here and in other advanced capitalist countries. Rising affluence, and in some countries also a temporary shortage of skills, has made them raise their sights to more important, more responsible, more prestigious jobs, and to acquire the requisite training. Unfortunately, the upgrading of the labour force ran ahead of the upgrading of jobs. The resulting excess supply of higher skills and qualifications has already depressed the relative earning power of the college trained, raised their unemployment rates, and lengthened their search periods. At the same time, the lowly, dirty, unpleasant jobs at the other end of the skill scale would go begging were it not for the large inflow of Puerto Ricans and Mexicans to this country, Pakistanis and Indians to Britain, Algerians to France, and assorted guest workers to the other affluent countries of Western Europe. By now, the number of foreign workers in the labour force of those countries is commensurate to the number of their unemployed, yet to send them home would be no remedy, because the indigenous unemployed disdain the jobs that ousted guest workers would relinquish. They prefer, and thanks to Social Security and accumulated savings are able, to stay unemployed rather than to accept jobs beneath their station. If labour markets nevertheless retain long-run flexibility, it is owing to the next generation's response to market signals.

All those were instances of the diminished response of buyers and sellers to price signals, which leaves unimpaired the second kind of flexibility—the shifting of the economy's centre of gravity. But the loss of people's and firms' responsiveness to prices is compounded by the diminished response also of prices to changing conditions; and that has not only diminished the second kind of flexibility but, by impairing the signalling and incentive functions of prices, has further reduced individual adaptation as well.

Price rigidity has many causes. Disparity between the number of buyers and sellers accounts for price setting by price makers; and the greater the disparity, the more rigidly bureaucratic the way in which price makers set their prices. For the asymmetrical downward rigidity of wage rates everybody seems to have his own explanation. Mine, of course, is by far the most plausible and sensible; but it is too long to repeat here. It has to do with the conflict between unequal incomes and equal bargaining strength on the two sides of the labour market.[3] Monopolistic and oligopolistic restriction is another cause of price rigidity; and it explains, for instance, the tendency of productivity growth to lead, not to price reductions, which would be anti-inflationary, but to wage increases, which become inflationary as they are extended across the board for equity's sake, and so spread from workers whose productivity has risen to those whose productivity lags behind. Another cause of price rigidity is society's increasing refusal to accept inequitable price constellations and price adjustments.

Capitalism never got high marks for equity, although it was good not only to capitalists. Its fast growth benefited the average person and with him the majority; but it did so at the cost of great fluctuations and a wide dispersion of incomes around that fast-growing average. It provided jackpots and fleshpots for a minority, inflicted misery and unemployment or bankruptcy and ruin on another, larger minority—most of it the outcome of the great rewards and high penalties capitalism distributed in the interests of flexibility. Flexibility and the system's viability were well maintained as long as the public accepted the inequality of incomes and the wide scatter of winnings and losses as manifestations of the immutable laws of the market.

In time, however, we learned how to correct, suppress, overrule, or supplement the distributive functions of prices and price changes; and the better we learned to divorce income distribution from market forces, the more reluctant we became to accept the economic inequalities imposed by the market.

A good example, in the Scandinavian countries, is their use of the periodic centralized and synchronized wage bargains as occasions for implementing the policy of the Trade-Union Confederation aimed at mitigating wage inequalities. Between those equitable wage increases, inequality sneaks back as employers raise the pay of the more highly skilled in response to their greater scarcity; and that tug of war between the forces of equity and marginal productivity is now recognized as an important inflationary factor.[4] A similar example here and in many Western European countries is the tendency for productivity-related wage increases to be extended, for fairness' sake, also to groups of workers whose productivity has increased less or not at all; and that too is a well-known and much-discussed inflationary force[5]

It is mostly government, however, that overrules market prices and suppresses competitive price adjustments. Farm price supports, airline regulation and the dead-ending of trucks are examples of government interference in favour of business; but there is much of it also for the sake of greater equity. Indeed, to intervene in the interests of distributive justice has become an important preoccupation of government under advanced capitalism. To mitigate the inequities of capitalism while preserving its efficiency is the great liberal compromise—but does it work? Since we cannot divorce the signalling function of prices from their distributive function, every modification of market-determined distribution is likely to weaken or falsify market signalling and thereby to weaken the economy's automatic tendency to adjust. That being the case, one may well ask how the capitalist State got itself into the business of undermining its own economic base?

The answer, I think, is that up to a point the liberal compromise worked pretty well, especially while it was confined to improving the static income distribution through general taxation and the provision of social services and Social Security benefits. Apart from lowering the incentive to save, those measures have little or no impact on choice: the choice of consumers, workers and producers between alternative commodities, services, inputs and outputs. They are supposed to diminish the incentive to work or to participate in economic activity; but in the beginning they had no measurable impact on that either.

That was not only beginner's luck. It helped that, in this country certainly and in many other countries probably, progressive taxation is a myth. Our taxes make a hardly noticeable change in the distribution of income, because the main effect of the progressivity of the income tax is to undo the regressivity of the other taxes.

It also helped that price signals are not the only vehicle of market communication and the earning of money to spend is not the only incentive to work. There is satisfaction in the work itself and in one's recognition of oneself as a useful member of society. In countries with strong puritan traditions, people value income not only for what it will buy but also for the status it gives, because they regard it as a measure of their own worth to society. That is measured, of course, by income *before* taxes; and there you have the one and only instance of the successful separation of the incentive function of earnings from their distributive function.

Those, probably, are the main reasons why the liberal compromise was so successful in the early stages—successful enough not to seem like a compromise at all and not to cause a noticeable decline in market efficiency. It is hardly surprising that we got carried away into believing that progress towards more equality and more security could proceed almost indefinitely without impairing market performance. Doubts are arising slowly and only *ex post facto* as the blunting of market rewards and penalties is increasingly focused on assuring fairness in a dynamic sense: in the incidence of *changes* in earnings and in the distribution of the rewards and penalties created by price *changes*.

By the first of those I mean the taxation of capital gains and profits and the Scandinavian and British near-confiscatory tax rates on the very top of the income distribution. They are much blamed for reducing the rewards for risk taking and for dampening the spirit of innovation. They usually go hand in hand with government's also taking over some of the risks: allowing tax deductions of business losses, footing the bill for research and development and occasionally bailing out companies on the verge of failure. Such reductions of the entrepreneur's risk would offset reductions in his reward for taking risk, were it not confined, the first to companies large and diversified enough to have profits to offset losses against, the last to corporations so large that their failure would rock the boat. Unfortunately, the government's sharing the risks of those firms does more to ossify the corporate structure than to raise its animal spirits, while the Schumpeterian entrepreneur, the imaginative newcomer who has to risk his all to realize his vision, is left out in the cold, relieved of the reward for risk taking, but not of the risk itself.

The second form of State intervention just mentioned usually takes the form of price control proper. This country's control of oil prices is an excellent illustration of both the depth of the conflict between equity and efficiency concerns and the magnitude of the problems created when government suppresses market forces and puts nothing in their place.

I made inflexibility the villain of the piece but, apart from a few passing references to such things as the inflationary effects of price rigidity, and the slowing by government regulation of technical change and progress, I have said very little so far to establish its villainous nature. Let me now make good that omission by discussing a much neglected function of market flexibility: its impact on macroeconomic problems and macroeconomic policies.

Flexibility is the ability and willingness to substitute one thing for another, including the changing of inputs in response to a change in output and the changing of expenditures in response to a change in income. That is why, in a flexible economy, any change, disturbance, or disequilibrium originating in one market spreads to other markets, why the different disturbances in different markets are brought together and evened out, and why market situations throughout the economy tend to become more nearly uniform.

By contrast, inflexibility separates markets one from another and locks in whatever disturbance or disequilibrium each of them may be having. In other words, inflexibility causes, or rather preserves, the fragmentation of the economy, which becomes manifest in a dispersion of degrees and types of market disequilibria across sectors and regions. Empirically, that is best measured by the dispersion of unemployment rates, data on which are available and suggest that, in the United States and the United Kingdom at least, there has been a secular increase in economic fragmentation.[6]

Such fragmentation, however, and the resulting disparities between disequilibria in different markets, are not necessarily a bad thing. After all, the diffusion of a disturbance through several markets does not usually dissipate it. In economics, when one change leads to another, a cumulative process is often generated which magnifies rather than dissipates the initial disturbance. The unemployment multiplier is the obvious example. Accordingly, there is something to be said in favour of inflexibility, which locks in and isolates a fall in effective demand. Indeed, social insurance, social services, and the affluent consumer's and worker's uppety behaviour, all of which I blamed earlier for impairing flexibility, also go by the name of built-in stabilizers. They have undoubtedly lowered the value of the multiplier and probably explain why these days, thank God, unemployment never reaches anywhere near the heights it used to scale in the heyday of capitalism, say, in the 1890s and 1930s.

Unfortunately, that same inflexibility is no stabilizer in the opposite direction: it fails to arrest the spreading of inflationary price increases. The reason is that inflexibility locks in the excess demand but not the resulting rise in prices, because excess demand is not the only carrier of the inflation virus. Wage increases, for example, spread from firm to firm and industry to industry by the principle of equity more than *via* the spreading of labour shortages—and the latter alone is prevented by the fragmentation of markets.

Inflexibility shows up in even worse light in the next case. When two markets or two parts of the economy suffer, one from an excess, the other from an insufficiency of demand, flexibility would enable those two contrary disequilibria mutually to offset and eliminate one another, inflexibility preserves both of them intact. That may explain why we have more economic troubles nowadays than there used to be in the days of flexible capitalism, and also why today they seem so much more intractable.

That brings me to the next and by far the most serious trouble that inflexibility creates: its tendency to render orthodox Keynesian stabilization policies ineffective or politically unacceptable. I mentioned that flexibility and interaction between markets integrate their disequilibria, offset one against the other, diffuse them and render them more uniform. That opens the way to cumulative processes; but it also has the inestimable advantage of greatly facilitating the use of stabilization policies by so-to-speak preparing the patient for the treatment.

Fiscal and monetary restriction and expansion are macroeconomic policies par excellence. They cannot be focused on only one sore spot in the body economic; their influence is broad gauged, diffused, and so acts on the economy's different sectors and industries more or less equally and with the same intensity. That is why they are the most effective and politically the most acceptable in an economy whose different parts and sectors all suffer from the same trouble and more or less to the same degree. Flexibility, of course, is what creates that kind of uniformity, because it leads to high elasticities of substitution, transformation, adaptation and thereby assures that the different parts of an underheated or overheated economy will have not too dissimilar temperatures.

That may well explain why, in the more flexible and therefore more uniform economic environment of a generation ago, when stabilization policies were first developed and applied, they were effective and acceptable; whereas in today's rigid, fragmented and heterogeneous economy they often seem both ineffective and unacceptable. Indeed, what can fiscal and monetary policy do against the kind of stagflation where insufficient demand in one part of the economy creates unemployment, and excess demand in the other part creates inflationary pressures, which, however, do not remain confined to that part alone. What can be done even in the much simpler case where one part of the economy is overheated and the rest more or less in equilibrium? You get inflationary pressures generated in the overheated part and spreading out from it to the rest of the economy; but try to contain them with restrictive macropolicies and you are sure to create unemployment much sooner than you manage to slow the rise in prices. Policy makers complain that the public has become oversensitive to the side-effects of anti-inflationary policies: is it not rather that the side-effects have become more severe, now that those policies are applied in a more fragmented, more heterogeneous economy than they were designed for? Perhaps the most ominous consequence of inflexibility is that by failing to homogenize the economy, it limits the effectiveness and acceptability of macroeconomic policies.

The relevance of all that for the question to which this lecture is addressed is obvious. If I assessed the role and the fate of flexibility correctly, then I have added strength to Schumpeter's argument. Capitalism is bound to lose drive and manageability if it is becoming less flexible and less adaptable.

Lest you find that thought too depressing, let me remind you that Schumpeter predicted the demise of capitalism at the very time when it was embarking on its longest stretch of uninterrupted fast growth and high prosperity. Had he known that, he might still have stuck to his prediction, which was based on sociological more than economic considerations; but I do believe that he failed to recognize the importance of Keynes' contribution and failed to foresee the success of Keynesian macropolicies in stabilizing the free enterprise economy without making it less free and less enterprising. One of my main points was that today's economy is too fragmented for the broad-gauged, diffused action of Keynesian policies to do much good; but perhaps I, too, am overlooking the emergence of a new way out.

Salvation could lie in recapturing some of that lost flexibility or in some new policy better able to deal with today's problems. We should really have both. But lost flexibility is hard to restore, because some of it was lost due to factors beyond our control, the rest was the side-effect of liberal policies, ignored or minimized at the time owing to the liberals' excessive faith in capitalism and its ability to fly, however much its wings are clipped. It is difficult to go back on those policies, because they secured important benefits, which the public is reluctant to give up, whether or not they are worth the cost.

Yet, difficult as it may be to recapture lost flexibility, we have taken a few steps in that direction already. One of them is the budget constraints California's Proposition 13 imposed on government, and not only in California. Another one is airline deregulation; and several other of our regulatory agencies are also under attack. A different example, but perhaps only to show that the old flexibility is not all dead, is the competitive pressure thanks to which progress in electronics has led to stabilizing price reductions instead of inflationary wage increases.

Now what about new policies to deal with our new problems, and our old problems in their new setting? Nothing, so far, approximates what happened in the depressed 1930s: the spreading like wildfire of Keynes' new ideas and their capturing the imagination and loyalty of an entire generation of young economists. I know of some good ideas and there must be many more; but none has caught on. One reason could be that, to deal effectively with today's economic problems, new policies may have to be too selective or too drastic to stay within the spirit of capitalism. The benefits could well be worth the costs; but that, unfortunately, is not enough, because the public, jealous of its accustomed freedoms, may refuse to give such policies a fair hearing.

For this country's faith in capitalism is very peculiar. We blithely pile regulation on regulation, imposing as many costs and fetters upon the functioning of our markets, with never thought of what that may do to their efficiency; and at the same time, we retain more faith even in the most hamstrung and ineffectual markets and market signals than in anything that would displace or bolster them or change their character. The danger with such an attitude is that we might end up with the worst of both worlds: stuck with capitalism's unattractive features but deprived of what I described at the outset as one of the system's great and redeeming virtues: its flexibility.

NOTES

1.   cf. M. L. Weidenbaum 'The big cost of government regulation', *Challenge,* (November/December 1979), pp. 32-9; and E. F. Denison 'Effects of selected changes in the institutional and human environment upon output per unit of input', *Survey of Current Business,* (January 1978), pp. 21-44.
2.   cf. the 1st 1979 quarterly report of the Pacific Gas & Electric Company; and *US News & World Report,* (November 12, 1979), p. 73.
3.   cf. my 'Asymmetrics in economics', *Scottish Journal of Political Economy,* Vol. 25 (1978), pp. 227-37.
4.   cf. O. Aukrust 'Inflation in the open economy: a Norwegian model', L. B. Krause and W. S. Salant, (eds.), *Worldwide Inflation—Theory and Recent Experience,* (1977), The Brookings Institution, Washington, DC.
5.   cf. J. Eatwell, L. Llewellyn and R. Tarling 'Money wage inflation in industrial countries', *Review of Economic Studies,* 42, (1974), pp. 515-523.
6.   R. G. Lipsey ('The relation between unemployment and the rate of change of money wage rates in the UK, 1862-1957: a further analysis', *Economica,* Vol. 40, (1960), pp. 1-31) seems to have first posed the question whether inflation might not also depend on the dispersion of excess demand and the consequent dispersion of unemployment across regions and sectors. His question was followed up by C. G. Archibald ('Wage price dynamics, inflation, and unemployment, the Phillips curve and the distribution of unemployment', *AER Papers and Proceedings,* Vol. 59, (1969), pp. 124-60) and by R. L. Thomas and P. J. M. Stoney ('Unemployment dispersion as a determinant of wage inflation in the UK 1925-66', *Manchester School* (1971)); they both found significant and quantitatively important positive relationship, and Archibald explained the upward shift of the Phillips curve by increased dispersion. For a qualification, *see* G. C. Archibald, R. Kemis and J. W. Perkins 'Excess demand for labour, unemployment and the Phillips curve: a theoretical and empirical study', in D. Laidler and D. Purdy (eds.) *Inflation and Labour Markets* (Manchester: Manchester University Press, 1974), pp. 109-63. My argument, of course, is quite different but clearly related.

8 Price Takers' Plenty: A Neglected Benefit of Monopoly Capitalism*— 1985

To understand the world around us, we theorize about it. We build simplified models of reality in order to bring into focus one or another of its important features and to abstract from confusing and distracting detail. The economist's standard model for explaining the workings of the capitalist economy is the model of perfect competition—justly admired for its elegant simplicity and great explanatory power in showing how market prices distil, summarize and transmit information about the urgency of demands and availability of supplies, how that coordinates different people's and firms' market behaviour and so brings about an efficient allocation of resources and distribution of goods.

The perfectly competitive model is idealized and unrealistic, of course, because real-life competition is far from perfect. Its main shortcoming, however, is not its lack of realism, nor its idealizing what it shows of the workings of the capitalist economy, but rather that it does not show enough of the latter's workings. It fails to show and even masks several functions of the economy that are not much less important than the allocation and distribution of resources and goods. I am not proposing to displace the perfectly competitive model with a better one, only to supplement it with another partial model that focuses attention on those neglected functions.

The desire for profit is the driving force of the capitalist economy; and ◄ the profits generated in the pursuit of that desire, or rather the income inequalities profits give rise to, are the cost capitalist society pays for the proper functioning of its economy. The model of perfect competition is an idealized picture, not only because it depicts the economy's allocative and distributive system as 100 per cent efficient, but also because it underrates the cost of achieving such efficiency. For the assumption that competition

---

* This is the revised version of a paper presented at All Souls College, Oxford, and before the Marshall Society, Cambridge, in November 1981. I am indebted to John Pencavel for constructive criticism but am solely responsible for all remaining shortcomings and errors.

is perfect implies that it tends to eliminate profits completely, so that they are earned only in disequilibrium situations, while the economy approaches but has not yet reached equilibrium. In an ever-changing economy, of course, equilibrium may never be reached; but that by itself would not prevent the elimination of profits, because departures from equilibrium create not only profits but losses as well, although profits may well predominate when the economy is expanding. Moreover, the windfall profits generated by disturbances and disequilibria don't accrue to capitalists alone but are distributed among all the participants in market transactions, producers and consumers, sellers and buyers alike. The model of perfect competition, therefore, which admits no other kind of profits, plays down their importance as a source of capitalists' income (as distinct from their other source of income, the return on capital). That is why the model underrates the driving force of profits and completely overlooks several important functions that capitalists perform in quest of monopoly profits.

One of those functions is innovation, the development of new products and superior manufacturing methods, which are the instruments of economic progress. Joseph Schumpeter pointed out that innovation, and the research and development needed for innovation, would hardly be undertaken without the innovators' being compensated for the risks they take by their monopoly of the profits to be gained if the innovation is successful. Indeed, most research and development is undertaken by large, monopolistic or oligopolistic firms; and patent rights, which establish at least a temporary monopoly, seem to be an essential condition of innovation in private enterprise economies.

Another valuable function capitalists perform in the capitalist economy, and the one this paper will concentrate on, is their tendency to ascertain, anticipate, and cater to consumers' wishes, thereby creating for them a buyers' market, in which the consumer is king, being made to feel like one by producers and sellers who go out of their way to please and serve him and to ease and minimize his share of the chores and effort of marketing. The first to note and stress the value to the consuming public of shopping in a buyers' market was Professor Janos Kornai. That is hardly surprising. After all, Kornai is the foremost theoretician of the socialist economy, which patently fails to provide its consumers with a buyers' market; and it is a law of human nature that the good things in life are always the most noticed and best appreciated by those who lack them, while those who have them hardly notice the fact because they take them for granted. Indeed, visitors from the capitalist countries always deplore what they believe to be a lack of consumer goods in the socialist economies, not realizing that part, perhaps the main part of the trouble is the inadequacy of a communication and transportation system between buyers and sellers, consumers and producers, that puts the main burden of communicating on the buyers. although all the advantages and economies of scale in providing good communication happen to be on the sellers side.

Kornai was also the first to fault the perfectly competitive equilibrium model for its inability to deal with such (and similar) functions of the economy. Note his choice of the title, *Anti-Equilibrium,* for his book in which he treats the subject.[1] In his view, a particular kind of disequilibrium—by which he means a particular kind of departure from the perfectly competitive equilibrium—is characteristic of the capitalist economy and responsible for creating the buyers' market. I don't disagree with that view but prefer to analyse the cause of that kind of disequilibrium, and so the basis of the buyers' market and its amenities, in the framework of an imperfectly competitive model in equilibrium, rather than in Kornai's framework of the perfect competitive model out of equilibrium. Let me proceed to set up such a framework.

THE RELATIONSHIP BETWEEN PRICE MAKERS AND PRICE TAKERS

Market transactions freely entered into yield a gain to both buyer and seller. When higgling and bargaining determine the price and, with it, the division of the gain from trade between the two sides, then the side with the better market information and superior bargaining skill secures the greater part of the gain. That is usually the side with the fewer competitors because, with each of them making a larger number of similar transactions, they have not only more alternatives to choose from but more opportunity to acquire the requisite knowledge and expertise as well.

When specialization renders very great the number of markets and so the disparity between the number of people on the two sides of each market, then those with the fewer competitors find themselves concluding so many market transactions with so many people that it becomes profitable for them to set their prices on a take-it-or-leave-it basis, and thereby to sacrifice some of the gain from their advantage in bargaining for the sake of saving on the cost of the time and skill it takes to bargain. That accounts for the asymmetrical relationship between price makers and price takers, which is the dominant form of market organization in all the advanced economies.

The price maker-price taker relationship has two characteristic features: one simple, straighforward and obvious, the other complex, not at all obvious but central to the argument of this paper. The first characteristic is that the symmetrical position of buyer and seller in bargaining situations and in a perfectly competitive equilibrium is replaced by an asymmetrical relation, in which the price maker, who often but by no means always is the seller, takes the initiative in making all the marketing and production decisions and so reduces the price takers facing him to playing the purely passive role of quantity adjusters, who are free merely to accept or reject the offers they face and decide on the extent to which they make use of them.

The difference between the two roles is important, because those who take the initiative exercise the power; and since the price makers in the capitalist economy are independent businessmen and corporations run by businessmen for the owners of capital, the price maker / price taker relationship characteristic of most of our markets gives capitalists the enjoyment of power and the privilege of running the economy. Those are valuable advantages, because the exercise of initiative and power are important sources of satisfaction, irrespective of whether they are well or ill used, for selfish or for unselfish purposes, and also, because such power usually secures monopoly or monopsony profits.

Since price takers face the same situation that both parties would face in a perfectly competitive market, wheras price makers face the less-than-perfectly-elastic demand or supply of imperfect markets, it is easy to see how the welfare implications of their asymmetrical relationship differ from those of the perfectly competitive model. To begin with, market prices continue to reflect and transmit information about the urgency of demands and the availability of supplies when looked at from the price maker's side of the market; but they become unreliable indicators of social opportunity costs or demand urgencies when viewed from the price taker's side. In short, even the market's signalling functions favour the price makers. Second, the efficiency of markets remains undiminished as far as the allocation and distribution of goods and jobs among price takers is concerned; but it is impaired with respect to resource allocation among price makers. Third, income distribution among price makers now becomes a function also of their relative monopoly power, and the division of income between price makers and price takers becomes tilted in favour of price makers, as will be argued below.

The other characteristic feature of the asymmetrical relationship between price makers and price takers, and the one which is crucial for the argument of this paper, is the contrast between the very limited use price makers make of their ability to change prices and the very great and active use they make of all the other competitive weapons at their disposal.

Since the price maker always faces less than perfectly competitive markets, he can always set his selling price (p_s) above marginal cost (MC) and his buying price (p_b) for his inputs below their marginal value product (MVP), to establish thereby a margin of profit between selling price and MC and/or between buying price and MVP. We are not concerned here with the size of that margin. It may be the one implied by the well-known formulae for maximising profits:

$$p_s = \frac{e}{e+1} \, MC \quad \text{and} \quad p_b = \frac{e}{e+1} \, MVP$$

where e stands for the price elasticity of the market. In practice, of course, MC and MVP are approximated to, e is guessed at, and most price makers must also pay attention to their competitors' already established prices and refrain from setting their own selling price either much above those prices (for fear of pricing themselves out of the market) or much below them (lest they precipitate a mutually ruinous price war). Symmetrical considerations govern the price maker buyers' pricing policies.

Whatever the level, however, at which the price maker has set his price, empirical evidence shows that once it is set, he tends to keep it unchanged for a while. In particular, he seldom changes prices in response to changed demand conditions, though he usually (but by no means always) adjusts output prices promptly in response to the changing costs of inputs. In short, prices set by price makers tend to be sticky.

There are at least three reasons for this. First, the price maker may have no inducement to change his selling price in response to changes in demand and sales, because his estimates of neither MC nor e, nor for that matter the prices of his competitors, need be affected by ordinary fluctuations in sales.

In addition, however, to often lacking a reason for changing his prices, the price maker also has reasons for keeping them unchanged. One stems from his desire to gain and keep his customers' (and suppliers') goodwill. Price takers rely on the price makers they face to provide them with the market information they need for making their choices; and since they naturally put a premium on information that can be depended on to remain valid for some time, they also put a premium on market offers and sources of market offers to which such dependable information pertains.

The price maker's other reason for keeping prices unchanged—and the third explanation of sticky prices—is his fear of upsetting the delicate equilibrium of an oligopolistic (oligopsonistic) situation and starting a mutually ruinous chain reaction of all-round price reductions if he is a seller, or price increases if he is a buyer. As is well known, there exists for every group of oligopolists a joint-profit-maximizing price or price structure the level of which changes, of course, with every change in input prices and production methods, but which is relatively easy to establish and adjust (OPEC's experience notwithstanding) in cases where an explicit cartel agreement is possible. It is much more difficult to achieve an approximation to such an oligopolistic price structure through tacit collusion, and even more difficult to adjust it to changing market conditions, because every price change, however motivated, is automatically suspect as an oligopolist's attempt to gain at his co-conspirators' expense, and so threatens to precipitate a price war that can end a profitable collusive agreement. That is why oligopoly prices tacitly agreed to are especially sticky and only change in the framework of some coordinating convention like price leadership, rule-of-thumb or focal-point pricing.[2] The argument is symmetrical for oligopsony prices.

I stressed those three explanations of the price maker's observed tendency to keep his selling prices unchanged, because, with none of them inhibiting his active use of the other competitive weapons at his disposal, they also explain the contrast between the stickiness of prices and the variability of most of the other terms and attributes of the price maker's offer. After all, while a change in a price maker's volume of sales seldom changes his most profitable price, it often induces him to change his advertising and his offer of various fringe benefits. Similarly, price, as by far the most visible and important attribute of the price maker's offer, is also the one whose fixity is the most important for assuring price takers' goodwill.

As to oligopoly as a cause of price stability, it positively encourages non-price competition. Every oligopolist is tempted to undercut his competitors to gain at their expense and is only kept from doing so by his fear of its or its effects' being noticed and leading to retaliation. But price reductions are singularly conspicuous and easy to imitate; whereas many, perhaps most other competitive moves easily go undetected for long periods of time and are not nearly so easy to match. Accordingly, it is no exaggeration to say that oligopoly encourages the substitution of non-price for price competition.

The purpose of the foregoing argument was to explain in rational terms why the price maker adds a profit margin to MC (or subtracts one from MVP) when setting his price but then considers that price given as he proceeds to use various forms of non-price competition in his efforts to maximize profits. The first of those, price above MC (or below MVP), imparts an expansionist bias to all the price maker's actions; the second, price regarded as given, limits his expansionist efforts to non-price competition.

A BUYERS' MARKET FOR CONSUMERS

From now on, it will be convenient to analyse separately the nature of markets in which the sellers set prices and the nature of those in which the buyers are the price makers. To begin with the former, the price maker always finds it profitable to make additional sales at his set prices, considering that every additional sale adds to his profit or diminishes his loss. Accordingly, he will welcome new customers, try to accommodate them and cater to their needs and desires and will find it profitable to stimulate demand through all the many forms of non-price competition. Moreover, he is also likely to find it profitable to combat falling demand through stepped-up advertising, special sales, special conveniences, etc. That is so, because the profit margin between his price and marginal cost measures not only his monopoly power but also the worth to him of the marginal transactions he makes and the marginal customers he sells to. The greater his monopoly power, the more he gains from additional sales or the more he loses by losing some of his established customers, and the greater therefore his inducement to hold on to the market he has and to expand it if possible.

Compare that to the seller's very different situation and market behaviour in the perfectly competitive market, where he pushes or is supposed to push all transactions to the margin of indifference, where—making no profit at all on the marginal transaction—he is correspondingly indifferent to the marginal customer facing him. The contrast is important, because just as price is determined on the margin, so are all other aspects of the market relationship as well. Kornai was very right in arguing that a buyers' market has no place in perfectly competitive equilibrium; but it is the market's imperfection and the monopolistic or oligopolistic nature of price determination in it that brings about the conditions which render the creation of buyers' markets profitable.

Indeed, when I introduced the concepts of price maker, price taker, and their asymmetrical relationship in my *Welfare and Competition,*[3] my sole aim was to provide a realistic and suitable framework for analysing the motivation and determining factors of non-price competition, the many forms of which are palpably more important than price competition, but which, until then, had a place neither in the economist's perfectly competitive model nor in his theories of imperfect and monopolistic competition. At the time, I also dealt with the allocative and distributive implications of the price maker-price taker relationship but was blind to the benefits that non-price competition among price makers confers on the price takers facing them. That aspect of it was first noted and discussed in Professor Martin Weitzman's *The Share Economy.*[4]

It is well worth listing some of those benefits, because we, who live with them during all our lives, tend hardly to notice them. To begin with, the mere fact that price makers are willing and even anxious to acquire new customers and generally to increase their sales is itself an advantage, which will be evident to all who have ever lived in a country or during a time in which it was absent. A second and related benefit is that once price makers are able to profit by an expansion of their sales at their set prices, they prepare to meet such additional demand by holding adequate inventories, stocking a full selection of brands, sizes, colours and styles, and by making that fact known through advertising and window displays.

A third benefit, or set of benefits, that price takers enjoy is the whole gamut of conveniences and attractions, which are known as the tools of non-price competition, and with whose aid price makers try actively to attract customers and increase sales. Beautiful shopwindows; attractive and comfortable premises, well heated or air conditioned, conveniently located, and kept open for long hours; easy terms of payment and of credit; friendly and polite sales clerks who are ever ready with advice and information, make refunds with a smile but never apply pressure to buy; and finally the frequent introduction of improvements and new models with which manufacturers try to meet and anticipate buyers desires, are some of the elements that render shopping—which after all is an adversary relationship—a completely frictionless and even enjoyable task in our economy.

Needless to say, the price maker will always keep the cost of offering those conveniences smaller than the extra profit he hopes to make with their aid; but from the price takers' point of view, they may well be worth the price they pay for them by paying more for the merchandise they buy than what its perfectly competitive price would be. Indeed, the fringe benefits that price takers get in exchange for the price makers' extra profits can be looked upon as a secondary transaction, separate from and additional to the purchase of the merchandise but linked with it in a package deal. Because it is so linked, one would never know whether it is mutually beneficial, except for two things. First, many of the benefits in question are cheaper for price makers to provide than for price takers to procure for themselves. Information, for example, is usually cheaper for those to disseminate who have it than for those to procure who need it. Also, if consumers could not count on having ready access during all reasonable hours to the well-stocked inventories of food and clothing stores, they would have to invest in much larger inventories of their own, whose sum would probably exceed by a wide margin the inventories that shopkeepers keep. In short, the social cost of those benefits is minimized when provided by sellers rather than buyers.

Second, there is some evidence that most buyers are willing to pay the price of those fringe benefits. For, while they cannot be bought separately from the merchandise, the emergence of discount stores, which sell the same goods at a lower price but without the fringe benefits, has enabled consumers to conclude the primary transaction without also taking the secondary transaction with its fringe benefits into the bargain. The fact that the greater part of the public continues to buy the package reveals their preference for the fringe benefits and proves that they do consider the attractions of a buyers' market worth their cost.

The term 'buyers' market' brings to mind the consequences of the sellers' having an excess supply of goods they want to get rid of. An excess of supply in the literal sense, however, can only occur in a market for labour services or, in product markets, as a result of gross miscalculation on the part of sellers. The buyers' market I am talking about is the consequence of the sellers' being price makers and, as such, able to set prices above marginal cost. The two kinds of buyers' markets are almost identical because—price policy apart—price makers on the selling side of such markets usually behave *as if* they had an excess supply to get rid of.

If the argument presented above is correct in maintaining that most consumers in the capitalist economy get extra benefits in exchange for the margin of profit they pay over the perfectly competitive price and that most of them consider that a worthwhile exchange, then the standard practice of calling the price maker's pricing policy monopolistic or oligopolistic exploitation may well be wrong. Price makers do, indeed, earn monopoly or oligopoly profits, but they often provide services in exchange; and it remains to be decided in each particular case whether the exchange is 'fair' or 'exploitative'. After all, the services and benefits offered can be more or less adequate, more or less numerous, or completely absent. In time of war or other emergencies, for example, physical shortages may render impossible any expansion of sales, thereby depriving price makers of all incentive to provide the benefits we were talking about. Even in normal times, when output can be expanded, sellers may engage in little or no non-price competition and offer correspondingly few or none of the benefits it confers if they find cheaper ways of expanding their markets and increasing sales. An important example of that is the opening up of foreign markets. Historically, that may well have been the earliest and certainly one of the most effective means for expanding price makers' markets; and a recent book on Britain's economic problems blames the backwardness of British producers' product design on the ease with which 'the Empire and the British sphere of influence in Latin America provided markets for the products they should have updated'.[5] By contrast, exports have never been more than a minor outlet for America's manufactured products, which may explain why non-price competition, which alone can expand the *domestic* market, had its greatest flowering and provided the most benefits in this country.

To conclude this section and sum up its argument, let me first reiterate that the position of producers and merchants as price makers in the markets where they sell their products is, indeed, a dominant and privileged position, which gives them power, a monopoly or oligopoly margin of profits, and usually enough goodwill to keep newcomers from entering and eliminating their oligopoly profit. Competition among them, however, which is mostly though not always present, diminishes their profits; but in view of the imperfect and incomplete (i.e. non-price) nature of competiton among price makers, it favours the consumers facing them, not so much by lowering the prices they pay but rather by providing them with a variety of fringe benefits, some more others less useful, but the lot clearly valuable and more highly valued by the majority of consumers than the money they pay for them.

WHY A SELLERS' MARKET FOR LABOUR HAS FAILED TO DEVELOP?

Having dealt with the benefits that the price maker-price taker relationship confers on consumers by creating for them a buyers' market, it is natural to ask why workers are not enjoying the corresponding advantages of a *sellers' market*, considering that the market for labour could be, and before the rise of labour unions may well have been, almost the exact mirror image of the market for consumer goods. After all, the disparity in numbers between employers and employees has originally enabled the former to set wages on a take-it-or-leave-it basis, thereby putting employees, the sellers of their labour, into the position of price takers; and oligopsonistic relations among employers, rendering wages sticky, should have encouraged non-wage competition among them, leading to fringe benefits for workers, corresponding to those enjoyed by consumers.

The reasons why market relations in the labour market have developed so very differently are not far to seek. To begin with, the conflict between the employer's and his employees' interests appears to be much greater than that between the interests of consumers and their suppliers, simply because a given percentage change in a worker's wage makes a very much greater difference to his real income than does the same percentage change in the price of any one of the many consumer goods he buys. As a result, workers resent their subordinate position as price takers in the labour market much more than their similarly subordinate position in the markets for consumer goods. Their resentment is all the greater because the fringe benefits which non-price competition among sellers creates in the consumer's favour, and which soften and mask his subordinate position in product markets, have had no chance to develop in the labour market. For there, the employer's need to incur the cost of competing workers away from competitors through the offer of fringe benefits was rendered unnecessary by a fast-increasing labour supply, provided for them free of charge by the enclosure movement in eighteenth-century England, and by mass immigration into the United States until not long ago. On a diminished scale, the same rise in the labour supply continues even today, with continued immigration, inflow of guest workers, and the steady rise in labour productivity. With the price makers' much lesser need to compete against one another in labour than in product markets, it is no wonder if labour saw the only chance for increasing its share of income and improving working conditions in collective action to secure the countervailing power with which to offset management's monopsony advantage.

The above argument applies mainly to unskilled and semi-skilled labour. Skilled workers, and those who have to exercise judgement, discretion and/or initiative in their work, possess some bargaining strength individually, even without collective action. The reason is not so much their conscious control over the quality of their work as the latter's dependence on how well satisfied they are with their pay and their position and treatment in the workplace. That fact, and the employer's awareness of that fact, gives them a hidden but important bargaining strength and so mitigates (when it does not completely offset) whatever bargaining advantage the employer derives from his position as price maker in the labour market.[6] This factor, together with organized labour's say at the bargaining table, has diminished or eliminated the employers' monopsonistic profit margin between wages and the *MVP* of labour, and along with it the sellers' market for labour as well.

Labour's gain, in terms of its increased (and capital's diminished) share in income was probably considerable. To my knowledge, the United Kingdom is the only country with reliable statistics on income distribution that go back in time to well over a century. They show that the share of capital in the part of the *GDP* (gross domestic product) generated by the private sector has been almost halved, having fallen from a little less than one-half of the private-sector *GDP* in the 1850s to about one-quarter by the early 1980s.[7] That is a tremendous redistribution of income from capital to labour, which probably had several causes, but the great increase in labour's countervailing power in the labour market is bound to have been a very important one.

THE BENEFITS OF A SELLERS' MARKET FOR LABOUR

As already mentioned, the advantages of a sellers' market for labour were the price paid for the increase in labour's share of income. It was not a negligible price, because the advantages of a sellers' market for labour are more important and more valuable than those of a buyers' market for consumers, even without the fringe benefits that would result from non-price or non-wage competition. It is well worth while, therefore, to discuss those advantages.

As already mentioned, a price maker buyer—here the employer—finds it profitable to set the wage he offers below the marginal value product of labour to him by a profit margin that depends partly on the elasticity of the labour supply he faces, partly on the set wages of his competitors. And as long as the *MVP* of his workers exceeds their wage, all his non-wage policies and responses to external shocks will be biased in the direction of increasing employment and activity. In other words, just as the price maker seller behaves as if he had an excess supply to sell, so the price maker buyer of labour and other inputs behaves as if he had an excess demand to buy.

For example, if he can find unemployed workers willing to work for him at his set wage, he will find it profitable to employ them and anxious to do so. Of course, if the wage he set was the equilibrium wage, he will already be employing all the workers willing and qualified to work for him. But changing tastes and conditions may have released workers in other firms, or the end of the school year may have suddenly increased the size of the labour force, and the price maker employer will find it profitable to employ such newly available workers as long as their *MVP* exceeds their wage.

Needless to say, the new workers will produce additional output, which has to be sold, but the excess of labour's *MVP* over its wage indicates that it is profitable to employ more labour even though advertising expenditures have to be increased or product prices lowered in order to sell the extra output. That is so, because the *MVP* of labour measures the receipts from selling the output of the marginal worker *net* of the cost of marketing and selling it.

If the argument sounds unrealistic under present conditions, that merely shows how far removed we are today from a sellers' market for labour. For the situation depicted is the exact counterpart of the buyers' market for consumers, and there is nothing unusual about a seller's welcoming new buyers, anxious to sell as much as he can and making a good profit on his extra sales.

The price makers employer's excess demand for labour is limited, of course, because the *MVP* of his workers is a decreasing function of the number he already employs, and as it falls to equality with the wage, it eliminates the marginal profit, which created the excess demand. The falling *MVP* function indicates partly the physical limits of the firm's productive and employing capacity, partly the limited size of the market for his output. As to the former, let me recall E. Chamberlin's celebrated theorem that competition among price maker sellers—whom he called monopolistic competitors—creates excess capacity.[8] In the framework of his static model, he called that a blemish, but in a changing, growing world it should be considered an advantage: a source of flexibility.

As to the negative slope of the demand curve for the product, which is the second reason why the *MVP* of labour declines as the firm's workforce grows, the nature of that is obvious and needs no discussion here.

However, it limits the employer's scope to offer additional employment only in a microeconomic setting, when he alone is acting and the rest of the economy stands still. In a macroeconomic setting, when a change affects the whole or a large part of the economy and many employers respond to it, then the ordinary microeconomic demand curve no longer limits the economy's capacity to absorb unemployed labour profitably.

Let me enlarge on that statement. If employers in most sectors were price makers and found workers looking for work at going wages, their inducement to hire them would be limited to a much lesser extent. For, if most of them employed additional workers, the additional income so generated would add to consumers' demand, thereby greatly diminishing the need for additional sales effort to sell the output of those newly employed workers. Indeed, the resulting increase in capacity utilization might well stimulate investment as well and so set in motion an expansionary multiplier process. In short, an economy-wide availability of unemployed labour sets in motion much more sustained forces to make the economy absorb that labour than is the case with sporadic unemployment.

So far, we were concerned with the price maker employer's inducement to employ additional workers when they become available. The same inducement, however, will also make him respond to a decline in sales by trying to restore them through stepped-up advertising, special sales, hidden price reductions, etc., rather than by reducing output and firing workers. That conclusion follows from the fact that since the *MVP* of labour is initially higher, perhaps quite a bit higher than the wage, the fall in sales and consequent leftward shift of the *MVP* curve may still leave the *MVP* of the undiminished workforce higher than the wage. If so, then the above policy is the best available, even though it leads to a fall of profits, since it reduces revenues or raises advertising expenditures in the face of unchanged production costs.[9]

To summarize the argument of this section, a sellers' market for labour, created by the dominant position of employers as price makers and powered by their monopsony profits, sets in motion market forces that tend to maintain full employment in the face both of a rise in the labour supply and a fall in consumers' demand, with profits rather than employment or wages absorbing the impact of external shocks. It should be apparent from the argument that the employers' inducement to maintain full employment is the greater, the larger are their monopsonistic profit margins (the gap between *MVP* and the wage). The most remarkable feature, however, of the equilibrating mechanism is that the tendency towards full employment does *not* depend on the flexibility or reduction of wages. Indeed, the whole argument was based on the assumption of sticky wages.[10]

In the heyday of capitalism, when the early industrialists enjoyed the dominating position of price makers in both labour and product markets, there probably was a sellers' market, especially for semi-skilled and unskilled workers; but it is hard to tell at this late stage how well it worked. The fact that the economists of the time were such ardent believers in the economy's automatic tendency to full employment suggests that it did work, even if their theoretical explanations of that tendency exaggerated the role of prices and overlooked that of monopsony profits.

Note that the above argument does not depend on and has nothing to do with non-wage competition among employers, which, when it exists, is a separate and additional force that generates such fringe benefits for labour like pleasant working conditions, medical care, cheap housing, pension schemes, etc. As already mentioned, there was nothing or very little of that in early capitalism, and the miserable condition of the workers of the time have greatly contributed to their resolve in fighting the bitter and bloody battles that gained them access as equal parties to the bargaining tables of the labour market.

A SELLERS' MARKET FOR LABOUR WITHOUT EMPLOYERS' DOMINATION

The advantages for labour of having a sellers' market are valuable enough to raise the question whether they could be recaptured today, when employers no longer enjoy a dominating position and a comfortable monopsonistic profit margin in the labour market. An affirmative answer to that question was provided by Martin Weitzman in *The Share Economy*.

At the beginning of this paper, I criticized the model of perfect competition for its inadequate and incomplete representation of capitalism—especially for its failure to deal with monopoly and monopsony profits both as an important source of capitalist income and as the motivating force of some valuable services that capitalists as price makers render to the price takers they confront: consumers in product markets and workers in labour markets.

In modern times, the workers' increasing bargaining strength in labour markets has deprived capitalists of some of their monopsony profit and, with it, also of their motivation to perform some of those services. As we have seen, an important part of those services was employers' efforts to maintain full employment and stabilize wages in the face of changing economic conditions, with their monopsony profits acting as a kind of buffer to absorb the impact of changing conditions. With monopsony profits in the labour market abolished or greatly diminished, their ability, and the profit earners' motivation, to cushion labour against the shocks of economic fluctuations have also come to an end or been greatly diminished.

Weitzman's proposed remedy for that new situation is to substitute for part of the workers' fixed wages a commensurate share in their firm's variable profits, thereby making them share in the task of absorbing the impact of changing economic conditions. Such an arrangement is in force in today's Japan, where semi-annual variable bonus payments constitute, in a good year, one-third of the average worker's annual remuneration. The same arrangement on a smaller scale exists also in South Korea and Taiwan, and the custom of an increasing number of West German firms to give their employees dividend-yielding shares in the company's stock is not significantly different.

Such arrangements have two advantages over the traditional system of fixed wages. One is that when workers' pay automatically rises and falls with demand for the firm's output the cooperative element in the employer-employee relation is stressed, which makes for improved labour relations and so can increase labour productivity to the two parties' common benefit. Also, the automatic reduction of labour costs when revenues fall diminishes the magnitude of the problem to which management must make often painful adjustments, while labour finds some compensation for the fall in pay in the expectation of rising pay when revenues rise.

More important is the other advantage. Since the hiring of additional workers creates not only additional output but also the need to sell it at the cost of additional sales effort or a small price reduction, it is almost certain to increase revenues in smaller proportion than it increases the workforce. With a part of workers' remuneration consisting of their fixed percentage share in revenue, that causes also the wages bill to rise less than in proportion with the workforce, which implies that by hiring added workers, the employer reduces, however slightly, all his workers' average pay. As a result, the cost to him of his marginal worker is less than the latter's pay, because part of that comes out of that slight reduction in all the other workers' pay.

In the long run, of course, workers' pay is determined by bargaining between labour and management, and labour's strong bargaining power is likely to put employers into or near a perfectly competitive position, thereby inducing them to equate labour's *MVP* to its pay.[11] In the short run, however, the arrangement that makes workers share in the firm's revenues lowers their marginal cost to the employer to below their pay, and thereby also to below their *MVP*. The resulting gap between the *MVP* and the *MC* of labour creates the same profit motive for management to hire the unemployed that was discussed in the previous section; and it does so without handing management monopsony profits and the dominating position in the labour market.

That result is not quite as perfect as it looks. Labour does gain the benefit of enjoying a sellers' market without giving a *quid pro quo* to capital; but the unemployed workers' improved chance of finding employment is obtained at the expense of the employed workers, who all have to chip in to paying part of every newly enrolled worker's pay. That cost, very thinly spread, weighs lightly on the individual worker, who can look upon it as an unemployment insurance premium. That kind of insurance was paid out of employers' monopsony profits as long as they existed, it is not inappropriate that it should now be financed out of the workers' share of monopoly profits.

NOTES

1.   Janos Kornai, *Anti-Equilibrium,* (Amsterdam, North Holland, 1971).
2.   For an excellent summary of the whole subject of oligopoly pricing, see F. M. Scherer, *Market Structure and Economic Performance,* (Boston, Houghton Mifflin, 1980).
3.   Tibor Scitovsky, *Welfare and Competition,* (Homewood, III: Irwin) especially Chs. 2, 11, 12 and 13 in the 1951 first edition, or Chs. 2, 16, 17 and 18 in the revised 1971 edition.
4.   Martin L. Weitzman, *The Share Economy,* (Cambridge, Mass: Harvard U. Press, 1984).
5.   Andrew Tylecote, *The Causes of the Present Inflation,* (London: Macmillan, 1981), p. 26.
6.   The argument concerning the skilled and responsible worker's individual bargaining strength comes from Arthur M. Okun, who developed it and its macroeconomic implications in several of his writings. *See* his discussions of the 'invisible handshake' and the 'implicit wage contract' in Joseph A. Pechman (ed.), *Economics for Policymaking: Selected Essays of Arthur M. Okun* (Cambridge, Mass: MIT Press, 1983) and Arthur M. Okun *Prices and Quantities: A Macroeconomic Analysis* (Washington: The Brookings Institution, 1981).
7.   I wish to thank Maurice Fg. Scott for letting me have those estimates, which are based on C. H. Feinstein *Statistical Tables of National Income, Expenditure and Output of the UK, 1855-1965* (Cambridge: Cambridge U. Press, 1972), brought up to date from official statistics.
8.   Edward H. Chamberlin, *The Theory of Monopolistic Competition: A Reorientation of the Theory of Value* (Cambridge, Mass: Harvard U. Press, 1947), Chapter 5.
9.   Another, perhaps simpler way of looking at the same thing is to imagine that the fall in sales renders a part of the workforce redundant and to think of the workers made redundant as unemployed looking for work at the going wage. Then the earlier argument applies: it is profitable to rehire the workers just made redundant if their *MVP,* though lower than before, is still above the wage.
10.   So far, I assumed tacitly that wages are sticky for the same reasons that render product prices sticky. An important additional source of wage inflexibility, however, is the employer's desire to maintain good labour relations.
      Employer-employee relations are a mixture of cooperation and conflict:

cooperation in creating a common gain, conflict over how to divide that gain. Good labour relations call for employers to stress the cooperative and play down the conflict element; and since quantity (output and workforce) adjustments affect the common gain while wage adjustments change its division, employers naturally prefer quantity to wage adjustments, especially in the downward direction. That is an important cause of the downward rigidity of wages; and the expectation of that downward rigidity is a cause of upward rigidity as well.

11. Note that being reduced to the role of a price taker puts an employer into more or less the same perfectly competitive position as does bargaining between equally matched opponents.

Part IV
What Progress Leads To

9   Can Changing Consumer Tastes Save Resources?—1979

1. THE NEED TO SAVE RESOURCES

In the past, economic progress has mostly taken the form of a rise in labour productivity based on the substitution of mechanical for muscular energy and of material for human resources. The automatic forces of the market reinforced and speeded up that trend by raising the prices and so discouraging the consumption of all those sources of satisfaction that depend solely or mainly on human interaction. An example of these is the performing arts, whose prices rose and use declined with the rise in wages, except where public policies and subsidies slowed or arrested the process.

The spectacular mechanical and material development of the West was a welcome and necessary phase, which paved and showed the way that others are still following and are likely to follow for a long time yet. But as far as the developed countries themselves are concerned, their material development may well be close to having run its full course. For one thing, even as we continue our materialistic pursuits, we seem increasingly to reach out for their non-material rewards—a trend I shall deal with in the following. For another thing, the great increase in world population has made us realise that nature's bounty is not quite as lavish as it once seemed; moreover, as the poor nations of the Third World increasingly assert their claim to the same lifestyle that today is the privilege of a small minority, the globe's exhaustible resources appear not only exhaustible but insufficient.

The US share in the world's consumption of energy and mineral resources is six to seven times as great as her share in the world's population. If the remaining 95 per cent of the world's population raised their consumption to the US level and pattern, the globe's known fuel and mineral deposits would be used up in a single generation. Calculations of that sort, of course, are notoriously treacherous, because they assume too many factors as given. But they do indicate orders of magnitude and also serve to warn us that many of those givens will have to give. We will have to develop new sources of energy, new ways of saving energy and other resources, as well as ways to eliminate waste and wasteful lifestyles. This paper focuses on the problem of wasteful lifestyles.

Our present consumption pattern was moulded by very different scarcities and price ratios from those likely to prevail in the future. Already in the light of today's much higher energy prices, it seems to provide consumer satisfaction in a wasteful way. It is wasteful, not only in that the productive system uses up too many resources to produce what consumers want, but also in the sense that consumers choose an excessively expensive lifestyle to achieve satisfaction. Changing prices and scarcities can be counted on to change consumption patterns; but the process is sluggish and painful, partly because the automatic forces of the market are sluggish, partly because consumers get addicted to their accustomed ways, and partly also because the accumulated stock of still usable producers' and consumers' durables imparts a lot of rigidity to our lifestyle. That raises the question whether policy, and what kind of policy, could speed and facilitate matters by inducing the public to change its expenditure pattern in ways that would reduce resource costs without reducing consumer satisfaction.

II. CAN RESOURCE COSTS BE REDUCED WITHOUT REDUCING CONSUMER SATISFACTION?

That is a delicate question, which economists are not in the habit of asking, let alone answering. The following argument therefore is highly tentative and speculative—put forward with great caution and humility, but in the hope that it will stimulate more thinking on the subject and ultimately lead to more and better answers than I can hazard at this early stage.

Economists have rightly been reluctant to engage in social engineering and tamper with consumers' preferences; yet it ought to be possible to save material resources while detracting neither from the consumer's satisfaction nor from his sovereignty. After all, the input of exhaustible resources, though correlated with the level of living, bears no fixed relation to it. There are tremendous differences in different countries' consumption pattern and resource utilisation that have nothing to do with differences in their levels of living and seem fortuitous or due to differences in national tradition, explained in turn by historical accident. Sweden, Switzerland, Western Germany and Norway, for example, are countries whose standard of living is estimated to be higher (certainly no lower) than that of the United States, yet their per capita consumption of energy is less than half that of the United States—as is also their per capita generation of household waste, a good index of the consumer's use of exhaustible materials other than energy. To compensate, those countries consume twice the quantities we Americans consume of such other good things of life as vacations, active sports, the performing arts, whose input of exhaustible resources is small. I am not advocating the forcible imposition of one country's expenditure pattern on another; but the persuasive force of market opportunities and prices is surely a permissible weapon, and the example just given illustrates the scope for change which ought to be achievable by persuasion.

For a more rigorous discussion of the scope, nature and means of change, it is useful to subdivide the consumer's needs and sources of satisfaction into three categories. First, one can distinguish between comforts and stimuli. Stimuli are anything the consumer values for the novelty, variety, excitement, challenge, surprise, or stimulus interest it provides. Comforts are whatever eliminates, relieves or prevents pains and discomforts, or anticipated pains and discomforts. Comforts may further be subdivided into personal and social comforts. Personal comforts cater to biological needs, make one physically comfortable, save time and effort in the performance of various chores, or provide for the future satisfaction of such needs and desires. Social comforts are satisfactions derived from one's membership and standing in society, in professional and social organisations, in one's workplace, and in any other formal or informal, permanent or *ad hoc* social group, as well as from whatever titles, objects, possessions and activities symbolise such membership or standing.

That classification into personal and social comforts and stimuli is comprehensive, comprising all forms of human satisfaction; and it classifies satisfactions, not goods and services. For many satisfactions, including some of the most important, do not depend on economic goods and services for their fulfilment; and many economic goods and services yield more than one of the three types of satisfactions listed. Let me stress that man's need for social comfort and stimulation is no less essential and no less urgent than his need for personal comfort. That fact needs stressing, because consumers and economists alike focus their attention on personal comforts and barely give grudging recognition to man's other needs. The probable reason is that, while the need for each of our personal comforts is highly specific, the need for social comfort and for stimulation can be filled in many ways by a great variety of activities and objects. As a result, none of these is indispensable, any one of them can easily be given up in favour of one of the many available substitutes; and that makes the need for all of them seem unimportant, however essential the need for *some* social comfort and *some* stimulation. Also, personal comforts are generally the most expensive in terms of economic goods and exhaustible resources, which is further reason for their claiming the centre of attention. Indeed, with so much attention lavished by the consumer on how best to obtain his personal comforts, and by the economist analysing the rational budgeting of resources needed to provide them, one wonders why their consumption and use should have become quite so wasteful in the developed countries.

One reason, much discussed and well known, is external diseconomies, the incidence of which has greatly increased with the increasing density of population and the rising standards of personal comfort. The production and consumption of many personal comforts generate pollutants, causing discomfort to others or necessitating the use of further resources to eliminate those pollutants, prevent their generation, or offset their harmful and unpleasant effects.

Other reasons, no less important, for the seemingly excessive cost of our personal comforts have to do with our failure to face up squarely to our need for the other satisfactions, social comfort and stimulation. As a result, we tend to be less rationally calculating when we cater to those needs—we obtain most of them jointly with personal comforts, in ways that add, often substantially, to the cost of our personal comforts.

An obvious example is conspicuous consumption: the acquisition of goods and services ostensibly for personal comfort but in quantities and at prices geared not so much to our need for personal comfort as to our desire for the status their use or ownership secures. One must accept man's need for status, recognition, and the other people's respect, as an essential human need; and conspicuous consumption is just one, an expensive but not the most expensive, way of satisfying that need. Titles, decorations, medals, citations are another, virtually costless, way of catering to some of that same need; and they are much used in the communist countries, somewhat less in Britain and France, and hardly at all in other Western democracies, which seem unable to forget and forgive the system's feudal origins. Our faith in market selection makes us seek social comfort in conspicuous consumption, already mentioned, and in that potentially most expensive source, job importance.

III SOCIAL COMFORT AND JOB IMPORTANCE

Most people's main source of social comfort is the importance or seeming importance and usefulness of their job, its place in the economic or political hierarchy, the title it confers, the functions it involves, the number of people over whom it gives control, and the extent of that control. People's demand for job importance rises with the rise in their real income; hence the rising demand for education, which is, or seems, the prerequisite for the more prestigious jobs. The proportion of such jobs, however, does not increase just because the supply of education and the proportion of highly trained people in the labour force are increasing; it depends mainly on the hierarchical organisation of society and the economy. That is why the rise in incomes and education in the developed economies are increasingly creating an excess demand for job importance. That excess demand is being filled to some extent by the creation of top-heavy hierarchies and an ever-increasing proportion of administrative positions. Even so, part of the demand for job importance seems to remain unsatisfied. Witness the frustration, amply documented in the United States, of the many highly qualified people placed in positions that provide insufficient outlet for the exercise of their qualifications yet unable to find more suitable jobs. Witness also the high unemployment rates of professionals and highly skilled workers, which so often exist side-by-side with staff shortages and unfilled positions on lowly levels, so that many humble but necessary jobs never get performed, because most people prefer to remain unemployed to working beneath their station, provided that adequate unemployment compensation or accumulated savings give them the choice.

That the existence of excess demand for job importance is harmful and costly is obvious enough; but the remedies so far mentioned are also costly. Perhaps the most costly is the direct catering to the demand for job importance: the creation of professional and administrative positions in government, education, the social services and the administration of private business beyond the requirements of efficient organization. In Britain and the United States, there has been a great redistribution of manpower in that direction for several reasons, of which the increased demand for job importance is only one. Whether that redistribution has gone beyond the requirements of efficiency and, if so, how far it has gone and at what cost to society is difficult to estimate. In a formal sense, the marginal social cost of creating job importance is the excess of a person's wage or salary over the value of his or her contribution to output: the difficulty lies in estimating that contribution and its value. Britain's great economic problems are increasingly attributed to the shift of manpower away from the more productive down-to-earth occupations; and if that is a correct diagnosis, then the cost of that shift is enormous.

That raises the question how, and by what kind of policy, could people be helped to obtain at lesser cost the social comfort of regarding themselves and being regarded by others as important and useful members of society? The first and obvious answer is educational planning: the better matching of the number of people who acquire given productive and administrative skills with the foreseeable number of positions that will require those skills. I am not for providing less education than the public wants, only in favour of its better distribution and possibly also (in some countries) of channelling people away from production skills, towards more consumption skills. An additional reason for that will become evident later.

Second, policies designed to give production workers more initiative, more challenge, as well as more responsibility and sense of responsibility ought to diminish both the frustration and the striving for higher positions so prevalent at present. Several countries are currently experimenting with such policies.

Finally, the overwhelming importance people attach to their job and its place in the hierarchy as a source and token of status is likely to diminish if consumption skills get more attention and become more prevalent. That brings me to the next subject, our tendency also to obtain stimulation jointly with personal comforts and at high cost.

IV. STIMULATION AND HUMAN SATISFACTION

Stimulation as a source of human satisfaction is, at least from the economist's point of view, a new and largely unexplored subject. Psychologists have clearly established the essential nature of man's need for stimulation and studied the additiveness of stimuli from different sources, the satiability of man's need and desire for stimulus, as well as the pathology of stimulus deprivation. They have also gained some understanding of the nature of the stuff that provides stimulus, and have begun to quantify it.

The number and variety of sources of stimulation is tremendous—as one would expect, considering man's almost continuous need for stimulation during most of his waking hours. Many are free, such as conversation, games, physical exercise and most active sports, while others, such as spectator sports, commercial entertainment, performing arts, art objects and vacation travel, are economic goods produced and sold expressly for the stimulus they provide. TV and radio programmes are public goods, whether public corporations or private advertisers provide them. The stimulus and satisfaction of work is the free by-product of creative and productive activity; many others are by-products or joint products of goods and services that also provide personal comforts. Obvious examples of the latter are window-shopping, the acquisition of new possessions, driving for pleasure, the plaything aspect of many consumer durables, and the novelty of fashion, new gadgets, and new models of old gadgets and consumer durables.

With so great a variety of stimuli, some free, others costly, some available by themselves, others only as joint products or as part of package deals, the resource cost of obtaining a desired amount of stimulation varies tremendously with the source or sources from which it is obtained. It makes a great deal of difference therefore how, where, and in what form people get their stimulation, whether they get what they want, and whether they get it in optimum quantities, at minimum cost. We know that differences in different people's freely chosen stimulus patterns can be enormous, and differences in the resource cost of those different stimulus patterns are just as great. Why is there quite so great a variety of choices?

A basic postulate of economics is that the individual is the best judge of what gives him satisfaction and a pretty good judge also of how to obtain that satisfaction. With minor qualifications, that postulate is generally accepted in the realm of personal comforts; but when it comes to stimulation as a source of satisfaction, there arises a logical difficulty which seems to rule out consumer rationality in the sense in which we know and accept it as the governing principle of consumer behaviour in other areas of consumer choice.

The stuff on mental stimulation—the main form of human stimulation—is novelty. It is the mental processing of novelty we enjoy, provided it comes in the right quantity, with neither too much nor too little redundancy, i.e. relatedness to the familiar. Now rational consumer choice depends on knowledge, advance knowledge of the nature and amount of satisfaction that can be expected from the various alternatives available. But knowing in advance how much stimulation to expect from a particular source of novelty inevitably destroys some of its novelty and reduces its ability to stimulate. Moreover, acquiring the knowledge necessary for informed customer choice is inseparable from acquiring or increasing the redundancy needed for enjoyable stimulation; and that too creates a problem, related to, though different from, the previous one. This second is much the more serious of the two problems; but I shall illustrate both, with two simple examples.

The enjoyment of a detective story depends on the suspense and surprise it provides. But to make an informed choice and select from among several detective stories the one I would most enjoy reading is virtually impossible, because such choice would have to be based on information whose very acquisition would diminish the suspense and surprise. I am better off if I choose to remain ignorant of the contents and make my choice by trusting friends' advice, reviewers' judgement, or authors' reputations.

My other example has to do with music. To enjoy music one must know something about it and that something has to be learned. Ideally, the learning process itself could be enjoyable, but mostly it is not, because inspired teachers are rare and because part of the learning process consists in listening *before* having learned to enjoy what one is listening to. That is why acquiring a musical education is usually as dull and strenuous as most other learning. One is tempted to liken the strain (and cost) of one's initiation to music to the cost of an investment, incurred for the sake of the future returns it is expected to yield. The two cases, however, are fundamentally different. An entrepreneur can estimate investment costs and expected future profits with some degree of confidence, calculate the probable rate of return, discount for risk, and make a reasonable rational decision. By contrast, the would-be music lover, who is trying to decide whether to acquire a musical education, cannot make an equally informed decision, because he would need to have that education not only to enjoy music but even to judge the nature and desirability of musical enjoyment. In other words, he is in the impossible situation of having to have musical knowledge to be able rationally to decide whether that musical knowledge is worth acquiring. Nor is that problem confined to music; it is common to all forms of stimulus consumption that require a skill for their enjoyment.

Those examples illustrate the insuperable difficulty that confronts the consumer in the realm of stimulus satisfaction when he wants to make an informed, rational choice. In the usual sense of the term, therefore, consumer rationality with respect to stimulus satisfaction is impossible. Possible, though of limited usefulness, is retrospective consumer rationality. After the event, with the benefit of hindsight, one can judge which story was the best and whether it was worth investing the time, pain and money into learning to appreciate music. Before the event, the best one can do is to follow the judgement of others who have the benefit of hindsight, in the hope that one's own retrospective judgement will coincide with theirs.

V. THE ORIGINS OF DIFFERENCES IN TASTES

The above argument throws new light on the origin of differences in tastes. In the past, economists accepted these unquestioningly and considered them sacrosanct. In the realm of personal comforts, however, where rational consumer choice is possible, tastes vary but little and most differences in consumption patterns are explained by differences in income and relative prices. What these fail to explain are differences in different people's patterns of stimulus enjoyment; and in that area, the impossibility of rational consumer choice is by far the simplest explanation. In other words, variety of tastes, confined as it is to sources of stimulation, is best explained by the difficulty of using prospective rationality with respect to stimulus satisfaction.

National differences in living habits and consumption patterns, where not due to income differences, are also largely confined to differences in patterns and sources of stimulus enjoyment; and those differences are again best explained by the impossibility of rational consumer choice in that area. But, while national characteristics differ greatly between countries, they are quite stable and persistent within each country, owing, probably, to what I called retrospective rationality. Each generation knows, with the benefit of hindsight, the advantage of possessing its own consumption skills; and the next generation benefits by that knowledge and acquires the same consumption skills if it respects tradition or submits to the authority of its elders.

Indeed, the paradox I am discussing, the logical impossibility of rationally choosing the best pattern of stimulus enjoyment, must seem a tame and largely academic paradox to many people, because it is so very easy to resolve by providing a humanistic education. A humanistic education is mostly training in consumption skills which prepares people for the enjoyment of a variety of stimuli; and by making it a compulsory part of the school curriculum, we can save our children the ordeal of an impossible choice. That solution, however, is better at preventing regress than at promoting progress; and besides, it is often not practicable.

In the US, the requirements of imparting production skills and a good grounding in science and technology have largely crowded out the humanistic and cultural part of the curriculum. Also, the individual's freedom of choice is an article of faith with us, which has kept the influence of tradition to a minimum and has even led to children being allowed freely to choose a large part of their school curriculum. That explains why we have few characteristic national pastimes; but it does not mean that our choice of sources of stimulation is random. The impossibility of rational choice means that one cannot weigh the benefits of having against the costs of acquiring each consumption skill and then choose those with the most favourable benefit/cost ratios, because one cannot ascertain the benefits. In such a situation, it is reasonable to minimise one's investment in consumption skills; and that is exactly what happens. Many stimuli require for their enjoyment little or no consumption skills or skills already acquired for some other purpose; and it is natural for the unskilled consumer to seek stimulation from these. If that proves costly or yields less stimulation than he wants, he will never know it, unless by chance he later acquires some of the consumption skills he has spurned in the beginning and so can exercise retrospective rationality.

VI. THE UNITED STATES CONSUMPTION PATTERN

How can we, as outside observers, judge the US consumption pattern and tell whether it provides the desired amount and kind of stimulus, and whether it provides stimulus at minimum cost? The first is too complex and difficult a question to deal with here,[1] but something can be said on the second.

The sources of mental stimulation whose enjoyment requires the least skills are shopping, window-shopping and otherwise learning of market opportunities, following and keeping up with changing fashions, using as playthings and sources of variety vehicles,[2] appliances and other aids to personal comfort, light entertainment, and spectator sports. Those that involve the most skills are music, literature, the arts, conversation, and problem-solving, which last ranges from puzzles and bridge to scientific inquiry. Those in the latter group require labour inputs and little else; those in the former have other inputs as well and, when they are by-products of or joint products with personal comforts, can be inefficient and costly sources of stimulation.

Unfortunately, we have no estimates of the cost of stimuli that are jointly produced with personal comforts, except for a single study of the cost of annual model changes in the US automobile industry.[3] That study has estimated the annual extra cost to society of cars following fashion in appearance, size, power and gadgetry, over and above what producing and running the same number of cars would have cost had they merely 'been built with the developing technology'. Over the period 1956–60, that extra cost is estimated to have averaged $4845 million p.a., 1.3 per cent of the net national income and well over a quarter (28.1 per cent) of total consumers' expenditure on conventional recreation. Since all it paid for is the stimulus of variety in the appearance and gadgetry of cars, it well illustrates the high cost of stimulation when that comes in a package deal jointly with personal comforts. The remedy is not, of course, to deprive consumers of a stimulus they opted for but to put them into a position where they can opt for something better.

If retrospective choice is to be trusted, consumption skills are worth having, and the satisfactions they render accessible are greater and longer-lasting than most of those unskilled consumers have access to. Yet such skills and satisfactions seem confined to a minority, which is very much smaller in the US than it is in most of Europe, although the average American has more education than the average citizen of any European country. The reason, almost certainly, is that our educational superiority is confined to production skills and does not extend to consumption skills. Our predicament in this respect is cause for concern not only to us, because the pattern we set is widely followed by others. The supply of education is rapidly increasing everywhere and the stress is always on production skills. I am pleading for an increase also of consumption skills, both because it would increase satisfaction and because it would lower the cost of satisfaction.

Education is cheapest in schools, which ought to exploit the increased demand for schooling, however much that is focused on production skills. Just as effective, however, and just as important, is informal learning by doing, trying, experimenting. That is the justification for subsidising the arts. But to get the public to learn consumption skills by practice is a lengthy and difficult process, whose success depends on ease of access not only in terms of cost. The price of elasticity of demand for the performing arts is very low—estimated at 0.25 in the US. That is supposed to measure the response of consumption to a price change, *given people's preferences;* but it also gives an inkling of the difficulty of changing those preferences—at least of changing them by price change alone. Yet the difficulty can be and has been overcome. The demand for theatre and music is three to four times, perhaps even five times, as great in the countries of Eastern and Northern Europe, where the price of admission covers 30–40 per cent of cost, than it is in the US, where the ticket price pays for 60 per cent of expenses. So great a difference in demand clearly reflects a difference in tastes much more than in price, probably explained by the communist and Scandinavian countries' greater success in making the arts popular. Credit may be due to the much longer period over which they have subsidised the arts or to the way they have done it.

The US subsidy programme has not been too successful so far in enticing the wider public into appreciating the performing arts; and while it is too early to pass judgement, two likely reasons for its failure are worth mentioning. One is the desire to minimise losses by selling every seat. That has led to so great a reliance on subscribers that, today, access is mostly limited to old-established enthusiasts, who alone are willing to plan and buy subscriptions weeks ahead; and access is denied to those who merely want a taste to find out if they like it. The other reason is that subsidisers take serious art, and the limiting of subsidies to serious art too seriously, and tend to sharpen the dividing line between it and light entertainment. That renders it that much harder for the public to stray across that line. It is so much easier to pick up a liking for the arts by trial and experiment in, say, Copenhagen, whose main concert hall is in an amusement park, next door to the roller coaster, with tickets usually available at the entrance when you want to go in.

The question posed in my title was raised more than answered in this paper. That was the easier part but it, too, had to be done. I am content to leave the difficult part to others.

NOTES

1. I have tried to deal with it in my *The Joyless Economy.*
2. Cars are aesthetic objects and a complex of gadgets to play with, additional stimulus stems from driving for the exhilaration of speed, for exercising one's skill, and for the fast-changing visual image one gets from being on a moving vehicle.
3. cf. F. M. Fisher, Z. Griliches and C. Kaysen 'the costs of automobile model changes since 1949', *Journal of Political Economy,* (Oct. 1962).

10   The Desire for Excitement in Modern Society—1981

Excitement is an important form of human satisfaction, which can be sought and obtained in many different ways, from many different sources. Looking at newspapers, movie and television screens, books of fiction, advertisements, etc., one gets the impression that today, the advanced economies of the West cater to a greatly increased public demand for excitement; and I shall offer some US statistics as evidence that bears out that impression. Yet, excitement is a primitive emotion, whose enjoyment seems to be an essential part of unchanging human nature. If that is so, then the desire for it ought not to be a matter of changing fashions. How can one reconcile that notion with the apparent increase in our need and tolerance for excitement? I shall offer such a reconciliation; but for that we need first of all a definition and a better understanding of the subject.

Excitement is the sensation due to the increasing arousal of the nervous system that accompanies the process of being stimulated when the stimulus is fairly strong—strong enough to pose a challenge or threat and so demand one's active response. The challenge is to one's skill, strength, endurance or intellectual capacity; the threat can be to life, limb, health, economic well-being, as well as to one's prestige, status or self-respect. In short, there are many different sources of enjoyable excitement; but the challenge or threat is an important precondition in all of them, and so is the uncertainty: the possibility of failure and the less-than-certain expectation of being able to cope.[1] Like all or almost all sensations, excitement can be pleasant or unpleasant, depending on its intensity; and it is subject to Wundt's Law, which says that the sensation is the most pleasant for an intermediate degree of intensity. Too much excitement is unpleasant and can be unbearable; too little excitement is boring and so unsatisfying. Enjoyable excitement lies between those extremes. Another dimension which can also make the difference between pleasant and unpleasant excitement and in which Wundt's Law applies is the duration of the excitement and the underlying uncertainty. Continued uncertainty leads to chronic excitement or tension, which is almost always unpleasant. In general, people dislike uncertainty and go out of their way to remove it. Only when either one's

128

stake in the outcome or its futurity is strictly limited and under control is it actively sought (as in gambling) or accepted as pleasant.

Most people want and enjoy some excitement; but tolerance for excitement and the desire for it vary greatly from person to person, and even in the same person they vary over time and decline sharply with age, being the greatest in the young. Indeed, their much greater desire for excitement and correspondingly greater acceptance of danger is perhaps the most important distinguishing characteristic that separates the young from the old. That is all I can say in this short paper on what may be called the demand side.[2] Let me now turn to dealing with the supply of excitement and with the changes in the form and sources of its supply.

The thesis I am proposing is that social, economic and scientific progress in modern society have greatly reduced our main sources of excitement; and that that reduction, combined with our unabated need for excitement, has caused the public to go out in search for more excitement in entertainment, travel, dangerous sports, violence, active participation in collective action, and much else besides.

What then are those sources of excitement that are being closed off by modern progress? The one most often mentioned is challenging, interesting, creative work. Increased specialization, mechanization and automation have taken the fun and excitement out of much work whose difficulty and hazards were once a source of challenge and satisfaction. Yet the number of people who have lost that source of excitement cannot be very great. For one thing, quite a few of the exciting jobs retain their exciting quality even today: they range from exploration to research, from the work of policemen, pilots, Alpine guides, undercover agents to that of some surgeons, teachers, social workers, not to mention artists and craftsmen for whose handiwork there is a revival of interest. For another thing, not all satisfying work is exciting; and there probably never was a golden age when more than a small fraction of people enjoyed exciting work. Accordingly, one must look elsewhere for the main reason of today's great increase in the public's desire for excitement.

That can probably be found in another consequence of progress: our greatly increased physical safety and economic security. The hazards of everyday life, the dangers of the workplace, and the insecurity of one's livelihood provide plenty of excitement. That excitement is far from pleasant; but it is just as exciting as the dangerous sports and games of chance people engage in deliberately. Indeed, considering that the main difference between pleasant and unpleasant excitement is the latter's greater intensity or longer duration, the unpleasant excitements and tensions of a rough life, a dangerous shopfloor, or an unstable economy can easily give people such a surfeit of excitement as to leave them without any desire for other, more enjoyable sources and forms of it.

What I am arguing therefore is that at an earlier stage of development, the ordinary routine of a more difficult existence imposed as much excitement as most people could take; but that progress since then, by reducing the intensity of those unwanted excitements and tensions, has created, for the first time in many people's lives, a positive need for more excitement, which they seek to fill for enjoyment's sake.

The extent of that reduction in the sources of tensions and unwanted excitements shows up well in US statistics. Work injury rates in manufacturing and mining have been reduced by one-half between 1926 and 1970; and fatality rates in mining show much the same trend. Life expectancy increased, since the beginning of the century, by more than 50 per cent; the death rate from all accidents has fallen by 25 per cent, that of accidents other than automobile accidents by 60 per cent.

Economic insecurity has also diminished greatly. The annual number of business failures as a percentage of the total number of businesses has fallen to less than a quarter of what it once was, from almost 2 per cent in the 1850s to between a half and a third of 1 per cent in the years since World War II. Unemployment statistics do not go back far enough to show a secular trend; but they show a great decline in the amplitude of fluctuations. The high unemployment of the great depressions of the 1890s and 1930s have not even been approximated to in recent depressions.[3] Equally important but harder to quantify are the greatly increased and much more effective safeguards pensions schemes, social insurance, and the various social services provide against economic insecurity.

In short, we have enjoyed an impressive increase in safety and security. That is bound to have affected the public's psychological state, reducing tensions and anxiety and so creating an excitement deficit for many people: a feeling that life is too empty, too uneventful, and a consequent desire for more excitement. The excitement people deliberately go out and get is, of course, enjoyable excitement; and such a substitution of pleasant for unpleasant excitement seems, at first sight, to be a good thing. Unfortunately, however, the matter is more complex, because one person's freely chosen enjoyable excitement is quite often a source of excitement also for others; and for them it is not always voluntary excitement, and not always pleasant. For a critical appraisal therefore, one must look carefully at the representative list of the activities people take up in their search for excitement.

What are desirable sources of excitement for those who enjoy boringly high standards of safety and security? Having mentioned challenging work as a source of enjoyable excitement now diminished, I must list first do-it-yourself activities as a substitute—at least when the particular activity chosen is sufficiently difficult and demanding to provide excitement. Reliable statistics are lacking; but we know that there has been a great increase in do-it-yourself activities and hobbies during the post war period and that much of that is handicraft and art work, which is the kind best suited to generate a feeling of excitement.

A second, probably more generally available, source of excitement is sports, especially competitive and dangerous sports. Statistics show a great increase of interest in all sports; but part of that must be due to our expanding population, the rise in per capita real incomes, and the increase in people's free time. To correct for the first factor, all figures quoted and to be quoted in this paper are rates per head of population. The influence of the other two factors cannot be so easily separated; but it is worth noting that the average annual rise in per capita expenditure on all recreation has been 3.5 per cent in real terms during the post war period and quite a bit less before that. The supply of most sources of pleasurable excitement has increased at very much faster rates, which suggests that more time and money are not the only influences at work.

The annual incease in admissions to spectator sports has been the lowest: 1 per cent for baseball, 2 per cent for professional and collegiate football, 4.4 per cent for horse and greyhound racing; and please note that the excitement of the last and fastest-growing is greatly enhanced by betting. Much faster has been the increase in active participation in competitive sports: 4.1 per cent for golf, 4.9 per cent for bowling, the two tamest sports, 7.8 per cent for softball and 11.5 per cent for tennis, the only ones among the more active sports for which data are available. Very similar are the average annual rates increase for what may be called the daring sports: 5.5 per cent for parachuting, 9.6 per cent for soaring (sail-planing), 15 per cent for motorcycling.[4] Participation in such recently developed, newly fashionable sports like hang gliding and hot-air ballooning is increasing very much faster; but that must be partly due to the fascination of their novelty.[5]

A third source of enjoyable excitement is gambling, which, like sports, offers many varieties which, again like sports, can cater to different people's very different needs for excitement. Almost half (48 per cent) of the adult US population participates in some form of organized gambling, on which its net expenditure is about 8 per cent of total spending on recreation. (The total sums wagered come to five times as much, or about 40 per cent of recreational expenditures). The annual increase in parimutuel net receipts has averaged 8.4 per cent in real terms over the half century since 1929; but that is an average of 14.4 per cent annual increase until 1950 and a 3.5 per cent increase since then. That last figure, however, understates real growth, because the period saw the establishment of national lotteries and other forms of legal gambling in many States as part of an unsuccessful attempt to displace and reduce illegal gambling, and also as a means to increase State revenues. The 6.6 per cent annual increase therefore in Nevada's net gambling receipts (in real terms and per head of US population) is probably a better index of the growth of gambling.[6]

The mention of illegal gambling brings me to the next source of enjoyable excitement; crime. Children are well known to get pleasurable excitement out of defying parental authority and doing what they were told not to do. Breaking the law is the adult equivalent. Experts are now agreed that the failure of legalized gambling to displace illegal gambling was probably due to people's enjoyment of the added excitement that the illegality of gambling provides.[7] Indeed, one of the purposes of the criminal law is to render the fear of punishment exciting—but to a degree where it becomes so unpleasant that it acts as a deterrent. Unfortunately, that purpose too often fails to be realized. Not only is our desire and tolerance for excitement on the increase; other factors are the greatly diminished probability of being punished and the tendency for sentences to become milder and shorter and for prisons to become less unpleasant.

Statistics to document those trends are few but those few are telling. Data on the diminished severity of sentences are lacking, except for the fall in executions, from 199 in 1935, the peak year, to zero by 1968. As to a criminal's diminished chance of being punished: between 1957 and 1970, the number of serious crimes known to the police increased fourfold, the number of arrests increased only three-fold, and the number of people sentenced to prison (or death) did not increase at all. By now, only one out of three serious crimes becomes known to the police, of those less than one in five are resolved and lead to arrest, and the chance of a person arrested being found guilty, either as charged or of a lesser offence, is less than one in three. All told, only one out of forty-eight serious crimes leads to conviction; and many of those convicted get suspended sentences or are detained in juvenile homes. No wonder if the deterrent effect of the criminal law has greatly diminished and turned into tolerable, for some even enjoyable excitement. After all, almost any unpleasant excitement can be made pleasantly titillating by a suitable reduction of its intensity. For a person without moral scruples, the remote chance of being punished for rape, or mugging, or purse snatching merely adds a thrill no different from a rock climber's thrill when he exposes himself to physical danger equally remote. The danger creates excitement while it lasts and a feeling of elation when it is over and one has escaped unscathed. The crime rate has been rising at the average annual rate of 7.6 per cent between 1957 and 1974—presumably the result of the public's diminished fear of punishment and of its increased desire and tolerance for such excitement as the fear of punishment.[8]

Somewhat related, certainly as far as statistical documentation is concerned, is the next source of enjoyable excitement: violence, which may be subdivided into vicarious violence and violence proper. Many people seem to enjoy vicarious violence: violence seen, heard, or read about in news or fiction. The great increase in the public's demand for violence on the screen and in fiction over the past two decades is only too obvious; but I know of no data to indicate its rate of increase. Since the enjoyment of vicarious violence stems from the spectator's or reader's identifying with one of the actors in the drama, being one of the actors must be even more exciting, and enjoyably so for those with an appropriately greater desire for excitement. Owing to the fact that most violence is a criminal offence and qualifies as 'serious crime', statistics, the same ones quoted in the last section, are available. They show that violent crime has increased about one percentage point faster than non-violent crime against property. Considering that the chances of getting away with it unpunished are very much greater and have increased very much faster in the case of non-violent than in that of violent crime, the faster increase in the incidence of violent crime is very puzzling and hard to explain, except on the ground that the combined thrill of violence and breaking the law is greater than that of the latter alone.

That short list of sources of pleasurable excitement focused on those statistically measurable; it omitted such items like drugs, dangerous driving, competitive games of skill (e.g. bridge); and I have yet to deal with what is by far and away the most popular source of enjoyable excitement: participation in collective hazardous action. Political campaigns for a cause and for the election of a candidate, demonstrations, protest marches, strikes, scientific expeditions, team sports are examples; and the ease with which mass enthusiasm can be generated for wars, revolutions and uprisings suggests that enjoyable excitement plays a role there too.

The team spirit is essential for that source of excitement, not only because the feeling of belonging to a group and sharing its fortunes is enjoyable in itself, but even more because, by being a member of a group, one supports more easily whatever uncertainty, danger or hardship that particular enterprise involves.

Recall that all excitement hinges on the presence of some difficulty or hazard; and the pleasure comes first from the building up of tension and then from its resolution and the elimination of the initial uncertainty concerning one's (or the group's) ability to overcome it. The dislike of uncertainty is a universal human trait. People will nevertheless deliberately expose themselves to uncertainty for the pleasure of its successful (or even the relief of its unsuccessful) resolution. In dangerous sports, the uncertainty is rendered bearable by its relatively short duration, in gambling by one's control over the amount of one's possible loss; but many sources of excitement involve prolonged periods of uncertainty and so are usually restricted to the few willing to bear that much uncertainty for the sake of the eventual feeling of triumph and sense of accomplishment.

Now, participation in a collective hazardous action has two important advantages. One is that different people can make greatly differing contributions to the collective action, according to their differing talents and temperaments. The other is that the uncertainty, the difficulties, and the possible setbacks are faced collectively by the group; and since there is a feeling of safety in numbers, people can bear hazards more easily in a group than singly. At the same time, differing contributions and the sharing of hazards do not seem to reduce the participants' pleasurable feelings of suspense, excitement and elation. It is well known, for example, that the emotional impact of a political campaign can be as great on the humble campaign worker who addresses envelopes as on the candidate himself—a fact which explains the ease of recruiting campaign workers. In short, to seek excitement in collective action is to reduce its cost without also reducing its benefits. That explains why participation is the most accessible source of excitement for those many people who are too timid or anxious to take the risks that independent sources of excitement require.

Statistical data are unfortunately lacking; but it is generally believed that the 1960s and the first half of the 1970s saw a great increase in the American public's interest in political causes and public concerns. Interestingly enough, the decline of that interest in the second half of the 1970s is matched by a decline also in motorcycling, sailplaning, violence and non-violent crime. Could the great increase in economic insecurity, due to depression *cum* inflation, be their common cause?

I presented a hypothesis and assembled a few statistics in its support but said nothing so far on policy and broader implications. They are, of course, simple and almost too obvious to mention; let me nevertheless at least point out two of them. First, an underlying assumption of this paper is that different sources of excitement are good substitutes for each other. If true, that points the way to reducing violence and crime by providing socially more acceptable sources of risk, danger and excitement. There is no reason to believe that the poor practice violence rather than dangerous sports because they prefer it and not because it is cheaper. Also, if criminality is due to poverty, why does it increase when poverty diminishes? City officials in the United States are very slowly beginning to recognize man's need to face danger and take risks for excitement's sake, and the absurdity of 'honey and milk toast' activities in urban recreation programmes. To quote one official, 'What an indictment against our programs that almost everything children do that is risky and fun is done off the playground'.[9]

The other lesson I want to point to is political. In recent years, we have seen groups of citizens of one authoritarian country after another taking great risks to assert or defend various human rights. Political scientists hail that as evidence of man's innate love of freedom and decency; and they are probably right. But if the argument of this paper is valid, then it must also be due to those very regimes' success in providing greater safety and economic security for their citizens.

NOTES

1. Where, you may ask, is the threat in a child's excitement while waiting for its birthday or Christmas present? The excitement, in this case, hinges on the surprise. The child expects something new and unexpected; and having to cope with the unexpected is always a threat, however slight.
2. For a more detailed account of the subject as well as for references to its literature in physiological psychology, *see* my *The Joyless Economy,* (New York: Oxford University Press, 1976).
3. All statistics come from the *Historical Statistics of the United States* and the *Statistical Abstract of the United States.*
4. Motorcycling in the United States is definitely a sport, very seldom a means of locomotion.
5. The data for spectator sports, golf, bowling and softball come from *Historical Statistics* and the *Statistical Abstract of the United States.* All other data come from private communications from the national associations of the respective sports; and I should like herewith to thank them for their prompt and helpful replies to my enquiries. Most of these data refer to approximately the last two decades.
6. The parimutuel data come from *Historical Statistics* and the *Statistical Abstract;* all others from *Gambling in America,* an excellent and very detailed official survey of the subject published in 1976 by the Commission on the Revision of National Policy Toward Gambling (Government Printing Office, Washington).
7. cf. W. R. Eadington (ed.), *Gambling and Society: Interdisciplinary Studies on the Subject of Gambling,* (Springfield, Ill: Charles C. Thomas, 1976), p. 17; also *Gambling in America,* p. 71.
8. All the data come from *Historical Statistics* and the *Statistical Abstract of the United States;* and they refer to the seven serious crimes (murder, forcible rape, aggravated assault, burglary, larceny-theft and automobile theft) for which the FBI collects and publishes nationwide statistics. The estimate that only one in three of such crimes become known to the police comes from the 1974 survey of the US Bureau of Census, *Criminal Victimization in the United States, January-June 1973.*
9. cf. J. H. Naylor, 'Honey and milk toast', *Journal of Physical Education and Recreation'* (Sept. 1975), pp. 18-19; quoted in D. R. Dunn and J. M. Gulbis, 'The risk revolution', *Parks and Recreation,* (August 1976), pp. 12-17.

11 Excess Demand for Job Importance and Its Implications—1981

From a distance, economic progress seems to be a good thing without qualification. But when a society actually experiences prolonged and substantial economic progress on its own skin, so to speak, then people become very much aware of its costs and undesirable side-effects. I propose to focus on just one of those side-effects; but it may be helpful to preface it by a very short discussion of the general nature of the costs of economic progress.

A rise in income is often identified with a rise in the standard of living. It is more correct to identify it with an increase in personal comforts, which are only one component of the standard of living. Moreover, it is only some, never all, the personal comforts that increase and can be increased. Accordingly, how a rise in incomes affects the standard of living also depends on what happens to its non-increasing components.

Incomes rise when improved technology raises labour productivity and renders possible the increased production of some goods and services. This rise in incomes in turn increases the demand for goods and services; but those for which demand increases are not always those whose availability is increased by the rise in productivity. For there is a class of goods known as positional goods, whose availability can be increased neither through a rise in productivity nor through a transfer of resources from sectors where productivity has increased. Land, natural scenery, clean air, clean water, antique furniture, the paintings of the Impressionist School are some examples of positional goods. Since their supply cannot be increased, a rise in the demand for them will either raise their price or worsen their quality, or do both. Any of those effects will divert the additional demand away from positional goods and towards those other goods whose supply can be augmented; but the process usually creates a feeling of loss. The reason for that feeling is partly that the increase in people's incomes leads them to expect increased access to all goods and services but their expectations are subsequently disappointed as far as their hoped-for increased access to positional goods is concerned; and to create expectations only to disappoint them is worse than having neither expectations nor disappointments.

136

Another, perhaps more important part of the reason is that when rising incomes raise the demand for positional goods, the redistribution of the available supply and the lag with which price and quality respond to the rise in demand, enable many people to get a foretaste of new satisfactions which they are later forced to renounce. In other words, the money illusion created by rising incomes and rising prices is not pure illusion. Usually, there is a real gain; but it is temporary and soon followed by its permanent loss. That explains why rational people will often pursue money illusion, and why pursuing that illusion creates a loss. It is a well-established psychological law that habits, including consumption habits, are much more easily and quickly established than they are relinquished. Drug addiction is the extreme example; but evidence shows the asymmetry to be pretty nearly universal. That implies that the pain of the withdrawal symptoms exceeds, in the subject's estimation, the initial gain. Indeed, cured addicts always maintain that with the benefit of hindsight they would not have become addicts. It seems likely therefore that the increased demand for positional goods is not only thwarted but often leads to a net loss of satisfaction as well.

Very similar problems are created also by another component of the good life: social comfort, because the sources of social comfort are either positional goods or closely resemble positional goods. Social comfort is the satisfaction one derives from one's status in the community to which one belongs or wants to belong. At a minimum, people want to consider themselves, and be considered by others, members of the community—a desire satisfied by a level of personal comfort exceeding a certain minimum known as the poverty line, which is determined in relation to and so moves with the community's median level of personal comfort. A proportionate rise therefore in everybody's income increases the personal comforts of the poor but does not render them any the less poor, because it does not reduce the gap between their and other people's levels of comfort. The only way to reduce poverty, and the proportion of poor people in the population, is to reduce inequalities of income; and that is not an inevitable, not even a probable outcome of growth.

In most developing countries, economic growth has increased inequalities of income and therefore increased poverty—at least on the definition just given. Perhaps the only countries whose growth went hand-in-hand with diminished inequalities were Great Britain and the Scandinavian countries—that is, countries where to mitigate inequalities was an important separate goal of social policy.

To avoid the stigma of poverty, however, is only part of people's desire for social comfort. Another, no less important part is the desire to rank high in the hierarchy of one's community. That part of social comfort is again an example of a positional good, whose total availability cannot be increased. The scramble for status is a zero-sum game: for me to gain I must outrank others, on whom my gain in rank inflicts a loss. A rise in people's incomes almost certainly raises their demand for status, which, frustrated by its fixed supply, creates a feeling of frustration. In addition, it often has side-effects, which may create further losses.

One such side-effect has long been known, deplored, and unsuccessfully fought against. Ostentation or conspicuous consumption is one of the oldest ways of seeking status. It can be quite costly; but, since it cannot increase the supply of status satisfaction, its cost is a wasteful side-effect. That fact had been fully recognized already by the ancient Romans and, at a later stage, by the citizens of many Free Cities in medieval Germany. That is why they enacted sumptuary laws, which tried but mostly failed to limit ostentation and its costs.

Today, most peoples' main status symbol is the ranking of their jobs in the economic and administrative hierarchy. The ostensible requisite for the more important jobs is more education; and the demand for education—education as training for those important and more responsible jobs—has greatly increased with the rise in incomes. In the developed countries, the rise in the demand for education has been fully met by the rise in its supply; as a result, the proportion of more highly trained and skilled people in the labour force has also risen. It has risen in relation to both what it was before and what the economy's needs are.

In the United States, the percentage of managers, administrators, technical and professional workers in the total labour force has increased from 17 per cent in 1950 to 26 per cent in 1978;[1] in Great Britain their proportion in the industrial labour force was 11 per cent in 1961, had risen to 15 per cent in 1971, and is expected to reach 22 per cent by 1981.[2] Those are very great and very rapid increases, yet they do not tell the whole story. After all, the labour-force statistics reflect the supply of jobs, not the demand for them. The ratio of the number of managerial and administrative jobs to the number of college graduates in the United States has fallen from 2.33 in 1952 to 1.6 in 1974. That suggests that the demand for such jobs must have increased even faster than the already very fast increase manifest in the labour-force statistics (see Figure 11.1) The increase in the excess demand for high-level jobs is also confirmed by some of its economic consequences. For one thing, unemployment among college graduates has increased faster than average unemployment for the whole labour force; for another, the average earnings of college graduates have declined relatively to the average earnings of those with grade school only. In the 25 – 34-year age group, for example, male college graduates working full time earned 38 per cent more in 1968 but only 19 per cent more by 1977. Another figure, which shows much the same trend, is the rate of return on capital invested in a college education, whose best estimate fell from 11 per cent in 1963 to 7½ per cent in 1974.[3]

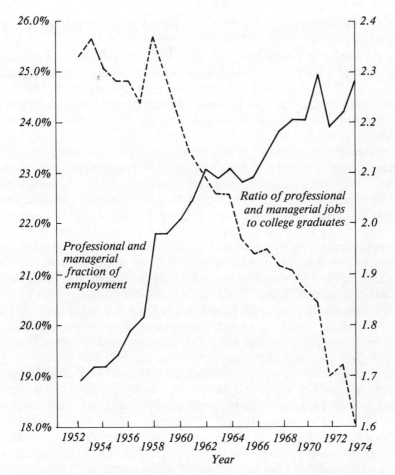

Figure II.1: Professional and managerial jobs, 1952 – 74 (data on professional and managerial employment from US Department of Labor, Manpower Report of the President (1974), Table A-11, p. 267, Manpower Report of the President (1963), Table A-7, p. 143; updates from US Department of Labor, Employment and Earnings (June 1975), Vol. 21, No. 12, Table 1, p. 7; data on college graduates, Manpower Report of the President (1974), Table B-9, p. 299, with interpolations; updates from US Bureau of Labor Statistics, Educational Attainment of Workers (March 1974), Special Labor Force Report No. 175, Table 1, p. A-17).
Source: Richard Freeman, The Overeducated American, p. 17.

Those are the US figures, but the corresponding data for the UK are very similar. The starting salaries of university graduates in the humanities and social sciences, expressed as a ratio of manual workers' average earnings, fell by 21 per cent, from 0.91 per cent in 1961 to 0.72 in 1976. The rates of return on capital invested in university education fell from 12.1 per cent in 1966 to 8-9 per cent in 1971; and the percentage of bachelor-of-arts and bachelor-of-science graduates still seeking permanent employment 6 months after graduation rose from 3.0 per cent in 1962 to 11.6 per cent in

1976. Total unemployment at those two dates was 2.2 per cent and 4.9 per cent respectively.[4]

A reduction in income disparities between college graduates and others is not such a bad thing, of course; but the other effects are. The higher than average and still rising unemployment rates of college graduates are one of those bad effects. The misinvestment of educational resources into the occupational and professional training of people unable to make use of that training is another bad effect.

One might argue, of course, that education in itself is a good thing, quite independently of whether or not it leads to more prestigious or better-paying jobs. Education, after all, develops people's potentialities and turns them into better citizens, more interesting and stimulating human beings, teaching them how better to enjoy life. I would agree that what is known as general education is largely an education in citizenship and consumption skills, and so well worth having irrespective of what it does to one's status and earning capacity. But that is not the kind of education most people want and get. The public's demand is for training in productive and administrative skills. That is especially evident in adult education, where the consumer's choice makes itself strongly felt; and in the United States, the whole educational system caters to that demand. As a result, most people get specialized, often quite narrowly specialized training in administrative and specific technical skills which, without jobs in which to put them to use, are largely wasted.

Here again, the statistics are striking. In 1958, only 5 per cent of people with bachelor's or master's degrees ended up in non-professional, non-managerial jobs, by 1978 that proportion had risen to 23.5 per cent for men and 28.1 per cent for women.[5] That clearly represents a waste of educational resources; but that is not the only waste. One would expect people who are overtrained or overeducated for their jobs to feel frustrated as a result; and that expectation is borne out by statistical evidence.

Many questionnaire surveys have been made in the United States of workers' job satisfaction and its relation to a variety of factors. One of those factors is the amount of education; whose relation to job satisfaction seemed, at first, to be very puzzling. Of sixteen different studies of the relation between those two factors, five found a positive association, three a negative association and eight either no association or an equivocal one. The key to the puzzle seems to be that general education probably increases people's ability to derive satisfaction from whatever they do, including their work; but that specific training for particular occupations or types of work can be excessive; and when it is, then the workers overtrained or overeducated for the work they do find that work not demanding enough and therefore not very satisfying.[6]

To test that last hypothesis a survey was carried out where workers' mean overall job satisfaction was related not to the number of years of their education but to the difference between their actual years of schooling and the years of schooling appropriate to their particular job and occupation. Four different norms of appropriateness were used: (1) the amount of schooling the worker himself believed appropriate for his occupation, (2) the amount of schooling listed as appropriate for that occupation in the *Dictionary of Occupational Titles* published by the US Department of Labor, (3) the median level of schooling of all workers in that occupation, and (4) the mean level of schooling of the immediate work group to which the worker belongs. Table II.1 shows the mean work satisfaction scores of workers with different amounts of schooling in relation to each of those four norms. The scores are the so-called z scores, their origin shifted to the mean, so that higher-than-mean satisfaction is denoted by positive, lower-than-mean satisfaction by negative numbers. The data bear out the hypothesis and the correlation is significant at the 0.001 level for the first, second and fourth criterion of appropriate schooling. What is surprising perhaps is that not only does overtraining lead to job dissatisfaction but insufficient formal training seems to lead to positive job satisfaction. A possible explanation could be that learning by doing or on-the-job training is an adequate substitute for formal training in school, and that people's success at performing work for which they were not properly trained gives them an extra feeling of accomplishment and satisfaction.

It is worth adding that we are beginning to have, in the United States, time series data on job satisfaction. National surveys conducted in 1969, 1973 and 1977 asked workers several questions relating to their satisfaction with their work, from the answers to which an 'overall job satisfaction index' was constructed. The value of that index declined from 2 in 1969 to − 2 in 1973 and to − 24 in 1977. The surveys also suggest a decline in the extent to which jobs provide the opportunity for the full use of skills; but, surprisingly enough, they show 'no increase whatsoever in the proportion of workers with more education than their jobs required. Consequently, the increase in perceived underutilization of skills may have originated outside of formal education'.[7] Later on in this paper, I shall suggest a possible explanation.

This far, I was dealing with the economic waste, the unemployment, and the feelings of job dissatisfaction created when the supply of highly skilled and educated labour exceeds the demand for such labour. That, however, is not the end of the story. We have seen that, although the supply of high-level jobs has failed to keep up with the rapidly rising demand for them, the increase in supply has also been pretty impressive. The increase in administrative and similar types of jobs from 17 to 26 per cent in twenty-five years is a very great increase; and one might well ask whether that increase was really called forth by the new requirements of our new technology. For it could also be explained quite differently. After all, the

Table II.1: Mean overall job satisfaction (facet-free), by relative levels of education

Measure of level of education	Mean overall job satisfaction (z-scores)	Measures of association and significance tests
Worker's level relative to that which worker reports is needed for his of her job		
Worker has four or more years of education short of that needed ($N = 107$).....................	0.22	
Worker has two years of education short of that needed ($N = 182$)....................................	0.17	
Worker has the level of education needed ($N = 788$)...	0.07	eta $= 0.21$
		$F = 17.57$
		d.f. $= 4; 1475$
Worker has two years of education in excess of that needed ($N = 227$)...............................	-0.07	p　0.001
Worker has four or more years of education in excess of that needed ($N = 176$).....................	-0.54	
Worker's level relative to that which *Dictionary of Occupational Titles* indicates is needed for his or her job[a])		
Worker has four or more years education short of that needed ($N = 174$)............................	0.00	
Worker has two years education short of that needed ($N = 121$).....................................	0.15	
Worker has the level of education needed ($N = 457$)...	0.11	eta $= 0.14$
		$F = 6.39$
		d.f. $= 4; 1142$
Worker has two years education in excess of that needed ($N = 285$)................................	-0.12	p　0.001
Worker has four or more years education in excess of that needed ($N = 110$).....................	-0.34	
Worker's level relative to the median level of others in his occupation[b])		
Worker has three or more years education less than others ($N = 163$)................................	0.08	

Table II.1: Mean overall job satisfaction (facet-free), by relative levels of education
(Table continued)

Measure of level of education	Mean overall job satisfaction (z-scores)	Measures of association and significance tests
Worker has two years education less than others ($N=116$)......................................	-0.07	eta $= 0.00$ $F = 0.72$ d.f. $= 4; 1482$ n.s.
Workers education differs from others by less than two years ($N=1021$)...........................	0.00	
Worker has two years education more than others ($N=70$)......................................	-0.13	
Worker has three or more years education more than others ($N=117$)...............................	0.02	
Worker's level relative to the mean level of others in his immediate work group[c])		
Considerably less than that of others ($N=3139$)	0.24	eta $= 0.14$
Somewhat less than that of others ($N=3583$)....	0.03	$F = 84.64$ d.f. $= 4; 15670$
The same as that of others ($N=1651$)..............	-0.01	p 0.001
Somewhat more than that of others ($N=1601$)..	-0.07	
Considerably more than that of others ($N=458$)	-0.17	

[a] Based on the General Educational Development codes of the *Dictionary of Occupational Titles.*
[b] Based on three-digit 1970 Census occupation codes
[c] The educational deviation score of each worker was normalized with reference to the deviations of others in his or her work group. The deviation scores do not therefore translate conveniently into years.
Source: Same as that given in Note 6.

market economy is pretty good in making the productive system respond to an increase in demand for goods and services. Might it not be equally good at catering to an increase in people's demand for high-level jobs? How would that happen?

To begin with, when firms find a great number of highly qualified, highly trained people available for the asking, and for lower salaries than such people needed to be paid in the past, they may well be tempted to create a few extra administrative jobs, on the argument that it is worth stocking up on such highly qualified and excellent people while they are available. They do so in the belief that sooner or later they will find some work for them to do.

> There is also another mechanism, known as *Parkinson's* Law. The desire for more important jobs is universal, shared by people with important and unimportant jobs alike. Now, if a person who holds a supervisory position wants to increase the importance of his position, the way for him to do that is to delegate his supervising job to two assistant supervisors and concentrate on supervising *them.* That way, the same act which increases his own importance creates two additional, only slightly less important jobs for other people to hold.

In short, it is not too hard to think of the way in which the economic system does cater to that kind of demand. Is that a good or bad thing? One's first reaction is that it is a good thing. If people get satisfaction out of the feeling that they are important and do something important, why not let them have that feeling?

> But there are a couple of problems. To begin with, if everybody is given important jobs with high-sounding titles, who will perform the humble, lowly jobs, of which there are plenty and which the economy cannot do without? We seem to have developed two ways to solve that problem. One is the transfer to the consumer himself of some of the work that others used to perform for him. The proliferation of self-service stores and do-it-yourself activities testifies to the existence of such a trend, which can only be welcomed, because it reduces the number of personal services people perform for others; and most of the work resented as humiliating or demeaning is to be found among those services.

The other solution to that problem is the importation of foreign labour. We in the United States have Mexicans and Puerto Ricans, the British have Pakistanis and Indians, the Germans have Spaniards and Portuguese, the French have North Africans, the Swiss have Italians, Greeks, Turks, Yugoslavs—virtually every developed country in the West has imported large numbers of foreign workers to perform the lowest, humblest, dirtiest jobs, at which indigenous workers turn up their noses. The percentage of foreign workers in the labour force is usually a multiple of the percentage of the unemployed; yet no country could or would resolve its unemployment by expelling some of its foreign labour; not because governments are so very considerate toward the foreign workers, but because despite the high unemployment, it would be very hard to get indigenous workers to take over the lowly jobs that foreign workers would relinquish.

Accordingly, foreign labour does contribute to solving the problem. Not without cost of course, because the political and social problems and friction created by a large body of foreign workers are considerable. Moreover, the solution is strictly temporary, because as soon as the foreign workers get acclimatized and integrated into the community, they too adopt the values of the local population and look for more dignified and more important jobs.

Another and to my mind more important problem is whether it really is possible to create more job importance in an economy just because there is a demand for it. It happens all the time that a bank or firm, which originally had one vice president, creates three or even a hundred vice presidents. But most vice presidents are not content with the mere title, they also want something important to do, something in keeping with their status. So they must be given responsibilities, work to supervise, tasks to accomplish, decisions to make. But the number of decisions to be made in a firm cannot be increased at will. So if you put in more managerial personnel, you have to do either of two things. One is to dilute the managerial function. As you install more managers, you give each of them less managerial work to do, fewer decisions to make, a narrower part of the work to supervise, etc. The other alternative is to take away some of the choices, discretion and judgement previously exercised by subordinates and let the new managers make those choices and judgements for them.

Needless to say, either of those solutions has its drawbacks. In the first case, the thinning and narrowing of managerial responsibility may render the managers' job less satisfying and so conceivably lower managerial efficiency. In the second case, the subordinates are likely to suffer. Not only is some of their discretion and freedom of choice taken from them, rendering their work less fulfilling and more monotonous; in addition, they usually find themselves saddled with the new task of collecting additional information about their work and making it available to their superiors. After all, these need a detailed informational base if they are to make good choices and prescribe meaningful behaviour for their subordinates. The latter's job satisfaction, however, is bound to suffer doubly: both from the reduction of their responsibilities and from the additional paperwork and reporting requirements imposed upon them.

Indeed, I referred earlier to surveys which showed a loss of job satisfaction in the United States between 1969 and 1977, which was not to be explained by an increase in the proportion of workers overtrained for their jobs. Might not that loss of satisfaction be explained by the diminished demand jobs make on the people who occupy them? It is possible that our fast rising demand for job importance not only renders the labour force progressively more overtrained for the jobs the economy provides but that at the same time it also renders those jobs more mechanical and thereby less demanding and less responsible. In other words, the difference between what workers are trained and able to do and what their jobs require them to do may well be increasing both because workers are getting more qualified and because jobs require lower qualifications.

Such a division of labour between decision makers and the

implementors of those decisions, between the tasks of making choices and carrying them out, increases the input of labour into a given activity. If all goes well, it also increases the output of that activity; and depending on whether it increases output more or less than in proportion with the increase in labour input, it will raise or lower labour productivity on balance.

In the past, we never had a doubt but always took it for granted that any change in the composition and structure of the labour force and in the division of labour between decision makers and decision implementors can only have one outcome: a rise in overall labour productivity. We jumped to that conclusion, because we were convinced that all re-shuffling of tasks and increases in the division of labour can have only one cause: they are dictated by the new requirements of our new technology, which in turn springs from the search for more profit and higher productivity.

In this paper, however, I tried to introduce and render plausible an altogether different hypothesis; the notion that all those changes were introduced, not in response to the changing requirements of an ever more efficient productive system, but in response to the changing desires of an ever more affluent and more choosy labour force. If there is at least some truth to my way of explaining the changes we see happening around us, then their impact on *labour productivity* can no longer be taken for granted but must be the subject of a separate investigation.

I have not made such an investigation but would like, at least, to report to you what scattered information is available on the subject. To begin with, there has been a very great decline in *labour productivity* growth in both the United States and the United Kingdom, which, as you undoubtedly know, is a matter of great concern in both countries. It is also a matter of great puzzlement. No one really knows what has caused that great decline, although there are plenty of guesses. In the United States, *Edward Denison* has done the most careful and painstaking work on the subject;[8] and while he, too, admits to being puzzled, the most important single factor to which he attributes as much as one-third of the retardation of labour productivity growth, is the great increase in government regulation and government-imposed paperwork on industry and business. That is a different factor from the one I am concerned with; but it is similar and closely related. For government regulation and the collecting of information for the use of Government's regulatory agencies is a close parallel to the division of labour within the individual firm between the decision-making managers and their subordinates, the production workers, who are reduced to collecting the information on which those decisions are based and to carrying them out in too mechanical a fashion. There is plenty of evidence of the increased bureaucratization of business in the United States; but I know of no studies enquiring into either the causes or the consequences of it.

We do have many studies of the relation between the individual worker's *job satisfaction* and his productive efficiency.[9] Most of them show a weak but positive correlation between job satisfaction and job performance; but that of course is only one element among the many one would need to piece together in answer to the question posed. If it is true therefore that the productive process is becoming more bureaucratic and that the production worker's task is becoming less responsible and discretionary and therefore less satisfying, then it is all the more urgent to look directly into the possible relationship between increases in the firm's managerial and supervisory personnel as a proportion of its total workforce on the one hand and changes in the overall labour productivity of the firm's entire workforce on the other hand.

In closing, I should like to caution that the main hypothesis of this paper remains unproven. It fits the facts pretty well; but an alternative and perhaps simpler hypothesis fits them almost as well. People may be seeking more professional and occupational training simply because it is heavily subsidized and because it seems a better source of income. It is true that the rate of return to higher education is declining and so is the ratio of the income of the more educated to the income of the less educated; but it remains true that education secures the best entry to any particular job or occupation. (That statement does not conflict with the high and rising unemployment rate among the more highly educated, which may have to do with the reluctance of many of them to accept more humble jobs.) Indeed, as the proportion of the highly educated increases among job applicants, employers find it useful to raise the educational requirements for jobs—not because they really demand higher skills but merely as a cheap, simple and convenient way of screening job applicants. Hence the paradoxical situation that as the labour force gets increasingly overtrained for the jobs available, so overtraining becomes a necessary condition for obtaining those jobs.

NOTES

1. Calculated from Series D 218-19 of the *Historical Statistics of the United States.*
2. Calculated from V. H. Woodward's 'Occupational trends in Great Britain 1961-81' Mimeo'd publication of Department of Applied Economics, University of Cambridge, p. 28, Appendix Table 1.
3. cf. Richard Freeman *The Overeducated American* (New York: Academic Press, 1976); and his 'Economic rewards to college education', *Review of Economics and Statistics,* Vol. LIX, (1977), pp. 18-29.
4. The data were presented by Richard Freeman in a lecture in London in 1978.
5. cf. Richard Freeman *op. cit.* brought up to date in private correspondence.

6.   For all the data concerning job satisfaction and its relation to education, *see* Robert P. Quinn and Martin S. Baldi de Mandilovitch, 'Education and job satisfaction: a questionable payoff', Mimeo'd publications of Survey Research Center, The University of Michigan, Nov. 1975.

7.   cf. Graham L. Staines and Robert P. Quinn 'American workers evaluate the quality of their jobs', *Monthly Labor Review,* (Jan. 1979), pp. 3-12.

8.   cf. Edward F. Denison, *Accounting for Slower Economic Growth, The United States in the 1970s,* (Washington: The Brookings Institution, 1979).

9.   cf. Lawrence D. Prybil 'Job satisfaction in relation to job performance and occupational level', *Personnel Journal,* (Feb. 1973).

12 Subsidies for the Arts: The Economic Argument—1983

The arts and the general public's access to the arts are subsidized in just about all civilised countries. In most Western European countries, the State subsidizes the performing arts, maintains museums and, by accepting the payment of inheritance taxes in the form of art objects, contributes to enriching museums. The situation is much the same also in the socialist countries, where, in addition, the State also pays salaries to creative artists and subsidizes not only the performing arts but publishing, and with it the public's access to literature as well. In the United States, direct government subsidies to the performing arts are minimal but the indirect subsidy of tax exemptions for private donations to museums and the performing arts, though not nearly as large, is still substantial.[1] In short, if we judge people's preferences as revealed by their collective actions, we must conclude that almost everybody is agreed that the arts must be subsidized.

The main dissenting voice is the economist's. Welfare economics is replete with good arguments for providing free or below cost quite a long list of goods and services; but the arts are not on that list. Economic theory, as currently taught, favours charging concert-goers the full cost of concerts and play-goers the full cost of theatrical performances, however drastic may be the curtailment of demand that would result from such full-cost pricing. Economic theory and the public's revealed collective preference is clearly at variance on the subject; and it seems to me that in this case it is economic theory that needs to be revised. The aim of this paper is to initiate such a revision.

The conventional theory of consumer behaviour has not yet advanced beyond the stage of first approximation, where all consumer satisfactions and sources of satisfactions are treated as if they were alike and all of them modelled on the simplest examples of biological need satisfaction. That is not a suitable framework for dealing with consumers' demand for the arts, which is very different indeed from their demand for biological satisfactions. A more suitable framework is the classification of consumer satisfactions I tried to develop in a series of articles and a book, on the basis of the physiological psychologist's motivation theory.[2] For the benefit of those unfamiliar with my work on the subject, let me briefly enumerate and explain those categories.

It is convenient to distinguish three categories of human satisfaction, which may be called personal comfort, social comforts, and stimulation. Personal comforts are all the things that cater to our biological needs and desires. That includes the amenities of food, drink, clothing, shelter, heating, health care, as well as all the services aimed at reducing the time and effort required for the performance of our work and various chores, whether those services are rendered by people, equipment, appliances or gadgets.

Social comforts are the things that give us a sense, partly of belonging both to the wider community and to whatever special group within the community we wish to belong to, and partly of ranking in the hierarchy of those communities and groups. They include all status symbols, from job titles to civic decorations and memberships, from conspicuous consumption to positions of authority and responsibility.

Into the third category, stimulation, belong all sources of interest, entertainment and excitement. Danger and novelty, however minor, are essential conditions of stimulation: danger, because it arouses the nervous system, novelty, because what is new and unexpected always contains an element of danger. For the stimulation to be enjoyable, however, the danger must be limited and appear manageable; and the novelty must not be too novel but blended with the familiar. In short, danger and novelty must be of an intermediate degree. The sources of stimulation are too numerous and varied to enumerate: they range from news and gossip to enjoyable work and include such dissimilar things as literature and gambling, art and violence, sports and crime.

The three categories classify not so much goods and services as the satisfactions they give rise to. For many goods provide more than one kind of satisfaction. An automobile, for example, can provide all three. It provides great personal comfort; but in addition, it often confers also the social comfort of status and offers the stimulating excitement of speed and dangerous driving. The arts provide entertainment and excitement and so clearly are sources mainly of stimulation. Accordingly, we shall concentrate on the characteristics of the demand for stimulation; but it will be useful to contrast that against the very different nature of people's demand for personal comforts, because that is how the conventional theory of consumer behaviour pictures all consumer demand.

The argument of this paper hinges partly on what I believe to be a high long-run and a low short-run elasticity of substitution between different sources of stimulation. That is the exact opposite of the situation in the realm of personal comforts, where the short-run elasticity of substitution is high but the long-run elasticity of substitution is quite low. The difference is important, because our thinking about the consumer's welfare is based almost entirely on what we know about his response to personal comforts and discomforts and we tend, wrongly, to generalize from that to the consumer's very different behaviour in the realm of stimulation.

Our needs and desires for personal comforts have many dimensions; in other words, we have many separate needs and desires, each of which has to be satisfied to yield a feeling of perfect comfort. In the short run, we easily and readily substitute one comfort for another, putting up with inconvenience in one respect for the sake of extra convenience in some other; and we are quite willing to endure temporary hardships and discomforts for the sake of more durable rewards. In the long run, however, we are much less willing to compromise, perhaps because biologocally determined minimum requirements for rest, food, and a long list of nutrients and environmental conditions demand to be satisfied in the long run and so render the long-run elasticity of substitution much more restricted. There has been much scientific enquiry into the nature and quantity of man's biological needs; but economists have been wise to accept consumers' tastes for personal comforts as given and to regard the consumer himself as the best judge of what will maximise his satisfaction, with the proviso that he is informed and familiar with the results of scientific enquiry into what is good and what is bad for him.

The nature of man's desire for stimulation is very different in many respects. It is similar only in its urgency and continuity; for he wants perceptual or intellectual stimulation whenever he is not engaged in earning his living or filling some biological need. Since man's need for stimulation is continuous, he caters to it by keeping his ears and eyes open to all sensations and changes around him, taking in news, gossip, changes in scenery and the environment; and when nothing happens around him, he immediately picks up a paper or book to read or turns on the radio or television set. The urgency of man's need for almost continuous stimulation during all his waking hours is proved by the ordeal of solitary confinement with its utter lack of any stimulus.

In addition, however, to minimal stimulation just to keep our mind and senses continually busy, most of us also want a certain amount of more intense stimulation, strong enough to occupy our thoughts and take our mind off all else. I propose to call such intense stimulation, which grips our whole being and commands our full attention, excitement. It is for the sake of excitement that people gamble and seek entertainment, watch or engage in sports, often violent and dangerous sports, are attracted by accidents, fires, storms, scandals, quarrels; it is for excitement that people engage in violence or seek violence vicariously on film and in fiction; and the desire for excitement is an important motivation also of explorers, scientists, researchers, criminals, policemen, intelligence agents, and members of other hazardous and dangerous professions. All the arts cater to that same need; and it is worth noting the frequent use of the word excitement in the artist's and art critic's vocabulary.

Excitement, of course, being just a higher intensity of stimulation, also comes in different degrees; and there is ample evidence to show that the intensity and amount (duration) of excitement or high stimulation that people seek varies greatly from person to person. Extroverts need more and stronger stimulation than introverts; and there is a great difference in the demand for excitement between born gamblers, who love to expose themselves to danger, and the timid and anxious, who seem to shun all but the mildest forms of excitement. The desire for excitement is the greatest in the young and declines with age; and most people like to alternate between short periods of high excitement and long stretches of more sedate forms of stimulation.

All of the above has been much discussed and well established in motivational psychology; but I now proceed to a peculiarity of man's need for stimulation, which has attracted little attention so far but is crucial for the argument to follow. In contrast to the many personal comforts, each of which caters to a separate need and all of which are required for complete satisfaction, the different forms and sources of stimulation and excitement seem to cater to a single need, the need of one's nervous system to be aroused, which can equally be satisfied by any one or any combination of a great variety of sources of stimulation, provided that the intensity of stimulation and the alternation of that intensity conforms to the individual's needs and desires. In short, I am arguing that there is a high long-run elasticity of substitution between the different forms or sources of stimulation and excitement.

Everything we know about the way people seek excitement and entertainment bears that out. To begin with, many people and especially children, youngsters and people in groups, are known to be highly suggestible and open to other people's guidance when it comes to choosing a pastime or seeking excitement. Often, they even prefer someone else to make that choice for them—presumably, because they are indifferent between different sources of stimulation and enjoy the added excitement of the surprise of novelty of activities proposed by others. Also, differences between different people's favoured sources of excitement, entertainment and recreation seem to be determined by nationality, social class and education more than by anything else, which suggests that those differences are not due to innate human differences in susceptibility and tastes but depend on differences in training, habituation and exposure. All that leads one to believe that in the area of stimulus enjoyment there is exceptionally great scope for minimizing costs and maximizing satisfactions through a suitable choice of the sources of stimulation.

We economists usually consider the consumer himself to be the best judge of how to obtain maximum satisfaction at given cost or given satisfaction at minimal cost. Unfortunately, however, the area of stimulus satisfaction is an exception to that rule. For one thing, the consumer minimizes only the costs he incurs himself, sometimes only the more tangible part even of those costs; and they are all too often the lesser part of the full social costs in the realm of stimulus satisfaction and excitement. For another thing, not only is the consumer likely to ignore some of the costs, he may also be a bad judge of the benefits, because many forms of excitement satisfaction require skill and previous experience not only for their enjoyment but even for judging whether they are enjoyable and whether their enjoyment is worth the cost.

Let us start by looking at the costs. It is convenient to distinguish four types of costs. Costs quantified by the market may be called monetary costs; and one can distinguish internal and external monetary costs, according to whether they are paid for by the beneficiary himself or incurred by others. Costs not quantified by the market are usually called diseconomies, which again can be internal or external. The most important diseconomies of enjoyable excitement are dangers to life and limb, considering that some form and degree of danger is a necessary condition of all excitement. For example, the excitement of fast driving imposes all four of the costs mentioned: the internal monetary cost of running and maintaining the driver's car, the external monetary costs of policing and maintaining the highways, the internal diseconomy of the danger to which the driver exposes himself, and the external diseconomy of the danger his fast driving creates for others. Let me also mention yet another important internal diseconomy imposed by many sources of stimulation and excitement: the danger of getting addicted. Getting addicted is a process whereby an enjoyable stimulus gradually ceases to be enjoyable while at the same time its absence becomes painful, so that the inducement to seek that stimulus changes from the desire for its enjoyment to a desire to escape the pain of its withdrawal symptoms. The danger of that happening is clearly a cost.

Costs can also be negative. The most common form of negative costs is negative external diseconomies, better known as external economies. These again are especially important in the area of stimulation and excitement, because many of their sources depend on human interaction, which is often of a type that is enjoyed by all those who interact. Since it takes two people or more to interact, each person's actions and interactions to the others' actions provide enjoyable stimulus not only for himself but also for all those with whom he is interacting. In the language of welfare economies, each person confers external economies on the others. Such external economies are created by social games, competitive games of skill, competitive sports, most forms of gambling, and by virtually all the arts, considering that artist, art critic, connoisseur and viewer, or composer, performers and audience all obtain enjoyable stimulation not only out of their own activities but out of their reactions to each other's activities and enjoyment as well.

Another, no less important external economy of the arts is the part of the benefit that accrues to posterity. Art and the artistic element in ordinary objects is probably the most durable form of economic value in existence; and the benefit future generations will derive from a given art object is often not, or only very partially and imperfectly, taken into account by the creator of that art object. The first buyer of, say, a painting, or the person who commissions a painting, values it not only for the enjoyment he expects to derive from it but usually also as an investment and store of value. To the extent he does the latter, the price he pays for that painting includes the present capitalized value of the infinite stream of enjoyment future generations will derive from that painting—heavily discounted, of course, for a lot of uncertainty. In such a case therefore, and to that extent, the first buyer of an art object can be thought of as also acting as an agent on behalf of future generations of owners and beneficiaries of that art object.

The forward market for most art objects, however, is very imperfect and incomplete and for some of them—music, for example—it hardly exists at all; and it is the non-existence, incompleteness or imperfection of forward markets that turns posterity's future enjoyment of present art into an external economy.

In short, art creates plenty of external economies; and we as economists must see to it that they are properly taken into account and become inducements for the creation of art and art objects.

The significance of all externalities is that they cause the internal costs payable by the consumer to misrepresent the amount of the true and full social costs. Their presence therefore causes consumers' and producers' choices to be based on misleading cost information and so leads to inefficient consumption patterns and resource allocation. The best remedy is to internalize externalities; for example, by levying a tax or granting a subsidy equal in value to each externality. Considering that the arts and competitive sports are the main sources of stimulation that create sizeable external economies (i.e. *negative* external costs) and at the same time create no external costs or diseconomies, efficiency demands that they be subsidized so as to make their cost to the consumer reflect their true social cost.

That is only one, although the most obvious and straightforward, economic reason for supplementing the private market incentive through State subsidies or their equivalent in the realm of the arts. On the same principle we should also internalize the externalities of those sources of excitement that creates external costs and diseconomies. That is the ground on which violence, another important source of excitement, has been made a criminal offence. But the way we punish crime today is not only ineffective as deterrent but almost certainly counterproductive as well. Recall that danger is an essential condition of excitement, and that limited danger, with a good chance of mastering and overcoming the danger, gives rise to enjoyable excitement. Accordingly, if the punishment is small and the chance of being punished slight, then making violence a criminal offence might merely render it even more enjoyable by adding to the excitement of violence the additional excitement of doing the forbidden, hoping and trusting one's ability to get away with it.

Everybody knows that children enjoy doing what is forbidden, precisely because it is forbidden; and adults are no different from children in that respect. There is bravado in breaking rules; even ordinarily law-abiding citizens get a kick out of occasionally asserting their manliness by crossing against the lights, ignoring speed limits, or otherwise defying authority and breaking the law in some more-or-less safe and innocent manner.

Unfortunately, a combination of circumstances and policies has rendered the commission of serious crime in the United States almost as safe as the breaking of speed limits. The statistics of crime and law enforcement show that the probability of being caught, arrested, tried and punished for a serious crime is considerably smaller than hitting the jackpot in roulette;[3] and even that all-too-rare punishment is not very punishing, owing to our excessive concern for humaneness and fairness to the criminal. The excitement of violence therefore may well be rendered all the more thrilling by the opportunity it offers of showing off one's smartness in getting away with it—an opportunity that is rendered very favourable by the slender chance of mild punishment attached to crime. Indeed, the slight probability of moderate punishment might well render all crime enjoyably exciting to those who enjoy living dangerously and have no moral or religious scruples. That certainly would explain our soaring crime rate, for which we have no better explanation.

If the above reasoning is correct and the limited means and excessive leniency of our crime prevention system render it not only ineffective but counterproductive as well, then we have here a second argument for subsidizing sports and the performing arts.

The argument is based on the belief that man's need and desire for stimulation and excitement are limited. If that is so, and all evidence points to its being so, then people's increased enjoyment of one source of excitement is bound to diminish their demand for its other sources. Accordingly, the next best thing to discouraging crime is to encourage more innocuous, non-criminal sources of excitement, whose enjoyment is likely to crowd out crime. Municipal officials in large cities are well aware of the fact that providing free access to good facilities and ample opportunities for competitive sports is an effective way of keeping idle and unemployed youths off the streets and out of trouble.

The arts are similar to sports in providing a good source of stimulation and excitement at no external cost. By saying that, I am not trying to imply that free access to chamber-music concerts would reduce the incidence of mugging. Almost certainly it would not. For one thing, people with different temperaments need excitement of different intensities; and those who seek strong stimulation in music would probably look for it in rock concerts rather than in chamber music.[4] For another thing, the arts are a good substitute for other sources of excitement only in the long run. In the short run, their elasticity of substitution is quite low, because the average person underestimates or is even completely unaware of his ability to enjoy the arts.

To be stimulated and excited by the arts is an acquired skill, which to acquire requires, as a minimum, some familiarity with a particular art form and previous exposure to it. One must learn to enjoy the arts and learning involves a cost. Part of that cost is the admission fee to, say, a concert and—more important than the admission fee—the tedium of politely sitting through and enduring what on first hearing—or even the first few hearings—seems like a boring, interminable, meaningless and unenjoyable cacophony of sounds. Moreover, the cost of learning must be incurred not only in order to enjoy a particular art form but also to be able to judge whether one will ever learn to enjoy it and whether its enjoyment will be worth the cost of learning to enjoy it.

The cost of learning is an information cost; and the problem just mentioned is the familiar problem of how much information to acquire in order to render choice more informed and its outcome more nearly optimal. The standard resolution of the problem is to weigh the marginal cost of information against the expected marginal benefit to be gained from more informed choice; and the consumer or producer is usually presumed to be the best judge of how to balance the one against the other whenever he himself is the person who both incurs all the costs and enjoys all the benefits.[5]

The situation is very different, however, in the realm of stimulus and excitement satisfaction. There, uninformed choice is not merely less efficient than informed choice and so likely to lead to less enjoyable excitement, less benefit to the chooser; it is also systematically and strongly biased in favour of choices that involve high external costs and diseconomies. Since consumers ignore externalities, they cannot be trusted properly to weigh information costs against the benefits of better informed choice between different sources of excitement. In consequence, they are liable often to opt in favour of getting less information and less net benefit than would be optimal when all social costs and all benefits are taken into account.

Let me explain and elaborate upon that statement. Note to begin with that no skill is required to enjoy the excitement that comes from the feeling of superiority and exercise of power—whether it is power over people, things, or nature. That is why such feelings and activities are among the main sources of excitement sought after by the unskilled. Unfortunately, those among such sources of excitement that involve the least cost for the beneficiary are also the ones that inflict the highest external costs and diseconomies on others. I have in mind violence against persons and property.

It appears therefore that there is a second factor to bias the excitement-seeker's choice in favour of violence and criminality: his lack of skill in finding enjoyable excitement elsewhere. If choice is to be optimal, that factor must also be offset; and the best way to offset it is to make it easier and cheaper for the general public to acquire the skills needed to enjoy other sources of stimulation and excitement. In other words, because so many of the sources of excitement accessible to the unskilled create high external costs and diseconomies, it is desirable for society to subsidize and otherwise promote general education in the skills of enjoying all those forms of stimulus excitement that involve no external costs.

Note that the argument just presented favours subsidies, not to the arts or access to the arts, but to the process of learning to enjoy them. Such subsidies therefore should be immune to the criticism often levelled at public support for the arts on the ground that it represents a regressive redistribution of income from taxpayers to the elite that forms the bulk of theatre, opera and concert audiences. For the purpose of art education is to increase and keep increasing membership in that elite until it ceases to be an elite.

It is not always possible, of course, to subsidize the learning process without also subsidizing the enjoyment of those who already possess the skill of enjoying the arts. Education in art and music appreciation is clearly one item on the agenda, cheap and easy access for the young is another, to judge by audience studies, which show the importance of education and childhood interest. Those studies also show that 'prior attendance is one of the strongest determinants of future attendance' at symphony concerts and theatre.[6] Simple exposure therefore, at an early stage, when motivation to expose oneself is still lacking, seems to be an important condition of learning. That explains why the offer of second tickets at half price has been one of the most successful strategies for expanding the audience of the performing arts in the United States; and it justifies the criticism I voiced years ago of the misguided effort of American concert and opera managers to fill all seats with subscribers. Productivity is, indeed, maximized as a result but it eliminates or greatly diminishes the chance everybody should have of acting on the spur of the moment to fill in an empty evening by going to an opera or concert and so finding out what they are about and what enjoyment and stimulus thay have to offer. Learning through exposure is an essential condition of art appreciation and, if so, then the loss of revenue on a modest proportion of empty seats must be regarded as a subsidy well spent on eliminating one of the obstacles in the way of newcomers when they want to get introduced to the performing arts.

I should like to conclude this short paper with another quick look at the psychology behind it. I argued that the main justification for subsidizing the arts is to acquaint the general public with the artistic outlets to man's passion for excitement, adventure and stimulation, in the hope that as the existence and attraction of those outlets become more widely known and appreciated, they will help to displace the obnoxious and the more costly outlets to those same passions.

Let us face it, the argument sounds weak and unconvincing on first hearing, especially when stated quite so bluntly. For one thing, the process is bound to be a slow one, a matter of generations rather than of years. For another, we all remember how seemingly similar hopes pinned to education in the past had come to nought. Earlier generations had hoped that the spread of general education would reduce criminality and that hope was cruelly disappointed. The United States had become the country with the most education; it also is the country with the most crime.

But that earlier hope was disappointed, because it was based on a mistaken theory about an altogether different kind of education. Education in the United States became increasingly lopsided, narrowly focused on teaching the skills and instruments of rational behaviour; our mistaken hope was that greater rationality would lead to more reasonable, more public-spirited behaviour—not realizing that education will not change man's nature, the most it can do is to channel his undiminished drives into new channels.

We had learned how to think and calculate more rationally; and while that increased our productivity and promoted technical and economic progress, it has not diminished our drives nor lowered our desire for excitement. On the contrary, technical progress has rendered work less strenuous, less hazardous, and so also more boring and that has increased our demand for discretionary sources of stimulation, excitement and adventure. Our narrowly focused, one-sided education, however, failed to provide new outlets for those new demands. In other words, the increase in our production skills has increased our need for education also in consumption skills; and that education was not forthcoming. That is the kind of education decried as elitist, it is the kind that, according to all the audience surveys, seems essential for the enjoyment of the arts and it is the only kind that can ever hope to deflect our need for excitement from anti-social channels.

NOTES

1. Direct Federal aid to the arts and humanities and the estimated loss of Federal taxes due to the tax exemption of private contributions add up to about 0.05 of 1 per cent of the GNP. Federal aid plus the total private contributions of persons, corporations and foundations amount to 0.12 of 1 per cent of the GNP. (Subsidies from the States and municipalities add very little to that.) Those figures compare to a public subsidy of 0.22 of 1 per cent of the GNP in the German Federal Republic and of 0.38 of 1 per cent on the GNP in Sweden.

2. My two articles that bear most directly on the subject of this paper are: 'The desire for excitement in modern society', *Kyklos,* Vol. 34, (1981), pp. 3-13, and 'Can changing consumer tastes save resources?' in Irma Adelman (ed.) *Economic Growth and Resources. Proceedings of the 5th World Congress of the International Economic Association,* Vol. 4, (London: Macmillan, 1979), pp. 34-5. Chapters 9 and 10 of this book. For a summary account of the psychological literature, see my *The Joyless Economy,* (New York: Oxford University Press, 1976).

3. Serious crimes are the seven crimes, ranging from murder to automobile theft, for which the FBI collects nationwide statistics. According to the latest (1974) detailed survey, the chance of being convicted of one of those crimes was 1 in 48. For references and detail, *see* Chapter 10.

4. At the time of the Beatles' great popularity, it had been argued that they should be given credit for the decline in violence in Britain.

5. cf. K. J. Arrow, *The Limits of Organization,* (New York: Norton, 1974).

6. cf. National Endowment for the Arts, Research Division Report No. 14, *Audience Development,* (Washington, DC, 1981) p. 7. *See also* the Research Division Report No. 9, *Audience Studies of the Performing Arts and Museums,* (Washington, DC, 1978).

13 The Economy's Impact on Family and Social Relations in America*— 1984

The peculiarly American character of family and society is hard to capture because it is not very peculiar. Since World War II, the United States has been the prototype of modern Western society; and its peculiarities were usually just the forerunners of what was soon to follow in the other advanced Western countries as well. I shall take my illustrations from America, of course; but mostly they illustrate general tendencies characteristic of a larger group of countries.

Another advance warning I should like to voice is that you asked me, an economist, to speak on what is a sociologist's or psychologist's subject. I happen to be all in favour of economists' broadening their vision and widening the scope of what has become over the years their excessively narrow speciality. That is why I was glad to accept your invitation. Nevertheless, you will have to put up with my economist's bias and economist's ignorance of sociological surveys. I hope they will not be too damaging.

Economic conditions and human relations, including family relations, are closely interconnected in many ways. Causality runs both ways; but the more profound and more interesting influences are the ones that economic structures and technology exert on human and family relations. I propose to deal with some of those at length, in the sections dealing with the causes and consequences of low economic friction and high mobility; but I will begin by discussing the reasons and repercussion of women's entry into the labour force, the subject where scientific, economic, personal and social factors are the most intricately intertwined.

* Paper presented at the 1984 Sapporo Cool Seminar in American Studies in Sapporo, Japan, and printed in Japanese translation.

WOMEN IN THE LABOUR FORCE

The Western countries, by which I mean the United States, Canada, and the industrialized countries of Western Europe, experienced a—to them—unprecedented fast economic growth over an unprecedentedly long and unbroken period of time after the Second World War. Economists customarily and instinctively associate fast growth with fast capital accumulation; but growth, in this case, was associated with a fast accumulation also of that other important factor of production, labour. The labour force grew and continues to grow faster than the population.

The faster growth of the labour force than the population was again a matter of mutual interaction. Fast economic growth created a fast-growing demand for labour; and the labour supply responded to that growth in demand, thereby sustaining economic growth. The sources of the increase in the labour supply were twofold: the increased participation of women in the labour force and the immigration of foreign labour. In the United States, immigration laws kept the inflow of foreign labour to more modest proportions than in the other Western countries; but women responded all the more strongly to the pull of demand in the labour market.

The participation rate of women in the US labour force increased between 1940 and 1982, from 27.9 per cent to 52.7 per cent. That compares with the still much higher male participation rates, which over the same forty-two years fell slightly, from 82.5 per cent to 77.1 per cent. As a result of those changes, the average annual rate of increase of the US labour force was 1.6 per cent, as against the 1.3 per cent increase in the country's population.

Women have responded, of course, to an excess demand for labour also in earlier periods; but their present response seems to be faster and more massive; and, if appearances can be trusted, it seems to be more permanent as well. The factors to explain that are many and complex, having to do both with increased feasibility and with increased motivation.

The feasibility of women's joining the labour force has increased, partly because their workload in the home has diminished, and partly because their opportunities of finding work in market-orientated activities has increased. The main factor under the first heading has been the increasing use of contraception and the improvement in contraceptive methods, which have reduced the number of children per family and with it the burden of bringing them up. A supplementary factor has been the development of household and kitchen appliances, which has greatly lightened the load of householding. That last was very much an American development, not only because American ingenuity was more strongly focused on developing such appliances but also because Americans, thanks to their higher incomes, were able to afford time-saving appliances at an earlier stage. The importance of those factors, and especially of the first factor, is shown by the fact that the increase in female labour-force participation is mainly due to the increase in *married* women's entering the labour market.

As to women's increased opportunities in the labour market, they are explained by those elements in economic and technical progress that changed the economy's occupational structure and lightened the task of factory work. The increasing importance of administration within the firm as it grows in size, and the increasing importance of service industries in the economy as it grows in affluence, have greatly expanded the proportion of the kinds of jobs at which women are particularly good. Simultaneously, the increased substitution of mechanical power for human muscle has greatly diminished the number of jobs whose performance requires great physical exertion and which, for that reason, have been the natural domain of men, owing to their biologically determined larger and stronger bone structure and greater muscular strength.

At the same time that those changes have occurred, women's motivation to enter the labour force has also increased. One would expect that motivation to be the greatest where people are the poorest; and that expectation seems to be borne out by an international comparison of the relevant statistics. Women's participation in the labour force is the greatest in the communist countries and in those Third-World countries where the labour market for women's work is adequately developed. In the rich countries, well-paid men used to pride themselves on their women's not having to work, not being compelled to work by economic necessity.

All that has changed, however, or is in the process of changing, at least in the rich countries and especially in the United States. Economic necessity has become only one, and perhaps not even the most important one, of the many motives women have for entering the labour force. In the United States, for example, the largest relative increase in women's labour-force participation since 1960 has occurred in the top income groups, among wives of high-earning husbands. How can that be explained?

For one thing, the reduced burden of child rearing and householding has rendered women's, and especially educated women's, life boring—the more so because our educational system is biased in favour of developing production skills but neglects the skills of leisure. For another thing, the American puritan ethic, which is responsible for having created that bias in our educational system, is itself a strong motivating force for women to join the labour force. Production in the United States is considered a more important, more prestigious activity than consumption, just as the earning of money is more respectable, more honourable than the spending of it. The reason for that feeling may be that production is viewed as an altruistic activity, which benefits the whole community, with the income earned by production measuring society's appreciation of one's contribution to the community's welfare; whereas leisure and consumption activities seem selfish, benefiting only oneself and one's family, which makes the money, energy, and ingenuity devoted to making leisure and consumption enjoyable a measure of one's selfishness.

At an earlier stage in economic development, that puritanical hierarchy of values merely contributed to the greater prestige of men, who were the traditional producers and income earners of the family. But the situation changed once technical and economic progress lightened women's burden of child rearing and householding, created new occupations to which women had equal or even preferential access, and reduced the muscular-strength requirement of many jobs previously reserved for men. Women, after all, share the value system of their menfolk; and they too aspired to the more prestigious status conferred by the earning of money in market-related activities—especially so after their wartime experience in the jobs given up by the men drafted into the army made evident women's ability to hold their own against men in the labour market, even in such strenuous and hitherto exclusively male occupations like welding, riveting and truck driving.

Finally, another important motivation for women to enter the labour force is their increased desire for economic independence. Economic independence has always been a good thing. But once the new, cheaper, safer and more convenient methods of contraception led to more sexual experimentation and gave women greater sexual freedom, including a new freedom of choice and search in seeking the best marriage partners, their lesser economic independence became women's main obstacle to attaining full equality with men in the pursuit of happiness. Accordingly, to achieve greater economic independence became a much more important goal; and the way to achieve it was to participate, and to acquire the right to participate on equal terms and for equal pay in the labour force.

Women's right to equal pay and equal standards of admission is far from being won; and the fight for women's equality has been slowed, even set back by the conservative movement of the late 1970s and 1980s. By the late 1970s, the average earnings of women working full time in the labour force were only 60 per cent of the average earnings of men. One reason is that such low-paying occupations like teaching, social work and clerical work have traditionally been and still remain 'female jobs'. A second reason is that women's inroads into traditionally male-dominated occupations have been much more successful in low- than in high-paying categories. For example, women have quickly become the majority among insurance adjustors and real-estate brokers; whereas women lawyers, judges and physicians constituted only 14 per cent of those professions in 1981, although their advance was impressive even there, women having constituted only 4 per cent of the legal professions in 1972 and 10 per cent of medical practitioners in the same year.

Another reason for women's lower average pay is that married women are more likely than married men to take time out from the labour force, usually for family-related reasons. The final reason, already alluded to, is the tendency of many employers to pay women less than men for the same work in the same job, and men's reluctance to appoint or elect women to top executive positions. Such discrimination is being successfully fought but success is very slow in coming.

When women go to work in the labour market, they have to give up something for the sake of the income they earn; and time budget studies show that two-thirds of their worktime they save on housework, one-third of it encroaches upon their leisure. In households where wives specialize in housework and their husbands specialize in market work, the husband contributes 16 per cent of the family's total time devoted to housework, and his total working hours exceed his wife's by 10 per cent. In families where both husband and wife are full time in the labour force, the wife's working hours exceed her husband's by 30 per cent, partly because the husband of a working wife spends less time on his job than do the husbands of non-working wives but does not contribute to housework any more than they do. It is in families where the man works full time and the wife part time that the total number of hours worked by man and wife are approximately the same. The detailed figures are shown in Table 13.1.

Surprisingly enough, the sum of husband's and wife's total housework and labour-market work combined is virtually the same in all three cases, because the time wives spend in the labour market is taken not out of the

Table 13.1: Average total weekly work time of husbands and wives, 1967-8

	Labour market	House- work	Total time
		(hours per week)	
Homemaker families			
Wife	3[a]	57	60
Husband	55	11	66
Part-time employed wife			
Wife	18	47	65
Husband	51	11	62
Full-time employed wife			
Wife	37	34	71
Husband	44	11	55

[a] Unpaid volunteer work.

Source: Kathryn E. Walker and Margaret E. Woods, *Time Use: A Measure of Household Production of Family Goods and Services* (American Home Economics Association, 1976), Table 3.17.

family's total leisure but out of its total housework. The housework that is abridged is not so much cooking and cleaning but mainly the education and socialization of children, the care of elderly relatives and—to a much lesser extent—the care of clothing. The working wife's extra earnings are spent in much the same way in which her husband's earnings are spent, except for her work-connected expenditures on transportation and extra clothing and for additional insurance, pension plans and social security.

Table 13.2: Household size: 1790-1980

	1790	1900	1930	1940	1950	1960	1970	1980
Average number of persons per household	5.79	4.76	4.11	3.67	3.37	3.33	3.14	2.75

Source: Bureau of the Census, *Historical Statistics of the United States, Colonial Times to 1970,* Series A291 and *Statistical Abstract of the United States 1983,* Table No. 62.

Table 13.2 shows the gradual move from the extended to the nuclear family in the United States: the size of an average American household has shrunk by more than 40 per cent during this century. That strikingly illustrates both the main explanation of women's increased labour-force participation, fewer children, and one of its main consequences, the family's lesser willingness to house and take care of parents and elderly relatives. The other main consequence is illustrated by Table 13.3, which

Table 13.3: Child-care arrangements for children below six years of age of married working mothers

(in per cent)	1958	1977[a]
Care in child's home	56.6	28.6
by father	14.7	10.6
by other relative	27.7	11.4
by non-relative	14.2	6.6
Care in another home	27.1	47.4
by relative	14.5	20.8
by non-relative	12.7	26.6
Group care centre	4.5	14.6
Child cares for itself	0.6	0.3
Mother cares for child while working	11.2	9.0
Total	100.0	100.0

Note: The data refer to arrangements only while the mother is working.
[a] The data for the two years are not strictly comparable, because those for 1977 refer only to the two youngest children below five years of age.

Source: Marjorie Lueck, Ann Orr and Martin O'Connell, 'Trends in childcare arrangements of working mothers', *Current Population reports,* Series P-23, No. 117. 1982, Table A p. 2.

shows the relative importance of the different ways in which the small children of married mothers working full time are taken care of. Their much greater reliance in 1977 than in 1958 on group care centres and on care in another home shows the extent to which the supply of those facilities has been responding to the demand for them.

Table 13.4: Living arrangements of married and unmarried persons aged Sixty-five and over: 1900, 1962, 1975

(numbers in per cent)

	Married			Unmarried		
Living arrangements	1900	1962	1975	1900	1962	1975
Total	100	100	100	100	100	100
Alone or with spouse only	29	79	84	11	48	67
With married child	16	2	1	38	14	7
With unmarried child	42	15	10	27	20	10
With other relatives	7	3	5	13	12	13
With non-relatives	6	1	0	11	6	3

Note: Because data collection procedures used in 1900 differed from those of 1962 and 1975, it is possible only to make general comparisons between 1900 and the other two years.
Sources: Daniel Scott Smith, 'Historic change in the household structure of the elderly in economically developed countries' in Robert W. Fogel, et al (eds.), *Aging: Stability and Change in the Family* (New York: Academic Press, 1981) Table 5, A1, p. 110; Ethel Shanas, et al, *Old People in Three Industrial Societies* (New York: Arno Press, 1980) Table VII-2, p. 186; and Ethel Shanas, *Final Report, National Survey of the Aged,* University of Illinois at Chicago Circle, January 1978, Table 5-7, p. 55.

As to the elderly, Table 13.4 shows the extent to which they have changed their lifestyle over the first three-quarters of this century in favour of independent housing and living. The reason is not only their children's increasing reluctance to house and care for them; an important additional reason is their greater affluence and greater ability to afford a household of their own. That is partly due to a generous, even over-generous US Social Security system, which has halved the proportion of the elderly below the poverty line between 1959 and 1980.

Yet another factor that has also contributed to the diminishing size of households is the increased tendency of not yet married young men and women to set up their own households. Their main motivation is the desire for independence, although the wish to ease the burden of householding on working mothers may also play a part. Table 13.5 shows an almost five-fold increase over a thirty-two year period. For men, a shift to living alone or with unrelated persons of their own or the opposite sex accounted for all the increase. For women, the increase included an almost five-fold increase also in the percentage of never-married women heading a family household—a reflection of the increase in premarital and extramarital

Table 13.5: Never-married men and women aged twenty-five to thirty-four maintaining their own households: 1950, 1960, 1970, 1982
(number in per cent)

	Men				Women			
Living arrangements	1950	1960	1970	1982	1950	1960	1970	1982
Total maintaining own household	9.5	19.4	31.1	42.7	11.0	21.1	35.2	53.3
Living with family members	4.6	4.3	4.5	4.1	3.6	6.7	11.9	16.8
Living alone or with non-relatives	4.9	15.1	26.6	38.6	7.4	14.4	23.3	36.5

Note: 1950, 1960, and 1970 data come from decennial censuses, while 1982 data are from the Census Bureau's Current Population Survey and are not strictly comparable.

Sources: Bureau of the Census, 'Marital status 1950', *Population Census Report P-E,* No. 2D. Preprint of Vol. IV, Part 2, Ch. D. (Washington, DC: US Government Printing Office, 1953), Table 1, p. 18. 'Persons by family characteristics', *US Census of Population: 1960, Final Report,* PC(2)-4B (Washington, DC: US Government Printing Office, 1964), Table 2, p. 10. Persons by family characterstics', *US Census of Population: 1970,* PC(2)-4B (Washington, DC: US Government Printing Office, 1973), pp. 12 and 17, and 'Marital status and living arrangements: March 1982', *Current Population Reports,* Series P-20, No. 380 1983, Table 6, pp. 36 and 37.

childbearing, more single mothers rearing their own children, and their greater tendency to live apart from parents and other relatives.

Women's greater sexual freedom and economic independence have much to do also with today's high divorce rates. While only 5 per cent of all marriages ended in divorce in 1860, almost half of those contracted in 1973 can be expected to end in divorce. For the first 100 years, however, the rising divorce rate merely offset the rise in life expectancy, because the rate at which marriages were dissolved by divorce *or* death remained constant. Only since 1960 has the rise in divorce rates outstripped the rise in life expectancy; and the disappointment of both men and women is not with the institution of marriage but with their marriage partners, because two-thirds or more of those who divorce young remarry within five years.

It is a peculiar but common misconception to take the rising divorce rate for a sign of declining marital happiness. In reality, it signifies a decline in people's tolerance for marital unhappiness. Questionnaire surveys show that the proportion of people satisfied with their marriage is on the increase. According to one survey, the number of those who regard their marriage as very happy or above average rose from 68 per cent to 80 per cent between 1957 and 1976; although the same survey showed that the proportion of those who perceived problems in their marriage also increased: from 46 per cent to 61 per cent over the same period. The two findings are not incompatible—on the contrary. They imply that people now expect more of marriage and make greater demands on it; and that they find their marriage more satisfactory even by those higher standards. Women's greater freedom of choice is one explanation of their expecting more of marriage; another possible explanation could be the declining closeness of friendships and the declining number of close friends, which I will discuss later as one of the consequences of great mobility (see p. 177 below), and which makes people cast their spouse also in the additional role of close friend.[1]

THE LOW-FRICTION ECONOMY AND ITS REPERCUSSIONS

The increase in women's work and its social, economic and psychological implications are by far the most tangible and quantifiable consequences of scientific and economic progress. For lack of statistical support, I proceed much more tentatively to look at another consequence of progress; the reduction in the number and frequency of personal contacts between economic agents and the lesser amount of friction those contacts generate. I am setting out to show that that too has happened in the United States, and possibly to a greater extent than elsewhere.

The reason for that is simple enough. Economic progress means a rise in the earnings and cost of labour, which calls for economizing its use, including its use in market transactions and other personal contacts between economic agents. There is something paradoxical in that, because increased specialization and division of labour mean increased economic interdependence; and while that makes each individual's welfare depend on the cooperation of an ever-increasing number of people, it also reduces the number and extent of his contacts with them. Cafeterias, supermarkets and self-service shops provide much less time, opportunity and need for personal contacts between buyers and sellers than their predecessors did, and also renders those contacts less personal. The same is true also of the automated factory and office, where people have been thinned out and machinery crowded in, increasing nervous tension and distance and reducing the need for personal contact and the opportunities for a chat. Finally, our rising standard of living has reduced the occasions for personal contact also among fellow consumers. The substitution of the private car for public transportation, of hi-fi equipment for concerts, of television sets for live theatre, cinema and spectator sports are examples; and so is the equipping of every modern household with a whole battery of kitchen, household and garden implements and appliances, all of which diminish its members' need for personal contacts with people outside the household.

So far, I dealt with the diminution in the number and frequency of personal contacts. Let me now come to the diminution in the degree of friction. The functioning of the market economy involves millions of everyday personal contacts, whose peculiarity is that they are both cooperative and antagonistic at the same time. They are cooperative, because they are necessitated by the division of labour and render possible the gains from specialization that result from the division of labour. They are antagonistic, because they determine the distribution of those gains, whereby one party's share in the gain is regarded by the other party as his loss. That is true of the relations between buyer and seller, master and servant, employer and employee, as well as of the relations among rival claimants to shares in any one of a great many things, ranging from markets to seats in a bus or space on a crowded beach. All such relations can generate friction, the more friction the greater the scope for individual astuteness and aggressiveness in influencing the outcome. To live in the midst of such friction, continuously jostling and being jostled by others, asserting or defending one's rights and advantages, yet living in peace with those against whom one asserts them, is the essence of social existence.

Every society enacts and enforces laws to keep friction within acceptable < limits by limiting the scope for individual aggression but leaves the individual to fend for himself within those limits. Friction, of course, stems not only from the conflict of economic interests. Non-economic interests, along with differences in temperament, tastes, habits and upbringing are no less or more important as sources of conflict and friction, especially in a society like ours, with its great variety of religions and racial and national origins. This paper will deal only with the decline in economic and related sources of friction and its consequences; but these, unfortunately, comprise our declining ability to contain friction, including racial and national friction, of which we have more than our fair share.

Before dealing with the economic factors that have alleviated friction in our society, I must at least mention two others. One is the singularly classless nature of American society. Another non-economic factor, though economic in origin, is the great homogeneity of neighbourhoods, especially suburban neighbourhoods in the United States. Americans have a strong preference for living in one-family houses with each on its own plot of land; and, thanks to the low density of population, 70 per cent of all families are able to have such housing. That arrangement, along with zoning regulations concerning the minimum size of plot and the admissibility of multi-unit housing and industrial and commercial establishments, causes the cost of housing to vary within a narrow range in each neighbourhood (zone) but vary greatly as between more desirable and less desirable ones. That causes families to settle in neighbourhoods where other families in their own income class and in similar occupational groups have also settled. It hardly needs adding that homogeneous neighbourhoods are conducive to relatively frictionless relations among neighbours.

Education in America also has something to do with the elimination of friction—but more as a symptom than as a cause. Two examples are worth mentioning. In the United States, where competition was pretty rough and abrasive in the nineteenth century, most parents still want to bring up their children in the American tradition of rugged individualism. No sooner can children walk and do some fetching and carrying around the house than they are sent out to learn the ways of the world by offering their services for sale to the neighbours: minding babies, delivering newspapers, mowing lawns, washing cars, and selling magazine subscriptions, Christmas cards and girl-scout cookies. In today's America, however, those attempts at the practical education of the young are frustrated by the neighbours. They are all smiles, tend to overpay rather than shortchanging the youngsters, and educate them mainly by setting an example in the art of gracefully buying and paying for things they often don't even need. The entire operation becomes not so much a training for economic life and a habituation to its frictions as a demonstration of neighbourliness and the frictionless character of suburban American life.

American schools reflect that same frictionless character in the relations between teacher and pupil. To spare the children the supposedly traumatic experience of bad grades and competition against their betters, teachers try to grade their performance, not on an objective scale or in relation to other children in the same class, but on the subjective scale of each child's presumed capabilities. Increasingly, there is reluctance to grade at all or to tell the child its grade. (Even universities try to spare their undergraduates: some have abolished the failing grade, a few have abolished all grades).

Contrast to that the way French children are treated, which I believe is fairly representative of the treatment of children also in the rest of Europe. Middle-class parents would never expose their child to the rough and tumble of the French counterpart to the market place American ten-year olds operate in; but he gets a foretaste in school of what adult French society has in store for him. Not only are grades very important in French (as in most European) schools; but every child, from first grade to the baccalauréat, is ranked weekly or monthly on the basis of his grades in every subject, and all know at all times that he occupies the umpteenth place in his class. In some schools, he even wears a badge to show and for all to see his ranking.

To come now to the explanation of the increasingly frictionless character of the American economy, the primary factor is probably the increasing size of the firm and its increasingly impersonal nature. Historically, the earliest as well as the simplest and most obvious form of friction in economic life was haggling and bargaining between buyer and seller. It has been eliminated in most developed countries by the practice of sellers' setting their prices on a take-it-or-leave-it basis, initiated by department stores and large sellers as a means of saving the time spent in bargaining and the cost of training hired employees in the skills of bargaining. In the United States, the changeover to set prices began rather late, in the last decades of the nineteenth century, but has probably been carried further than in most other countries.

There remained some scope for friction in arguing about workmanship and quality; but much of that was again eliminated by the mass production of manufactured goods, which created uniform products of standardized quality, by the self-service store, where customers select the individual items they buy, and by the recent practice of manufacturers to economize on the high cost of quality control by offering customers who bought faulty specimens far-reaching guarantees of repair or replacement and easy ways of activating and making use of those guarantees.

Finally, the ability of sellers to set their prices unilaterally usually gives them a monopoly advantage in the form of a monopolistic profit mark-up added to cost, which renders it profitable for them to stimulate sales at set prices by providing all the facilities, choice, convenience, easy terms of payment and politeness that together make up a buyers' market. All those developments were dictated by the sellers' self-interest; but the elimination of friction and the obscuring of the conflict of interest between buyer and seller were important consequences.[2]

One would expect the elimination of friction in product markets, where people spend their earnings, to put all the more strain on the labour market, where the amount of their earnings is determined. Indeed, modern man is notorious for his preoccupation with money income; and equally notorious is the violence of collective bargaining in many of the industrial countries. On the other hand, the individual wage and salary earner is seldom in a position personally to bargain or to experience much friction—and for essentially the same reasons that explain the elimination of bargaining and friction in the consumers' market for products.

Economies of scale, the increasing disparity in numbers between the two sides of the labour market, and the displacement of the personal firm by the impersonal corporation, have all helped to depersonalize the employee's wage contract and the employer's authority over him. Wage and salary scales in the large firm are geared to a man's or a woman's functions, skill, training and length of experience, with little scope left for individual bargaining and taking individual differences into account. Similarly, every employee's rights and duties are exactly determined and narrowly circumscribed by impersonal rules and regulations equally obeyed by all. All that leaves little scope for personal friction and the direct exercise of personal power.

Wage scales and conditions of work are often subject, of course, to negotiation and renegotiation through collective bargaining; and that can be bitter and violent. Personal involvement, however, in its bitterness and friction is largely confined to the skilled professional negotiators who represent management and organized labour. The people whose incomes and conditions of work are at stake usually remain uninvolved. Their participation in the bargaining process is confined to occasionally manning picket lines and casting ballots for or against their union's stand—both of which are usually fairly peaceful activities in the United States, and so highly organized and institutionalized as to admit little personal animosity and friction. The stratification of management also helps to minimize friction on the personal level.

One must further bear in mind that labour unions, never very strong in the United States, are on the decline. According to the latest count, union membership has fallen to about 15 per cent of the non-agricultural labour force. In the great majority of firms and industries, management unilaterally determines wages, fringe benefits and working conditions, in ways and at levels that, surprisingly enough, are not significantly different from those negotiated by unions. The probable explanation seems to be management's fear that its lesser generosity would lower morale and so lead to a fall in labour productivity. For, as more and more of the purely mechanical operations are performed by automatic machinery, workers perform increasingly sophisticated and responsible technical and supervisory functions. In those new roles, discipline is not enough to make workers give their best; care, circumspection, interest in the job, pride in its satisfactory performance, devotion to the work and loyalty to the firm are also required. That renders labour productivity much more variable, much more dependent on the employees' morale and their satisfaction with their position. Accordingly, the firm's profitability has become a function of its workers' satisfaction; and that provides management with a strong inducement to offer good working conditions, fair wages, comparable to those offered elsewhere, attractive fringe benefits, and whatever else it takes to make workers feel well treated and to avoid labour-market friction.

The inflationary wage increases in the United States are increasingly explained in those terms, rather than by the militancy of organized labour.[3] US inflation therefore is, at least partly, the cost we pay for avoiding labour-market friction.

The frictionless quality of personal relations between buyers and sellers, employers and employees in the United States is matched by relations among competitors on the buyers' side of consumers' markets, although there is friction among the firms competing for market outlets on the sellers' side. Probably the most friction remains in non-economic competition for public facilities and collective services, especially in the large cities with their high density and diverse populations, where apartment-house living, public transportation by bus and underground, and recreation in crowded places, parks and beaches remain the rule. Indeed, the resulting friction explains the continuing exodus from the large cities into the garden suburbs and the resulting increase in the proportion of owner-occupied single houses, as the rising standard of living turns more and more families into self-contained independent units, each crowded onto its own plot of land, into its own house or house-trailer, and in front of its own movie or television screen. That may increase strains within the family but diminishes friction among strangers.

Such and similar changes have rendered American society relatively frictionless in most personal contacts. Those are fewer, shorter, less personal—and more friendly. The eternal American smile is not a sales gimmick or just a facade but a sign of the success with which we have eliminated friction and obliterated the basis for conflict between the conflicting parties in most personal relations. Salespeople not only smile at the customer—to the never-ending amazement of foreigners, they are genuinely nice and helpful even when no sale is involved.

Lack of friction, mutual trust and general friendliness are an important aspect of America's high standard of living. Most Americans learn to appreciate it only when exposed to the more abrasive quality of the corresponding contacts abroad. Being constantly on the alert, never yielding and always exploiting one's right or advantage, never taking anything for granted, never quite trusting the other party and never being trusted oneself, those are the proper rules of behaviour wherever differences in personal behaviour can gain or lose small (or not so small) advantages; and most Americans, accustomed to their own more frictionless environment, find them hard to observe. They often judge foreigners dishonest and are judged naive by them, although the difference is merely the adaptation of each to his or her different environment.

But a frictionless environment, however pleasant, friendly and relaxed it may be, also has its dangers and disadvantages. Up to a point, it reflects the diminution of conflict thanks to diminishing scarcities and rising standards of living; and that is a valuable achievement. The lesser friction, however, between contending parties and competitors can also mean the elimination not so much of conflict as of the personal element in its resolution and the substitution of impersonal elements. One party's gain is still the other party's loss; but the loser blames his loss not on the gainer's aggressiveness or personal advantage but on impersonal factors: the system. That eliminates friction but creates frustration instead. For it is frustrating to face only a rigid, impersonal, often even automated and computerized system, against which one is helpless, instead of a personal adversary with whom to fight or argue, with however little chance of success, and on whom, at the very least, one can vent one's anger.

Here, then, is the trouble with the frictionless economy. When the lesser friction means less conflict, well and good. But when the conflict persists underneath and is strongly resented, the lack of friction creates a feeling of impotence and shuts off a psychological outlet that would have made it easier to live with the conflict.

> Another drawback of the lesser friction generated by today's American economy is that it tends to make us lose the ability to stand up for ourselves, defend our interests, and assert whatever advantages or authority we may possess. A skill that in a simpler economy everybody possessed in some measure and needed for mere survival is in danger of being lost through disuse when everyday life ceases to be a training ground for self-assertion.

For the need to be able to assert oneself remains in quite a few situations and has created a demand for the professional tough bargainer. Union bosses, vice presidents in charge of industrial relations, public-relations experts and high-pressure salesmen are the high practitioners of an art that the average person has lost. Lawyers also, at least in the United States, are increasingly employed as professional tough bargainers. On a humbler level, agents or managers to bargain on their behalf are retained also by writers, artists, fashion models, and others who can gain a lot by bargaining but lack the skill to bargain. For the very fact that the average person has lost the ability to assert him- or herself has rendered its possession all the more valuable. A society in which few people are aggressive offers high rewards to those who are. Note the premium Americans set on a man's 'having met a payroll' which is considered *prima facie* evidence of his ability to press his advantage and assert his authority.

Another and more serious consequence of our lesser aggressiveness and lost skill in asserting and defending ourselves on the personal level is our diminished ability to assert authority not only on the personal but on the collective level as well. The unsatisfactory state of crime prevention in the United States is generally known and well documented. Our police and judiciary system leave an estimated two-thirds of crimes go undetected, catches less than one-fifth of the perpetrators of known crimes, and condemns not quite a third of those caught—often imposing excessively lenient sentences even on those condemned.[4] There may be several reasons for that; but an important one is bound to be the public's reluctance to exert authority, reflected in the leniency of courts and juries and in the inadequacy of resources devoted to law enforcement.

As a slightly different example of the way in which technical and economic progress lowers society's skill of handling conflict, let me cite the changing nature of relations between the police and the policed in the United States. The rising cost of labour has called for the motorization of the police, since a police car can patrol many times the number of blocks that a pair of policemen on foot can. But this rise in labour productivity has been obtained at the cost of diminished personal contacts between the police and the policed. Foot patrols establish human contacts with the policed: words are exchanged, faces remembered, names learnt, usually enough to remind each party of the other's humanity and for the police to learn when feelings run high and why. Also, the memory of past friendly relations might both temper and render more effective contacts when they are no longer so friendly. All that gets lost when the police are insulated in their shiny cars from the policed; and greater violence and bitterness in their clashes are the result.

As to our diminished ability to assert authority on the personal level, that is best exemplified by the changing nature of the relations between the generations. The lesser need and scope for exercising personal pressure in the relations between buyer and seller, employer and employees has led to a similar decline in the use of pressure also in other personal relations. The authority of parents over children, of teachers over the taught, tends less and less to depend on the personal assertion of authority. Parents and teachers are getting both more reluctant and less able to exert authority, and society less willing to tolerate its excesses. We tend to rely instead on the verbal tradition and institutional trappings of such authority, in the hope that in an environment in which most other personal conflicts are settled without the open exercise of pressure, the young will not challenge it. Trouble often comes when they do, thereby exposing their elders' lack of skill in exercising authority, which tends to be manifested by an alternation of undue harshness and empty threats not carried out. The student revolt of the mid 1960s at many US universities provided an example.

The most serious danger, however, of the frictionless society is that the lack of friction makes people forget the presence of the underlying conflict and tension, thus rendering them less able to understand and handle them when they come to the surface and require action. Friction can be a useful reminder that other people's interests, lifestyles and views on life differ from one's own and that, such differences notwithstanding, peaceful coexistence with them is possible and desirable. Smooth personal relations easily lead one into imagining a greater similarity of views and harmony of interests than exist in fact; and they also make one attribute the peaceful nature of personal relations to that supposed harmony and uniformity of one's environment. That explains why the friendly and frictionless atmosphere of rural and small-town life is so often the seat of conservatism, conformity and intolerance; and why the big cities, with their greater diversity and friction, are also the centres of liberalism and tolerance, where some differences are resolved, others accepted, and the possibility and desirability of the peaceful coexistence of diverse peoples, views and lifestyles are recognized. In the United States, with its great diversity of peoples and cultures, it is especially important to keep alive such tolerance; and we are in the process of enacting legal safeguards of non-discrimination, although they are better at complementing a spirit of tolerance than at serving as substitutes for it.

HIGH MOBILITY AND ITS IMPLICATIONS

> One more distinguishing feature of the US economy and society, which has important implications for personal relations and the family, is the population's great geographical mobility. Approximately 20 per cent of the US population moves each year, and about one-third of those move to a different county. Comparable data for Western European countries seem unavailable or hard to find, those that are almost comparable show significantly lesser mobility.

The economic reasons for high US mobility are apparent. Labour has been the scarce factor of production in the United States right from its beginnings, making it the land of high pay and great opportunities. For higher pay, better jobs and more job opportunities to move people, a well-organized and integrated labour market is also necessary; and that too has been an important feature of the American scene, at least since the days when American employers sent agents abroad to recruit immigrant labour. In addition, their high average level of education might also render Americans more willing than others to move for the sake of high reward and to follow in the footsteps of their forebears who must have been the most mobile and enterprising members of their countries of origin to abandon home, family, friends for a new land in search of a better life. There is some statistical evidence to suggest that while in the early days the poorest were the most mobile, the most willing to escape their poverty, in present-day America the migrants tend to be the more skilled, the better educated, and the white-collar rather than the blue-collar workers.[5]

To turn now to the consequences of mobility, it is pretty obvious that from the economy's point of view, mobility is a good thing. The geographical mobility of labour and the cheap transportation of material resources render the economy more efficient and more adaptable, and social mobility enables people to develop their potentialities more fully, which again is good for the economy. More complex and varied are the consequences of all that for human relations, human satisfaction, and the family.

The simplest and most obvious of those consequences are the gains. People's ability to go where their services are the most appreciated and best paid adds both to their income and to the satisfaction of their work. So does their ability to develop their potentialities more fully and so achieve a greater harmony between their potentialities and their achievement.

Such harmony, however, need not and usually does not imply a similar harmony also between expectations and achievement. For, if great mobility enables many people to better themselves, it also raises even more people's hopes and expectations of doing so. That may make the unsuccessful more discontented; but for the successful it is apt to create a lifelong tension between expectation and achievement and thereby a life-long spur to ambition and an enterprising life, which itself can be a source of additional satisfaction. There is plenty of evidence from psychology that the process of working towards a goal and trying to achieve it is often more satisfying than the achievement of the goal itself.

Having dealt with the benefits of mobility, we can proceed to discuss its costs, or what on the surface look like costs. They all stem from the fact that when people move to a new location in order to take up their first job or a new job, they break or weaken the strong ties of kinship and friendship formed in childhood and in school. The modern American family is a nuclear family, with ties between adult brothers and sisters, adult children and their parents and more distant relatives usually weakened by geographical, often great geographical distance between them, which also weakens the close and intimate friendships among schoolmates.

One loss that that leads to is the loss of the support that friends and family members still provide for each other in time of need wherever their ties happen to be close. For much of that support, however, the American economy has developed pretty good substitutes. The highly developed US market for consumer credit is more than a substitute for other countries' informal credit markets, in which family and friends help out people in need; similarly, the average American's frequent reliance on advice and help from social workers and psychotherapists is also often just a substitute for the services older family members and trusted friends perform in societies where family and friends are closer and their ties stronger.

Another loss inflicted by the weakening of early friendships and kinship is the loss of their close and intimate social relations, which are an important source of human satisfaction. A visible outward manifestation of that loss is the shifting of the centre of social activities from public places to people's homes. Schoolmates and young friends naturally prefer to meet in public places rather than in their parent's homes; and they continue that habit as adults in less mobile and more stable societies. Hence the importances of the English pub, the French and Italian cafe, and the Central and South European coffeehouses as centres of social activity, which people visit on an almost daily basis to meet their friends. In the United States, such places are used strictly for eating and drinking, except by the young; presumably their geographical dispersal ends that habit of the young along with the close ties of friendship between them.

Needless to say, Americans seek and find compensation for their loss of contact with relatives and early friends, partly in greater closeness and comradeship between husband and wife, and partly by their greater willingness to make new friends in adult life among colleagues, business associates and neighbours. Closer marriages are probably a good thing, although they are bound to put more strain on the relationship and may contribute to the high US divorce rate already mentioned (see p. 167 above).

As to the friendships formed between adults, they are usually different in kind from the early friendships formed in school. Early friendships are mostly *imposed* by years of daily physical proximity in the home, in school and in the neighbourhood. Because they are imposed, one's circle of early friends usually contains quite a cross-section of people with differing interests, abilities and backgrounds; and as time passes and the young friends grow into mature adults, those differences usually lead to even further differentiation also by occupation, income groups, social class, and political ideology. The deep and easy intimacy, however, that prolonged physical closeness creates among the young usually survives and remains compatible with the strains and friction that increasing differences in their circumstances and outlook are bound to generate between them as they become adults. That mixture of strain and easy friendly relations between ex-schoolfellows who have become different is part of the cement that holds society together.

By contrast, friends made in adult life seldom become so close and intimate; but because they are freely *chosen,* usually on the basis of common interests, common tastes, and similarity in occupation, income, social class and political views, one's relations with them are likely to be less strained and subject to less friction. Here, then, is another factor that contributes to the frictionless character of American society.

There is one more change in people's behaviour and relation to others that their great mobility and the consequent thinning out of their circle of early friends and relatives is likely to create. People's moral and social behaviour, their marital and family relations, the upbringing of their children are governed by a code of behaviour. Pressure to live by that code and impose it on others comes partly from one's knowledge that others around one live by it, and partly from one's faith in its rightness, which again depends partly on its acceptance by one's circle of friends. The increase in mobility therefore and the consequent breaking of ties with friends and relatives weakens both the outside pressure to obey the code and the inner conviction of its soundness. While approving the rule that governed one's upbringing, one may yet be reluctant to impose the same rules on one's own children in a totally new environment, if in that new environment one knows too few families that believe in and live by the same rules. One will have a vague feeling that the same code of behaviour cannot be applied in a different place, new social environment or a more modern age, even when one is at a loss to know what else to put in its place. The result is a general loosening of standards.

Such loss of faith in traditional values and desire to put new and better values in their place used to be considered typical of immigrant mentality and its importance in American society attributed to the high proportion of first-generation immigrants. But the argument applies just as well to internal migration. A New Englander moving to California, or a Californian to New England, is likely to experience the same weakening of faith in his inherited values as an Italian arriving in New York.

A relaxation of inherited standards need not be a bad thing. All progress hinges on a refusal to accept unquestioningly traditional ways of doing things and their subjection to critical scrutiny. Social and moral codes of behaviour are no exception to that rule. But reform must necessarily be tentative, because logic provides little guidance in such matters and adopting the different code of behaviour of one's new environment is also difficult, because it is difficult to ascertain—especially difficult to ascertain in a highly mobile and therefore diverse society, where each family may observe a somewhat different code of behaviour. As a result, most people compromise between their own inherited tradition and what they think is more sensible, their compromise is tentative, and their attitude shows it by the half-hearted way in which they enforce that code on their children.

FAMILY RELATIONS

That brings us back to family relations; and I should now like to broaden the discussion by also listing or recalling the various other ways in which the factors discussed in this paper impinge on the relations between parents and children, husbands and wives.

Parents, when they impose rules of behaviour, are in an antagonistic relation to their children, whose natural tendency is to defy or escape the rules imposed upon them. In that tug of war, the parents' authority is buttressed by the enforcement of similar rules by their friends' and relatives' families; the children have allies in the example and precedent of the more permissive homes of *their* friends and schoolmates.

In a highly mobile society, that balance of power is tilted in favour of the children. Mobility weakens the parents' own faith in the rules they impose and, by dispersing their relatives and close friends, it reduces the number of families in which the children could observe the maintenance of similar rules. At the same time, the children's bargaining power is likely to be strengthened by mobility, which increases the diversity of their schoolmates' family backgrounds and with it their chance of finding permissive precedents.

An added factor, referred to earlier (see p. 175 above), is the decline of people's skill in exercising authority. The tradition for mothers to threaten their children with disciplining by father probably had its origin not only in the male's superior physical prowess but also in his greater experience in asserting himself in the business of everyday life. If my argument made in the second section of this paper is valid, that last-mentioned factor has largely disappeared, which would explain why mothers' threats have such a hollow ring nowadays and have become so ineffectual.

Yet a third factor that may also have contributed to the shift in the balance of power between parents and children is the latter's lesser economic dependence on their parents. In the past, the children's economic dependence extended to their need for parental help in launching them on their careers: paying for their education and training and helping them to find and secure their first job. Today, education up to college is free and compulsory, many of the best students get fellowships and scholarships to college and university, and schools at all but the elementary level provide vocational guidance and all the facilities of a well-organized labour market for finding a job. All that renders young people's entry into the labour market very much their own personal affair; it has become the first truly independent decision of their lives.

The shift in the balance of power between husbands and wives is closely related and fairly similar. The days are long past when the husband was the family's undisputed head as its only breadwinner whose breadwinning involved fighting the elements and other breadwinners, and gave him dominance over wife and children whom he sheltered. Today, he no longer is the family's sole income earner, his job rarely gives him training in asserting himself and exercising authority, and his authority is further weakened by his diminished faith in the value system he is trying to impose.

On all those counts, his wife's relative position has become stronger, often even making her the dominant figure. Most important, perhaps, in establishing women's greatly improved status was their entry into the labour force, which gave them economic independence and equality or near-equality as a family breadwinner.

Second, the wife is becoming or has already become the person with the most skill in exercising authority. In today's frictionless economy, which is increasingly governed by impersonal rules more than by personal ascendancy, the family has become the main scene of friction and of the open exercise of authority; and family authority is imposed mainly by the mother over her younger children. Moreover, her skill in imposing authority is strengthened by her position in the labour force, because employers seem by preference to give women most of the jobs that involve personal contacts and direct dealings with people: customers, fellow employees or the general public.

Third, the wife and mother has remained what she has been already in the days when her husband held the reins: the upholder of manners and morals, social graces, family discipline and relations with the wider family. Mobility, of course, has weakened also her faith in inherited values; but less so than her husband's; and that for two reasons. First, because her ties to the wider family, always stronger than her husband's, are likely to remain stronger even across great geographical distances; and second, because among the new friendships formed in later life, the women's are usually the more intimate and many-sided, since they are likely to be based on their common interest in child rearing and in converting money income and money wealth into an enjoyable life.

That brings me to my last topic: women's traditional role as the family's generalist in American society. As was clear from the foregoing, when married women entered the labour force, they did not relinquish their inherited roles of keeping house and rearing children. Another role they also retained was that of family generalist.

Economic progress, which means ever greater specialization and division of labour, has not only made the husband the earner and his wife the spender of income but has also made him focus on the increasingly narrow speciality of his occupation, thereby forcing her to learn more about that ever-wider range of subjects one must know something about in order to make good judgements on how best to devote and apportion the family's resources to medical care, the children's education, vacations, travel, recreation, cultural activities, and all the other things that go into a good life and the family's bodily and mental well-being.

I have argued elsewhere that the division of labour between specialists and generalists is one of its undesirable forms;[6] and one should hope that women's entry into the labour market will ultimately force the men also to acquire more of the generalist's expertise and judgement needed for using and enjoying the income they earn thanks to their specialist's expertise. For the time being, however, women still excel in the area of broad general knowledge, men in that of thorough but narrow specialized expertise; and that has helped women to make some spectacular if still few inroads into the one occupation that, like householding, also calls for broad general rather than thorough specialized knowledge: politics. Public and private households are similar in requiring not only a general knowledge of every speciality but also good judgement and ability to choose, make decisions and tactfully exercise authority.

NOTES

1.   Many of the findings quoted in this section come from Arland Thornton and Deborah Freedman, 'The changing American family', *Population Bulletin,* Vol. 38 No. 4, (Oct. 1983).
2.   For a full discussion of buyers' markets *see* Chapter 8.
3.   For the argument that employers give inflationary wage increases freely and on their own initiative, *see* Arthur M. Okun, *Prices and Quantities: A Macroeconomic Analysis,* (Oxford: Basil Blackwell, 1981) and the section on 'Implicit contracts' in Joseph A. Pechman (ed.) *Economics for Policymaking: Selected Essays of Arthur M. Okun,* (Cambridge, Mass: MIT Press, 1983).
4.   For a fuller statement about law enforcement and its documentation *see* Chapter 10, especially p.132.
5.   Claude S. Fischer *et al., Networks and Places: Social Relations in the Urban Setting,* (New York: The Free Press, 1977), Ch. 9.
6.   In my *The Joyless Economy,* (New York: Oxford U. Press, 1976), Ch. 13.

14   How to Bring Joy into Economics*—1985

Most human actions are motivated by human desires. A person's actions are mostly responses to his own desires, but many of them cater to other people's desires, just as some of other people's actions satisfy or contribute to satisfying his desires. Interaction between different people's actions and desires may be assured by many things. First of all, by the mutually satisfying nature of many types of interaction, but also by coercion, convention, sexual drive, and emotional ties between relatives and friends, and very often it is a reciprocal exchange of one person's services to others for their services to him. That last type of interaction comprises economic activity, which constitutes an important part of the subject matter of economics.

Since desires are the motive force of all economic activity, they clearly are or ought to be of interest to economists. Indeed, the classical economists paid great attention to the nature of desires and their various sources. But as our knowledge of the economic system and its workings became deeper and more detailed, we paid less and less attention to the ultimate ends that economic activity is aimed at, and present-day economists find it convenient just to infer them from people's observed behaviour—on the assumption of man's rationality and the constancy of his desires. The system of desires so inferred is known as revealed preference.

Much can be explained with the aid of those simple assumptions but not everything, and as more and more examples were found of seemingly irrational behaviour or of inconsistent and inconstant preferences, a small

* The first half of this paper is also being published under the title 'Psychologizing by economists' in A.J. and H.W. MacFadyen (eds.), *Economic Psychology: Intersection in Theory and Application,* (Amsterdam: North Holland, 1986). Two earlier and shorter versions have been presented at the Tenth Annual Colloqium of the International Association for Research in Economic Psychology in Zell an der Pram, Austria, and at the Eighth Annual Conference on Economic Issues in Middlebury, Vt, under the title 'How to bring psychology back into economics. Its present version has greatly benefited from discussions at those conferences, comments by Kurt Rotschild and Paul Streeten, and most of all from Amit Badhuri's constructive suggestions.

but growing number of economists began to question those assumptions and look more deeply into the meaning of rationality and the nature of people's motivation.

As one of that small band of questioning economists, I sought the answers to such questions first in those tentative speculative writings of my fellow economists in which they tried to look beyond their own speciality at the broader issues of economics. There, I found a few scattered bits of answers to my questions; and when I next looked to physiological psychology for a more systematic and analytic treatment of human motivation, I was elated to find, in the work of Hebb, Berlyne and some others, a theory of motivation in terms of the brain's arousal, into which the economists' guesses and observations could be fitted like the pieces of a jigsaw puzzle to make a meaningful, coherent picture.

The close correspondence between the economists' insights and the psychologists' experimentally based theory seemed to indicate that I was on the right track. That is why I tried, in *The Joyless Economy,* to summarize Hebb's and Berlyne's motivation theory in simple language accessible to economists and other non-specialists, rounding it out whenever necessary in order to make it fit into the economist's frame of reference.

I still believe that I was on the right track, although I now know what I did not fully realize then, that the striking similarity between economists' thinking and psychologists' findings was at least partly due to their common historical origins. After all, economics and psychology were both part of philosophy until the end of the eighteenth century; and it was Jeremy Bentham, one of their common ancestors, who laid great stress on the role of pleasure and pain in motivating behaviour, arguing their measurability, and distinguishing fourteen kinds of pleasure and twelve kinds of pain as so many different sources of motivation. Accordingly, when psychology and economics split off from philosophy to become separate disciplines, they carried in their baggage the same inherited psychological insights, although they put them to very different uses.

The economists seemed to accept them unquestioningly as exogenously given psychological assumptions on which to base their models of the economy; but then, as they improved their models, making them more rigorous, more quantitative, and more elegant, they gradually simplified and whittled down those psychological underpinnings to almost vanishing point.

The psychologists regarded those same inherited insights as initial, tentative hypotheses and made it their business to design experiments for testing them and, if confirmed, to integrate them into a larger framework that would also fit in with the neurophysiologists' fast-expanding knowledge of the functioning of the brain. That was the kind of work I tried to summarize and adapt to the economist's needs in Part 1 of *The Joyless Economy*.

In this paper, I want to focus on the economists; but it would be too lengthy and tedious to trace the full history of their use of psychology from the latter's inception to its near expurgation. I propose instead to deal merely with the end points of that history, beginning with the Greeks of classical antiquity and proceeding directly to the three Cambridge economists of the twentieth century in whose writings one finds most of what little psychology is still used by the profession. On first sight, so great a jump over time may seem absurd; but it isn't really. For the Greeks, with their acute insight into psychology, left little for others to discover as long as introspection and wordly wisdom remained the only sources of psychological information; and thanks to the great stress on classical education in England, the Cambridge economists probably learned most of their psychology from the Greeks. Their references to psychology certainly seem to be in direct succession to the Greeks, with the addition only of a few economic implications.

THE GREEKS

The Greek philosophers were much concerned with physiological psychology. Plato was a relative latecomer to the subject; but in Book IX of *The Republic* he conveniently summarized his predecessors' and his own thinking on motivation. He sharply differentiated pleasure from the relief of pain and discomfort, and also distinguished an intermediate state in which both pain and pleasure were absent. Following Protagoras, he called this last rest or repose, and noted that both pain and pleasure are states of excitement and so involve motion, pain more, pleasure less motion, which he called 'motions of the soul'.

Plato also observed that the relief of pain and discomfort creates a pleasurable, often intensely pleasurable feeling, although it only brings one to that intermediate state, which is devoid of both pain and pleasure. Indeed, to the suffering, mere rest and cessation of pain and not any positive enjoyment appears as the greatest of pleasures; but they never knew it to be the greatest pleasure until they were ill. To distinguish that temporary but intense feeling of pleasure from the more enduring but less acute pleasures that do *not* depend on an antecedent pain or discomfort, he called the former illusory, the latter real or pure pleasure. The value judgement implicit in his use of those terms seems also to refer to the different durations of the two kinds of pleasure and to their differing impact on the individual's and society's welfare.

For Plato also distinguished three kinds of desire: the desire for wisdom and knowledge, the desire for honour, fame and power, and the appetitive desires, which include love of money because they are generally satisfied with the help of money. The satisfaction of all three kinds of desire is motivated and accompanied by pleasure; and, in the case of the second and third kinds of desire, those pleasures are 'necessary' up to a point for maintaining life and health or promoting productivity, but become 'unnecessary' and harmful when pursued to excess. Thus, the pleasures of food and drink can lead to gluttony and drunkenness, and an insatiable desire for power or fame can lead to tyranny.

The psychological insight of the Greeks and many of the categories they introduced have a very modern ring. Their sharp distinction between pain and pleasure presages the modern neurophysiologists' discovery of separate pain and pleasure centres in the brain; their noting the exciting quality of pain and pleasure and calling them 'motions of the soul' brings to mind the heightened arousal level or activation of the brain that today's psychologists have found to accompany both biological deprivation and pleasant stimulation. Plato's 'illusory pleasure' is the counterpart of what in modern psychology is known as the reinforcing effect of an ongoing activity (Hebb's 'salted-nut syndrome'), which can push its pursuit beyond the point of satiation to excess (at which stage it becomes what Plato calls 'unnecessary pleasure'). As to his three kinds of desire and their corresponding pleasures, the first corresponds closely to the enjoyable stimulus of novelty, complexity and information, which Berlyne analysed, the second and third have been distinguished by economists whenever they tried to separate satiable from non-satiable satisfactions; and the three correspond fairly closely to what I, ignorant of Plato's categories, have called personal comfort, social comfort, and enjoyable stimulation.

Those insights and categories of the Greek philosophers have been kept alive by the emphasis on the classics in eighteenth and nineteenth century education; only in economic theory has the increasing emphasis on formal mathematical models led to the progressive simplification and so the impoverishment of the basic psychological assumptions.

ALFRED MARSHALL

Mainline economics has often been criticised for that, and especially for focusing too exclusively on monetary gain and the relief of pain and discomfort. American institutional economists of the nineteenth century often attacked the 'British school of economists' for their preoccupation with the 'lowest instincts of humanity' to the neglect of 'nobler interests'. Interestingly enough, Alfred Marshall, the most distinguished British economist of the turn of the century, was not unsympathetic to that view.

He agreed with Thomas Carlyle's characterization of economics as 'the dismal science' and criticized Jevons, the most abstract and formalistic economist of his time, for his too one-sided approach.

In his *Principles of Economics,* Marshall discusses wants and activities and the relations between them. Wants are satiable desires, satisfied by the consumption of goods and services; activities either contribute to producing the goods and services desired for consumption or are desired for their own sake, because it is pleasurable to pursue or learn to pursue them and excel in their performance. He realizes that activities pursued for their own sake are not economic activities but notes that the desire for them:

leads not only to the pursuit of science, literature and art for their own sake but to the rapidly increasing demand for the work of those who pursue them as professions. Leisure is used less and less as an opportunity for mere stagnation and there is a growing desire for those amusements, such as athletic games and travelling, which develop activities . . . Desires of this kind exert a great influence on the supply of the highest faculties and the greatest inventions; and they are not unimportant on the side of demand. For a large part of the demand for the highly skilled professional services and the best work of the mechanical artisan arises from the delight people have in the training of their faculties and in excercising them by the aid of the most delicately adjusted and responsive implements. Broadly speaking therefore, although it is man's wants in the earliest stages of his development that give rise to his activities, yet afterwards each new step upwards is to be regarded as the development of new activities giving rise to new wants, rather than of new wants giving rise to new activities. . . . It is not true therefore (as Jevons argued) that 'The Theory of Consumption is the scientific basis of economics'.[1]

Unfortunately, Marshall merely stated those ideas but never developed them. In particular, he never explained exactly how and why the desire to exercise activities for their own sake also causes them to be performed for pay. He strongly criticized Jevons for ignoring the desire for activities and asserting the supremacy of consumption as if it were the prime mover, the 'scientific basis' of all economics; but his own writings are vulnerable to the same criticism, because he never incorporated the ideas just quoted into his own model of the economy. Marshall's *Principles* was the most influential and most widely read economics text for half a century (1890–1940), but the passages I quoted from it have been almost completely ignored and forgotten, because they were not integrated with the rest. They are echoed by two of his pupils, Keynes and Hawtrey, but they, too, fail, with one partial exception, to integrate those ideas into their workaday economics.

LORD KEYNES

Keynes dealt with activities engaged in for their own sake in two places. First, in his 'Economic Possibilities for our Grandchildren', where he predicted that without important wars and without too great a population increase, the combined effect of technical progress and capital accumulation could easily raise per capita incomes by an average of 2 per cent per annum or more, thereby increasing our standard of living eightfold within a century. He felt that so great an increase in material welfare would bring 'the economic problem, our struggle for subsistence' to a solution or at least to within sight of solution, and that then, 'for the first time since his creation, man will be faced with his real, his permanent problem—how to use his freedom from pressing economic cares, how to occupy the leisure which science and compound interest will have won for him, to live wisely and agreeably and well'.[2]

Keynes seems to equate the economic problem to the struggle for existence and to regard almost all wants as satiable. Although he explicitly mentions a second class of wants, 'our need to feel superior to our fellows' (Plato's desire for fame and honour), which is insatiable, he nevertheless expects an eightfold rise in labour productivity to increase our leisure time much more than our output, and thereby to ease our economic problem at the cost of creating one that is much worse:

the fearful problem for the ordinary person, with no special talents, to occupy himself. To judge from the behaviour and achievements of the wealthy classes today, (he calls them 'our advance guard for spying out the promised land of leisure and plenty') the outlook is very depressing. . . . For they have most of them failed disastrously . . . to solve the problem which has been set them.[3]

That is why Keynes speaks of the danger of a 'general nervous breakdown' and proposes as a practical solution 'to make what work there is still to be done to be as widely shared as possible. Three-hour shifts or a fifteen-hour week may put off the problem for quite a while'.[4]

The other context in which Keynes deals with activities pursued for their own sake is his discussion of businessmen's motivation for investment in *The General Theory of Employment, Interest and Money:*

If we speak frankly, we have to admit that our basis of knowledge for estimating the yield ten years hence of a railway, a copper mine, a textile factory, the goodwill of a patent medicine, an Atlantic liner, a building in the City of London amounts to little and sometimes to nothing . . . If human nature felt no temptation to take a chance, no satisfaction (profit apart) in constructing a factory, a railway, a mine or a farm, there might not be much investment merely as a result of cold calculation. . . . Most . . . of our decisions to do something positive, the full consequences of which will be drawn out over many days to come, can only be taken as a result of animal spirits—of the spontaneous urge to action rather than inaction, and not as the outcome of a weighted average of quantitative benefits multiplied by quantitative probabilities . . .

Enterprise only pretends to itself to be mainly motivated by the statements in its own prospectus. . . . Only a little more than an expedition to the South Pole is it based on an exact calculation of benefits to come.[5]

In short, Keynes fully realized man's psychological need to engage in activities to occupy him and regarded that need as the main motivating force of all creative activity, not only in the fields of science, art and leisure, but also in that of business investment and so of economic and technical progress. He assigned a subordinate role to the businessman's expectation of profit as a motive for investment, stressing instead his animal spirits, his urge to assume the risk of investment for its own sake, for the excitement of playing a daring game of chance and skill and creating something new and constructive in the process. Apart from his discussion of the businessman's animal spirits, Keynes said not a word about the way in which enjoyable activities might generate a demand for economic goods; but that, fortunately, is the subject on which Marshall's other pupil, Hawtrey, focused his attention.

SIR RALPH HAWTREY

In *The Economic Problem,* Hawtrey distinguished 'two broad classes of objects of consumption: on the one hand those products which are intended to prevent or remedy pains, injuries or distresses, and on the other those which are intended to supply some positive gratification or satisfaction'.[6] He called them defensive and creative products, warned that they are neither mutually exclusive nor exhaustive, and pointed to a:

> class of defensive product . . . which is intended to provide leisure . . . a form of power, like money, which people covet without necessarily having any clear idea of what use they wish to make of it.
>
> But is must not be supposed that the positive good which (the individual) is to pursue must necessarily take the form of objects of expenditure, or of marketable products. He might find it, for example, in human intercourse and the beauties of nature, without drawing any further on the productive resources of society. Or he might pursue artistic or intellectual activities which make very slight demands upon them. It may be indeed that the greatest good, for rich and poor alike, is of this kind. But that does not mean that it cannot at any rate be supplemented by what we have called creative products. And the almost universal opinion of mankind, if we may judge by their practice, is that creative products are a very important good.[7]

Hawtrey then proceeds to a detailed and very interesting enumeration and discussion of creative products, such as drugs, sport, humour, entertainment, literature, art, pleasurable intellectual pursuits, and the creative ingredients of defensive products, such as the skilled preparation and selection of food, the elegance and artistic element in clothing, and the decorative and applied arts. He also has interesting things to say on the difference between active participants in enjoyable activities and their passive spectators, on the defensive function of creative products in relieving boredom, on the need for novelty, originality and imagination to render creative products enjoyable, on the role of art patrons, on the rational function of consumers' inertia and convention, etc. His extensive discussion of all that and his many insights and shrewd observations provide most of the building blocks for a full and coherent theory of the subject.

ENJOYABLE STIMULATION

Remember that Hawtrey's creative goods, Keynes's animal spirits, Marshall's activities sought for their own sake and Plato's desire for truth and learning are just different names and aspects of the same enjoyable stimulation, whose many forms and manifestations are well described by Hawtrey and whose ever-increasing importance was stressed already by Marshall. Plato exemplified the pure pleasures, which require no antecedent of pain, by the pleasures of wisdom and learning, presumably because in his day they were largely restricted to philosophers; whereas Hawtrey's long and varied list of creative goods indicates their wider availability and the much greater demand for them in our civilisation today. Marshall, aware of their increasing importance, was right in wanting to see them included in the economist's universe of discourse; but before I outline a means of doing so, let us take a look at the reason, first, why their importance is increasing, and second, why economists have ignored them so far.

The first is simple. Economic progress frees some of people's time and energy from the task of earning their living and, by also increasing their physical safety and economic security, creates or increases their desire for stimulation. For the nervous system needs a minimum amount of stimulus, just as the muscular system needs a minimum of exercise; and when the tensions, anxieties and uncertainties of workplace and ordinary living are reduced below that minimum, people actively seek the stimulation of pleasurable activities in order to eliminate their stimulus deficit.[8]

As to why pleasurable activities have been excluded so far from the economist's universe of discourse, bear in mind that his main preoccupation is with the way in which people interact and cooperate for the purpose of satisfying their desires. The great economies of scale and advantages of specialization provide plenty of scope for such interaction in the production of the goods and services that cater to consumers' needs, where it also takes a rather simple and obvious form. Productive activity affects the welfare both of those who perform it and those who benefit by it; and since it usually affects them in opposite ways, it impels the two parties to engage in market transactions that enable both of them to influence the volume of production and makes them share in its costs and benefits alike. No wonder if economists made the satisfaction of consumers' needs the centre of their attention.

The satisfaction of people's desire for social comfort and for enjoyable stimulation also involves interaction and cooperation between them, which, however, is lesser, different and more subtle than those that economists are used to. In the area of social comfort, the nature of that interaction has been analysed in detail,[9] only its integration with the main body of economics remains yet to be done.

As to enjoyable stimulation, the nature of the interpersonal interactions it involves seems for some reason to have baffled economists, even Marshall, who advocated its inclusion into the standard economic model. Marshall's bafflement can perhaps be explained. He seems to have been mesmerized by the name he gave to enjoyable stimulation: 'activity pursued for its own sake'. That name implied that to perform the activity is pleasant instead of being unpleasant; and it could also be *mis*interpreted to mean that its beneficiary is always and *only* the same person who performs it. For, curiously enough, Marshall overlooked the rather obvious fact that activities pursued for their own sake are similar to productive activities in that they, too, have passive beneficiaries: the spectators who enjoy observing those who pursue them. The interaction between performer and spectator resembles the interaction between the maker and the user of a consumer good closely enough to make it possible to incorporate enjoyable along with productive activities into the economist's standard model. I proceed to substantiate that statement.

TOWARDS A MORE GENERAL ECONOMIC THEORY OF HUMAN SATISFACTION

As we have seen, many physical and mental activities are such that to engage in them is enjoyable and pursued for its own sake. One of the enjoyable mental activities is to expose oneself passively to the stimulation provided from outside, by one's environment; and an important source of such enjoyable outside stimulation is the spectacle or product of other people's enjoyable activities. Accordingly, an active person's enjoyable activity provides satisfaction not only to himself but mostly also to those others who passively contemplate his activity or benefit by its products.

Indeed, given the differences in different people's energies, inclinations and talents—and differences also in the same person's energy and inclination at different times—people seek stimulation not only from different sources but also in different ways and at different intensities. Some like to be stimulated by their own physical or mental exertions, through actively engaging in one or more stimulating activities; other people, and the same people at other times, prefer to be stimulated passively, by exposing themselves to other people's stimulating activities or to the products of those stimulating activities, as readers, spectators, or audience.

Music, for example, can be enjoyed by composing it, by playing other people's compositions, by analysing and criticizing other people's playing and compositions, by reading or listening to such criticism, or by just sitting back and listening to music, live, canned, or electronically transmitted. In short, musical enjoyment comes in many forms and on many levels, and it can be both active and passive. That last distinction is especially important, because while passive enjoyment generates *demand,* active enjoyment usually creates *supply* for others to enjoy as well.

What is true of music is also true of other arts and crafts (e.g. pottery, embroidery, jewellery making), as well as of literature, sports, learning, research, exploration, scientific activity, and many others. In each of those areas, there always are some who love to be active and creative at least part of the time; and there are others, more passively inclined, who prefer to take their enjoyment vicariously and love to watch other people's activity or to own the products of other people's activities.

Different people's satisfactions interact in virtually all those enjoyable activities. The passive recipients' satisfactions obviously depend on the active performers' activities; but interaction goes much further than that. For one thing, the active participants' satisfactions from engaging in sex, social and competitive sports, social games, gambling, etc., depend on the availability of equally active participants as partners; and that kind of interdependence, unlike the previous one, is symmetrical. But even the asymmetrical interdependence between active and passive enjoyers is seldom one-sided, because active participants usually get added satisfaction from their awareness of other people's appreciation and enjoyment of *their* activities or the products of their activities. Indeed that additional satisfaction has received more attention from economists than the active participants' primary satisfaction and will be discussed further later on.

To come back now to the supply and demand for pleasurable activities, note first that in social activities, like bridge, chess, tennis, football, or gambling, each active participant both needs partners and provides one. In other words, he creates both demand and supply, which complement each other and are mutually offsetting. That explains why most such activities do not go through the market, which, in these cases, only performs the ancillary services of providing the tools, the premises, the training, the bringing together of partners, and occasionally provides a standby professional partner when amateur partners are not available.

Note also that the mutual offsetting of the supply and demand created by gamblers, bridge players etc., is equivalent to what in the realm of consumer goods is called barter, because each player provides what the other wants in exchange for receiving from him what he himself wants. When economists discuss barter, they call that 'the double coincidence of wants' and stress its rarity; but when each of two chess players both seeks and provides a partner, then the double coincidence of wants and the matching of supply and demand is the normal and natural consequence.

Such automatic matching of supply and demand, which renders unnecessary the market's function of equating them, is absent or very rare in the relations between active performers and passive recipients. For the distribution of talent and nervous energy in the population seems to be highly skewed and such that those with ability and desire for the active pursuit of any particular stimulating activity are outnumbered, often greatly outnumbered by those who lack those qualities but want to be stimulated by the same activity as its passive observers or beneficiaries of its products. Moreover, I shall argue later (see p. 197) that in the capitalist economy, businessmen have a selfish interest in influencing the public's tastes in the direction of creating or enlarging the disparity in numbers between passive beneficiaries and active performers.

Whatever the reason, the demand for the passive enjoyment of enjoyable activities or their products usually exceeds their spontaneous supply—that is, the supply forthcoming even in the absence of an economic incentive. That accounts for the relative scarcity of such activities and explains the entry of economics into the picture. For the excess of demand over the spontaneous supply creates a market in enjoyable activities of their products and puts on them a price, payable by those who want to take their enjoyment in passive form and earned as an extra bonus by the more talented, energetic and business-minded among those who enjoy actively performing the same activities. The function of the price, of course, is to increase the supply over what would be forthcoming spontaneously for free, and to limit the demand of the passive recipients.

That, in a nutshell, is the role of pleasurable activities as causative factors in market exchange and economic production. To highlight its main features, it is best to contrast it against the economist's customary model, in which needs and wants give rise only to demand, and the supply to cater to it results exclusively from productive activity, involving a disutility and motivated only or mainly by the pay it earns. Pleasurable activities, as already mentioned, generate supply as well as demand, although a large part of that supply never goes through the market, consisting of amateur sports, social games, and dilettante music making, painting, sculpting and tinkering that people engage in for their own and their friends' amusement and pleasure. Only a part, usually but not always the best part of such activities or their products are in demand by those who enjoy them passively. and since such demand mostly exceeds the part of the supply that is available to cater to it, a market price emerges to enable and tempt amateurs to turn professional and to induce hacks to join their ranks.

While that is a somewhat more subtle and complex model than the economist's standard one, *its marginal implications are the same* as those of the standard model. For the passive recipients do equate the money value of their marginal satisfactions to the price they have to pay; and each practitioner of enjoyable activities—however much he enjoys them—does need the extra inducement of the earnings they yield to provide his marginal output, because they: (a) either compensate him for the disutility of engaging in more such activity than he would enjoy, (b) or enable him to quit earning his keep with less enjoyable work, or (c) provide proof of other people's appreciation and enjoyment of the fruits of his own pleasurable activity and so become a source of additional satisfaction.

THE CHANGED BALANCE OF EXTRANEOUS AND ENDOGENOUS INFLUENCES ON THE ECONOMY

Let me now mention some of the wider implications of the model I am proposing. To begin with, it stresses the fact that the motivation of many economic activities (the pleasurable ones) is not primarily economic. Thereby, it directs attention to the impact of outside influences on the economy; and at the same time it warns against attributing an exaggerated importance to economic incentives.

The first is important, because it shows the market economy to be a more open (and so less self-equilibrating) system than it sometimes is taken to be. Recall that modern macroeconomics originated with Keynes when he stressed the predominance of convention and animal spirits over profitability calculations as determinants of investment, thereby establishing the latter as an autonomous influence, *via* the multiplier, over the level of aggregate activity.[10] This paper points to the existence of yet further non-economic influences on the economy, which are similar but additional to the influence of businessmen's animal spirits, and which also contribute to rendering the economy more open.

As to the second point, it should be obvious that the more open an economy, the less effective are economic incentives in governing that economy. That too is well worth being reminded of, because the impact of economic incentives on activity levels is all too often overrated. Remember the overestimation of the stimulating effect of tax incentives on economic activity when the first Reagan Administration introduced its unsuccessful experiment with 'supply-side economics'.

One is tempted to underrate these consequences of the existence of activities pursued for their own sake. After all, the pleasurable activities that go through the market and so enter the economist's realm are still much less important than productive activities proper. But there are three arguments to counter that. First and as already mentioned (see p. 190), enjoyable activities are forever increasing in number and importance as rising labour productivity frees people's time and energy from making ends meet and rising standards of safety and security enhance their desire for enjoyable stimulation. Secondly, parallel to the increasing desire for enjoyable activities, the proportion of such activities that are subject to market transactions is also on the increase—for reasons that will be discussed in the next section.

Finally, the distinction between enjoyable activities pursued for their own sake and onerous work performed primarily to earn the income it yields is not as clear and sharp as the foregoing argument and my choice of examples might suggest. People derive at least some modicum of satisfaction from all jobs except the most unpleasant and most monotonous; and those are rapidly diminishing in number, thanks to modern technology, which puts robots into factories and computers into offices. Furthermore, many productive occupations are interesting and challenging enough to yield much more than some satisfaction. The prime example of those, of course, is Keynes's animal spirits, the excitement of creating something new or unique, whose importance is well borne out also by present-day empirical studies of entrepreneurial motivation.[11] The same also applies, however, if to a lesser extent, to much of the work of professional people and craftsmen. Note that empirical investigations of the effect of income taxation on the work incentive of the legal and other liberal professions have always come up with negative findings, which suggests that the challenge and inherent interest of their work is an important part of their motivation.[12]

In short, there are not two kinds of activities, the one motivated purely by pleasure, the other purely by pay: those are merely limiting cases of a continuous range of activities, most of which are performed partly for fun, partly for pay, with the relative importance of those two motivations varying greatly from one activity to another. The model here proposed therefore should accommodate all activities, not just the narrowly defined pleasurable activities I used in my examples.

THE DISTINCTION BETWEEN ECONOMIC AND NON-ECONOMIC ACTIVITIES

A second advantage of my model is that it deals with both the economic and the non-economic activities prompted by the same desire, so that the dividing line between them is endogenously determined within the model.

That is an important advantage, because that dividing line is continuously shifting as social, economic and technical factors change the ratio between the demand for various activities and their spontaneous supply, or change the passive recipients' access to the active participants' products.

News, for example, was hardly an economic product until the eighteenth century, because the demand for it was largely restricted to a very small literate public and, with letter writing a popular pastime of many of the literate of those days, its spontaneous supply was almost sufficient to satisfy demand. Only gradually, with the spread of literacy, faster communications, and the development of the fast printing press did the gathering and spreading of news become the *economic* activity of newspapers and professional journalists.

Another example is advice. Giving advice is usually more fun than taking it, which is why advice has been a free good for a long time and is still free today in many countries. In the United States, however, the great geographical mobility of the population has disrupted the closeness of family ties and early friendships, which has reduced the availability of spontaneous free advice on intimate personal and family matters and so created an economic demand for the costly professional advice of psychiatrists and social workers.

Technical progress has led to a similar shift also in the decorative and applied arts. In an earlier, more primitive and more self-sufficient age, ordinary people decorated many of the useful objects of their everyday life for their own amusement and pleasure. Only with the advent of mass production did decoration and product design become the differentiated economic activities of professionals, while the beautiful design and decoration of the handmade objects of the past acquired a scarcity value and became highly prized (and priced) as folk art.

In a similar way, technical progress in the electronic reproduction and transmission of sight and sound has greatly lowered the cost and increased the availability of the passive enjoyment of sport, music and the other performing arts, which had a number of consequences. To begin with, it has familiarized a much larger public with those activities, which has greatly increased the demand for their passive enjoyment and probably for their active enjoyment as well. Greater familiarity, however, has also made people more expert and therefore more choosy, concentrating the passive enjoyers' demand on the best performers and diminishing their demand for witnessing second and third raters. That has led to price discrimination but without greatly reducing the supply of less than first-rate performances, since even first raters have to begin modestly and acquire experience as they approach the top. The public's greater expertise and desire for excellence, however, is likely to shift the emphasis from informal activity watched or listened to by non-paying beneficiaries to formal performances before paying spectators or audiences and thus extend the scope of the market. The increased emphasis on excellence may also switch from active to passive participation those who cannot aspire to excellence.

The examples just cited also give an idea of the many ways in which enterprising businessmen have made a profit by increasing the disparity between the demand and spontaneous supply of some enjoyable activity, thereby to turn it into a marketable product. After all, the fast printing press was not developed without a view to taking news out of the hands of amateur gossip-mongers and turning it into a marketable product; professional sport would not be the big business it is without some deliberate wetting of the public's appetite; and many a charming folk custom and traditional festival has become a less charming but profitable tourist attraction thanks to a clever promoter.

Deliberate or not, the trend is definitely towards the increasing commercialization of enjoyable activities. But let me mention also a shift in the opposite direction, causing *spontaneous supply* to exceed demand. That has occurred in scientific writing, due partly to increased and increasingly narrow specialization in the sciences, which diminished the readership, and partly to the increased value to the scientific community of having published articles to their name, which increased the number of their writings. That is why scientific journals that used to pay for the papers they published have ceased to pay, or even demand to be paid for publishing them—thereby making the writers or their employers subsidize readers' access to their writings.

CONFLICT BETWEEN ECOMOMIC INCENTIVE AND INTRINSIC PSYCHIC MOTIVATION

So far, I have taken it for granted that the intrinsic motivation of the pleasure of engaging in an activity and the economic incentive to engage in it are additive and pull in the same direction. That, however, need not be the case. Often, perhaps even most often, the main effect of the economic incentive is to encourage the additional production of a *given* activity or its *given* product; whereas the intrinsic pleasure of engaging in that activity and creating its product is an inducement to qualitative excellence, always spurring one on to more difficult tasks and to creating something new, better, more original, and aesthetically more pleasing.

Indeed, psychologists have noted, deplored, and discussed at length the fact that monetary reward or other external motivation will often diminish a person's ability to perform a task and his satisfaction with his own work, sometimes because it interjects the influence of other people's preferences concerning his work and so diverts him from doing what he himself considers best, most worth doing, and would like to do.[13]

Their argument, while interesting, valid, and well documented, is not one that economists would or should make their own, because we—unlike psychologists—are concerned not only with the creative and active individual's personal welfare but with the welfare of society as a whole, which of course also includes the welfare of the creative person's public: the people who passively enjoy his activity and its products.

Indeed, from the economist's point of view, one must distinguish not two but three separate motivating forces: a person's enjoyment of his own activity, the monetary reward he earns from those willing to pay for their passive enjoyment of what he is doing or producing, and the fame his work acquires among professionals in his own field. Each of those reflects the preferences of a different segment of the people affected by the activity in question; and, while they may pull in three different directions, it is desirable from society's point of view that the interests of all those who are affected by that activity should have an impact on the way in which it is done.

The decision which to heed the most or what compromise to work out between their conflicting pulls is, of course, entirely in the hands of the person who actively engages in the activity. His or her activity therefore will contribute more or less to society's welfare, depending on the weights he or she attaches to intrinsic satisfaction, money, and fame, in making that decision. I know of no objective criterion for judging when an enjoyable activity is performed in the socially most desirable way but would like to illustrate the nature of the problem with a few examples.

Let me take as the first example business investment, the enjoyable activity that is crucial for economic development. It is fortunate that so many people should take pleasure not only in doing what they are doing but in doing it well, because the innate urge to excel is bound to be much more effective than any outside pressure. Recall that Keynes credited the entrepreneur's animal spirits, not the profit motive, for our technical and economic progress; and he was not alone in that. Schumpeter, who disagreed with Keynes on most other things, also believed that there would be no innovation, no technical progress under the incentive of the profit motive alone, without the creative entrepreneur's creative urge.[14]

The economic incentive of the profit motive, however, is just as essential as the entrepreneur's innovative spirit, because it indicates which innovations are likely to be appreciated by the wider public and causes only those to be selected for commercialization from among the much greater number of innovative ideas that are available. Less than 10 per cent of the patents registered in the US Patent Office ever reach the production stage; and readers of the surveys of new patents in the Saturday editions of the *New York Times* will probably agree that such selectivity is in the public interest. It seems therefore that as far as investment activity is concerned, profitability and the desire (and ability) to be creative are both necessary conditions of the social optimum.

Much more difficult is the question of the relative importance of those two conditions for optimal investment activity. Note for example that the far-reaching corporate tax reforms of the first Reagan Administration have greatly increased the profitability of business, with the aim and hope of encouraging investment activity; but they only led to higher profits, larger cash reserves and more takeovers, because businessmen lacked the creative desire and ability to improve upon existing products and productive methods and had no need for additional productive capacity.

For a different example of the same problem recall that some of the most famous and successful modern architects (Le Corbusier and Frank Lloyd Wright to mention just two) have often sacrificed the convenience and comfort of the future owners and residents of their buildings for the sake of aesthetic considerations that weighed more heavily with them than with the owners and residents themselves.

A very similar example is the tendency of many modern composers to ignore deliberately their contemporary audience's musical tastes and compose for their own and their colleagues' pleasure music which the concert-going public neither understands nor enjoys. One cannot judge whether such activity is optimal or suboptimal without being able to predict whether increased familiarity with their music will bring its enjoyment within the reach of future generations of audiences (whose number, of course, exceeds the number of the present audience).[15] Such and similar issues can be quite difficult and complex; and the proposed model, by explicitly introducing and keeping separate the several motivating influences on activity, is bound to be helpful in their resolution.

SOCIAL WANTS AND PRIDE IN ACTIVITIES

Yet another advantage of my proposed model is that it can accommodate social wants and deal with their economic aspects as integral parts of the model. The conflict between people's apparently insatiable desire for more income and the satiability of most human needs and wants has forced the early economists to pay special attention to the desire for social distinction, because it creates the inherently insatiable demand for positional goods, which are the outward manifestations of social distinction.

All that fits easily and naturally into a model that takes explicit account of activities as sources of satisfaction. For the individual's enjoyment of other people's appreciation of his own activities forms an integral part of the interaction between active performers and passive spectators; and his desire for distinction and for the privileges, titles, medals, trophies and other tokens of distinction, are as many manifestations of that enjoyment.

Since the appreciation of one's accomplishments inevitably involves one's being ranked against others, and since for me to rank high there must be others whom I outrank, it is patently impossible ever to satisfy fully everybody's desire for distinction and its privileges and trappings. That is the sense in which the demand for distinction is insatiable.

The meaning and implications of the insatiable demand for positional goods have been fully discussed,[16] and there is an interesting discussion also of the tradeoff between social distinction and monetary compensation.[17] The proposed model, however, should facilitate the subject's integration into the rest of economics and it fills a gap by explaining the insatiable nature also of that other important symbol of social distinction: conspicuous consumption.

CONSPICUOUS CONSUMPTION, NOVELTY AND FASHION

People like to be appreciated for their proficiency in enjoyable activities; but they also enjoy the status that comes with earning and having money, although earning one's keep is not always an enjoyable activity. The desire for the status that goes with money is special also in two other respects. First, since information about people's income and wealth is not usually in the public domain, they must advertise it themselves by conspicuous consumption if they want to enjoy the status that goes with it. Second, the desire for the status that money imparts comes at all income levels and may even be the strongest among the poor, for whom a consumption level and style of living comparable to their neighbours' and other peoples' around them is a valued symbol of their belonging to the society in which they live. That is a good reason for preferring more comprehensive terms, like social wants or social comfort, to the customary term, social distinction.

Because it caters to a social want, conspicuous consumption plays an important role in social relations. But why should the demand for conspicuous consumption be insatiable, in the sense of rising with the secular rise in incomes? The desire of the poor to emulate the lifestyle and appearance of the non-poor would be satiated sooner or later, were it not for the latter's similar desire (and ability, since their incomes also rise) to emulate the lifestyle of the rich. Their desire to emulate the rich would also approach satiation, of course, (and thereby lead to the satiation of the corresponding desire of the poor as well) if only the expenditure of the rich would remain unchanged.

The rich, however, aspire to outdo the non-rich and to increase *their* consumption with that aim in view, which raises the question how they can do that. For the rich, unlike others, have no superior example to follow and emulate[18] and few if any unsatisfied desires which to fulfil requires more spending. At the same time, mere excessive spending in careless and frivolous ways or on some eccentric hobby will not do, because that is mostly looked down upon more than up to. To secure status therefore, the rich must not only have the money to outspend others, they must also manage to spend it well: in ways that others regard as superior and desirable, and set an example worth following. To resolve that problem requires that crucial ingredient of many, perhaps most enjoyable activities: the right degree of novelty.

As is well known and amply documented, novelty—in art, entertainment, fiction, and the design and decorative element in housing, furnishings, clothing, and many other products—is the essential condition for mental stimulation.[19] For its stimulating effect to be enjoyable, however, the novelty must be limited in degree, different from the familiar and conventional but not too much so, because the familiar is dull but too much novelty is disturbing. People vary, of course, in the degree of novelty they enjoy and can tolerate; but because all novelty wears off with repeated exposure and habituation, the same novelty that only a few people can take and enjoy at first, gradually becomes more familiar and so gets to be accepted and enjoyed by virtually everybody. That explains the slowness of the process with which any given fashion starts and spreads, until it becomes generally accepted, only to be gradually displaced by a new fashion as time wears off all the novelty of the old fashion and the public's undiminished desire for mental stimulation calls forth the fresh novelty of a new fashion. The changing of fashions is a never ending sequence caused by the steady demand for novelty, which reminds one of the Red Queen's race in *Alice's Adventures in Wonderland,* where 'it takes all the running you can do to keep in the same place'.

I outlined that process, because the expenditure pattern and lifestyle of the rich plays an important role in it. To create new fashions—in art, architecture, design and decoration in furnishing, dressmaking, etc.—is an activity that requires imagination, taste and talent—qualities as rare among the rich as among the rest of us. But to recognize potentially new fashions and their creators, to launch them, display their creations, and make them and their products known to a wider public—in short, to act as leaders of fashion—that is something the rich can do better than others, given their superior financial resources, their self confidence, and their ability to hire experts to advise them.

It only has to be added that leaders of fashion enjoy the same privileged position as all other leaders, consequently the conspicuous consumption of the rich, which establishes their leadership in fashion, is a positional good, the demand for which is insatiable in the same sense and for the same reason as the demand for all other positional goods.

CONCLUSION

The main advantages, however, of the model outlined and proposed in this paper is that it would bring enjoyable stimulation within the scope of the economist's well-established theory of the market economy, and do so in a relatively simple and natural way. There was some truth in the old charge that economics deals only with man's lower instincts. His enjoyment of the stimulus in science, art, sport, entertainment, literature, learning, and exploring the unknown is surely the better part of his nature; and it is a very important part, which is forever growing in importance. Moreover, as has just been shown, its inclusion in the economist's area of discourse would make it possible to include along with it social wants as well. That would go a long, if not the whole way to incorporating the psychologists' insights into economics.[20] Finally, expanding the scope of economics along the lines suggested would also have the paradoxical but salutary effect of always reminding economists of the limits of their science by making the dividing line between economic and non-economic welfare one of the variables determined by the model.

NOTES

1. Alfred Marshall, *Principles of Economics,* Eighth (definitive) Edition, (London: Macmillan, 1930), pp. 88-90.
2. J. M. Keynes, 'Economic possibilities for our grandchildren', in *Essays in Persuasion,* (New York: Norton, 1963), p. 367.
3. Keynes *op. cit.* p. 368.
4. Keynes *op. cit.* p. 369.
5. J. M. Keynes, *The General Theory of Employment, Interest and Money,* (London: Macmillan, 1936), pp. 149-50 and 161-2.
6. R. F. Hawtrey, *The Economic Problem,* (London: Longmans & Green, 1925), p. 189.
7. Hawtrey *op. cit.* pp. 190-1.
8. *See* Chapter 10, especially pp. 000.
9. *See* Notes 16 and 17 below.
10. *See* especially J. M. Keynes, 'The general theory of employment', *Quarterly Journal of Economics,* Vol. LI (1937), pp. 209-23.
11. Joshua Ronen, *Entrepreneurship,* (New York: Lexington Books, 1982).
12. For an early study, whose findings have been confirmed but never contradicted by subsequent research, *see* G. F. Break, 'Income taxes and incentive to work: an empirical study', *American Economic Review,* Vol. 47 (1957), pp. 529-49.
13. Mark R. Lepper and David Greene (eds.), *The Hidden Costs of Reward: New Perspectives on the Psychology of Human Motivation* (Hillsdale, NJ: Erlbaum, 1978), especially the chapters by Edward L. Deci and by Deci and Joseph Porac.

14. Josef Schumpeter, *Theorie der Wirtschaftlichen Entwicklung* (München & Leipzig: Duncker & Humblot, 1935), Ch. 2, section 3.

15. For a detailed (but somewhat biased) discussion of the music example, *see* Henry Pleasants, *The Agony of Modern Music,* (New York: Simon & Schuster, 1955).

16. R. F. Harrod, 'The possibility of economic satiety—use of economic growth for improving the quality of education and leisure', in *Problems of United States Economic Development,* (New York: Committee for Economic Development, 1958); Fred Hirsch, *Social Limits to Growth,* (Cambridge, Mass.: Harvard U. Press, 1976). *See* also Chapter 11 for the discussion of a particularly important positional good.

17. Robert H. Frank, *Choosing the Right Pond: Human Behaviour and the Quest for Status,* (New York: Oxford U. Press, 1985).

18. For a different opinion, *see* Hawtrey *op. cit.* pp. 205-6.

19. My *The Joyless Economy,* (New York: Oxford U. Press, 1976), Ch. 3.

20. One subject not covered in the proposed model is the temporary pleasure of relieving a need or achieving a goal (Plato's 'illusory pleasure') and its potential conflict with comfort, which was discussed at length in Chapter 4 of *The Joyless Economy.*

Acknowledgements

The author and publisher are grateful to the following for permission to reprint: *Quarterly Review of Economics and Business* for 'The Place of Economic Welfare in Human Welfare' (1973): *Annals of the American Academy of Political and Social Science* for 'Inequalities: Open and Hidden, Measured and Immeasurable' (1974); American Economic Association for 'What's Wrong with the Arts is What's Wrong with Society' in *American Economic Review* (1972) and 'Can Capitalism Survive?—An Old Question in a New Setting' in *American Economic Review* (1980); *De Economist* for 'The Producer Society'; Academic Press, Inc. for 'Are Men Rational or Economists Wrong?' in *Nations and Households in Economic Growth,* c 1974; *Kyklos* for 'Human Desire and Economic Satisfaction' (1985) and 'The Desire for Excitement in Modern Society' (1981); The Macmillan Press Ltd for 'Can Changing Consumer Tastes Save Resources?' in *Economic Growth and Resources* (1979); Duncker & Humblot for 'Excess Demand for Job Importance and Its Implications' in *Wert- und Praeferenzprobleme in den Sozialwissenschaften* (1981); Association for Cultural Economics, The University of Akron for 'Subsidies for the Arts: The Economic Argument' in *Economic Support for the Arts* (1983); Elsevier Science Publishers for 'Psychologizing by Economists' in *Economic Psychology: Intersection in Theory and Application* (1986).

Index of Names

Arrow, K. J., 34n5, 80n1, 159n5, 34n5, 80n1, 81r
Becker, G. S., 78, 80n8, 81r
Beesley, M. E., 77, 81r
Bentham, Jeremy, 184
Berlyne, D. E., 184, 186
Carlyle, Thomas, 187
Carey, Henry, 14
Chamberlin, Edward, 108, 112n8
Dember, 21, 25r
Denison, Edward D., 146, 148n8
Domar, Evsey, 86
Easterlin, R. A. 23, 34n15
Fisher, F. 18, 25r
Freeman, Richard, 139, 147n3-5
Freud, Sigmund, 16, 25r
Galbraith, J. K., 10
Griliches, Zvi, 18, 25r
Gronau, R., 78, 81r
Hansen, Alvin, 86
Harrod, Sir Roy, 86, 203n16
Hawtrey, Sir Ralph, 66, 68n13, 187, 189-90, 202n6-9, 203n18
Hebb, D. O., 184, 186
Herrick, N. Q., *see* Sheppard and Herrick
Hobson, J. A., viii
Jevons, W. S., 187
Kaysen, Carl, 18, 25r
Kalecki, Michal, viii
Keynes, J. M., viii, 41, 50, 93-5, 187-9, 190, 194, 198, 202n2-5 & 10
Kornai, János, 98-9, 103, 112n1
Lange, Oskar, viii
Le Corbusier, 199

Lerner, A. P., 86
Lisco, T. E. 77, 81r
Marshall, Alfred, 86, 186-7, 190, 202n1
Marx, Karl viii, 4, 17, 30, 34n10, 80n3
Mill, John Stuart, 5, 26
Mitchell, Wesley, 50
Modigliani, Franco, 72-3, 81r
Molière, 72
Nader, Ralph, 15
Nordhaus, W. D., 22, 23, 25r, 34n6
Owen, J. D., 78, 81r
Pigou, A. C., 13
Plato, 185-6, 190
Plautus, 72
Quarmby, D. A. 77, 81r
Protagoras, 185
Robbins, Lord, viii
Rockefeller, John D., 72
Rothschild, Anselm, 72
Samuelson, P. A. 22
Scitovsky, T. 12n3, 33n1, 81n17, 81r, 89, 103, 112n3, 127n1, 159n2, 182n6, 184-5, 203n19-20
Schumpeter, Joseph, viii, 85, 92, 94, 98, 198, 203n14
Sheppard, H. L. & Herrick, N. Q., 32, 34n11
Simon, Herbert A., 15, 25r
Solow, Robert, 86
Steiner, E. A. 77, 82r
Stopher, R. R., 77, 81r
Swan, Trevor, 86
Tawney, R. H., viii, x
Thompson, Robert, 14

205

Index of Subjects

Activity, enjoyable, pursued for its own sake, x, xi, 79-80, 187, 190-1, 193-202
Addition, 153
Advertising, 47, 52-3, 102ff, 108-9
Animal spirits, 92, 188, 189, 190, 194, 195, 198
Alienation, 17, 30, 49
Arousal, 15-16, 128, 152, 184, 186
Art, 17, 37-46, 50, 51, 117, 119, 122, 126-7, 131, 149-59, 189, 192, 196
Authority, 174-5, 180

Balance of payments, 86, 89
Bargaining skill, 99, 174
Barter, 193
Buyers' market, 98, 102-6, 171

Charity, *see* Philanthropy
Collective hazardous action, 129, 133-4
Collective goods, 3, 27-9, 122, 173
Comfort, personal, 20, 24, 38-9, 119-20, 122-6, 136-7, 150-1, 186; *see also* Defensive consumption
Comfort, social, 119-22, 137, 150, 186, 191, 199, 200; *see also* Status
Companionship, 14, 17
Conspicuous consumption, 51, 120, 138, 200-1; *see also* Positional goods and Status symbols
Consumers' domination, 52-3, 57
Consumers' sovereignty, 18ff, 47, 50, 54, 118

Consumption skills, 40, 39-41, 51-2, 61-2, 123-6, 140, 153, 156-8, 162
Creative consumption and products, 60-2, 67, 189-90
Crime, 132, 134, 135n8, 150, 155, 157

Danger, 128, 129-30, 132-3, 135n1 & 9, 150, 153
Death penalty, 9
Defensive consumption and products, 41, 60ff, 189
Distribution of income, 3, 5, 18, 26-34, 87, 90, 91, 92, 100, 107
Divorce, 167
Do-it-yourself activity, 32, 64, 69n22, 75-6, 130-1
Drugs, 133, 137, 189

Effective demand, 50, 93
Egalitarian distribution, 6-10
Elites, xi-xii, 37-8, 157
Equity, 3-12, 87, 90, 92, 93
Excitement, 128-35, 151-8, 185, 189
External costs and diseconomies, 88, 120, 130, 153, 157
External economies, 153-4

Family relations, 179-81
Fashion, xi-xii, 126, 200-1
Flexibility and inflexibility of the economy, 86-95, 118
Foreign workers, 89, 106, 144, 161
Fragmentation, economic, 92-4
Friction, 168-76, 178, 180